Breastfeeding Naturally

Breastfeeding Naturally

A new
approach
for today's
mother

Hannah Lothrop

FISHER
er
BOOKS

Publishers: Bill Fisher
        Helen V. Fisher
        Howard W. Fisher

Managing Editor: Sarah Trotta

Assistant Editor: Meg Morris

Cover Design: Josh Young

Cover Photo: Larry Williams
        /Masterfile

Book Design
& Production: Randy Schultz

Originally published as *Das Stillbuch*,
Copyright © 1989, 1995 Kösel Verlag
GmbH & Co., Munich, Germany

Published by Fisher Books
4239 W. Ina Road, Suite 101
Tucson, Arizona 85741
(520) 744-6110

**Library of Congress
Cataloging-in-Publication Data**

Lothrop, Hannah, 1945-
  [Stillbuch. English]
  Breastfeeding naturally : a new
  approach for today's mother /
Hannah Lothrop.
    p. cm.
  Includes bibliographical references
  and index.
  ISBN 1-55561-131-1
  1. Breast feeding—Popular works.
  2. Lactation—Popular works.
  3. Breast milk—Popular works.
  4. Infants-Nutrition-Popular works.
  I. Title.
  RJ216.L8713 1998
  649'.33—dc21   98-43386
                      CIP

Printed in the U.S.A.
5 4 3 2 1

Note: The information in this book is true and complete to the best of our knowledge. In no way is this book intended to replace, countermand or conflict with the advice given to you by your own physician. The ultimate decision concerning care should be made by between you and your doctor. We strongly recommend you follow his or her advice. The information in this book is general and is offered with no guarantees on the part of the author or Fisher Books. Author and publisher disclaim all liability in connection with the use of this book.

Contents

DEDICATION

Dedicated to my children
Anya and Kerry
without whom this book would not have come about.

When children are small, give them roots.
When they are older, give them wings.

Part 1

Breastfeeding Naturally

Breastfeeding Is Worthwhile

The sight of a content, happy newborn touches every woman who has had a baby. Nothing in the world is more satisfying and healthy for a newborn than its mother's milk. But nursing is easier for some women than others. Without support, information and self-confidence, some mothers give up. They tend to remember their difficulties, and may feel sad and disappointed even years later that they couldn't give their baby this special gift. Women who *do* overcome their struggles with breastfeeding, on the other hand, are often strengthened in a way that enriches their relationship with their child for a long time to come.

Information and support can help you establish a happy nursing relationship with your baby. Even after many years have passed, you will remember the deep joy, warmth and connection you experienced with your baby during a wonderful, special time.

Why I Wrote This Book

Our daughter, Anya, was born in 1972 in a small hospital in Virginia. Although my husband, Rob, and I lived in the country, we drove 30 miles to town every week to attend childbirth-education classes for couples during the latter part of my pregnancy. Through these classes, Rob and I learned to trust in the natural processes of birthing and breastfeeding. Anya's birth, which I experienced without medication, with the help of my nurturing husband, was the most intense and enriching experience of my life. It laid the foundation for a very uncomplicated, natural nursing relationship.

Before we left the hospital, our pediatrician came by and congratulated me on our baby. He reassured me our daughter was completely healthy and had already regained her birth weight. I was told to nurse her at home as often as she was hungry, including at night.

Back in those days, I had read babies should be fed five times a day, with an 8-hour break at night. When I asked what I should do if my child slept through the night, my pediatrician said with a twinkle, "If that *really* happens, then let her sleep." It became clear this would be highly unlikely!

Soon I felt secure in caring for my child. It came naturally. Anya woke up several times a night, but I was prepared for that, so it didn't bother me a bit. I woke up a few minutes before she did. In the semi-darkness I brought her into bed with me or sat with her in my comfortable rocking chair and nearly went back to sleep myself. Looking back, I can't say how often Anya was hungry in the first weeks. Thanks to the calm and reassuring words of my wise pediatrician, I didn't think about schedules at all. I took my positive, unproblematic nursing experience for granted.

When Anya was nine months old, we moved to Germany. Talking with friends there, I was surprised to discover how many women who had wanted to breastfeed originally had discouraging and frustrating experiences with it. They believed they should advise other expectant mothers not to breastfeed! Their experience was far removed from *Stillen,* the German word for breastfeeding (and which also means *calming, soothing, appeasing*). What they had experienced was in stark contrast to what I had experienced. That puzzled me. I wondered how something as natural as breastfeeding could become such a problem.

It became clear there was a shocking lack of information available on the natural course of breastfeeding. This lack of information doomed breastfeeding success for many, many women.

I designed a research study and began questioning mothers systematically about their experience. I also questioned gynecologists, pediatricians, midwives, nurses and counselors at parent-counseling centers. It became clear there was a shocking lack of information available on the natural course of breastfeeding. This lack of information doomed breastfeeding success for many, many women. Indeed, I had experienced a little of this myself, with the counterproductive treatment I received at the birth of our son, Kerry. I nursed him successfully only because I deeply believed in myself and my body and because of my previous positive experience with Anya.

From all this, I decided to write a book to help others have as rewarding a nursing time as I had enjoyed. Back in the States, I spent many days at the Harvard Medical Library and later, at the La Leche League research library in a Chicago suburb collecting all the literature available on the subject at that time. I am grateful to have been welcomed by, and able to talk in person with, leading breastfeeding researchers and with the Founding Mothers of La Leche League. I started the breastfeeding support-group movement as the first German La Leche League Leader—now there are about a thousand support groups there. I am in total awe and so grateful that the book, which was inspired by the heart, founded on research and the thousand-fold contact with young mothers, has reached an estimated 3 million moms and dads and today is being translated into other languages.

Where We Come From

Few areas of human life have been influenced by fads and medical ideologies as much as pregnancy, childbirth, breastfeeding and parenting. Moms used to breastfeed their babies because there was no appropriate alternative. When they had too much milk, they sometimes would become wet nurses for someone else's baby, or they pumped their milk and donated or sold it to a milk bank. Mother's milk used to be a precious commodity.

When baby formulas hit the market, many people were enthusiastic. Finally, one could weigh, measure and allot how often and how much each child should drink—very scientific! It became more progressive to feed by bottle according to an exact schedule than to feed by breast following one's natural instincts. Suddenly *this* was the norm: delaying the very first breastfeeding, sticking to rigid 4-hour schedules, taking long breaks at night, limiting feeds, feeding babies by bottle before putting them to the breast, or weighing and supplementing with a bottle after the breastfeed (to make up the baby's "required" amount).

The many conditions put on breastfeeding helped make women so unsure of themselves that they could hardly ever nourish their babies by breastfeeding alone. What's more, the routine use of drugs during labor and delivery prevented mothers and babies from bonding to each other right after birth (see page 217), negatively affecting the breastfeeding relationship. And bottle-feeding may also have agreed with the inclinations of mothers who had been reared in such a way as not to have a good relationship with their own bodies.

Manufacturers of commercial baby formula played a significant part in the "bottle euphoria" that ensued. To push their products, they went so far as to claim their "milk" was *equivalent* to mother's milk. Through advertisements, they subtly and not-so-subtly influenced new moms to doubt their ability to breastfeed. They promoted and distributed their preparations in the developing world. The results of this were disastrous. Infants (in Africa, for example), who up to then were relatively well-protected from infection and malnutrition in the first year of life thanks to breast-feeding, began to die by the thousands when mother's milk was replaced by germ-ridden formulas incorrectly prepared in unsanitary conditions. Because family incomes were minimal, formulas were often diluted to last longer, and therefore did not provide these babies with adequate nutrition.

The World Health Organization (WHO) International Code for the Marketing of Breast-Milk Substitutes is trying to address this problem. One of its ten provisions for infant-formula manufacturers is to refrain from advertising with free-sample packs in maternity units. Unfortunately, this effort has not been very successful. Although the United States endorsed the Code in 1994, even progressive U.S. hospitals do not abide by its provisions. Women still receive free formula when they leave the hospital; the only difference is that women who will breastfeed receive a *smaller* formula pack than women who will bottle-feed!

Circumstances are more favorable today, but many anxieties, prejudices, practices and old wives' tales about breastfeeding are still alive. Many expectant moms would opt to breastfeed if they knew about its important health benefits. But they do not get enough of

The World Health Organization

The World Health Organization (WHO) was formed in 1948 and now has 191 member states, including the United States and Canada. It has been instrumental in providing worldwide guidance in the fields of health promotion and disease prevention. WHO supports breastfeeding in general as a means of promoting children's health, especially in developing countries.

Baby-Friendly Hospitals

The World Health Organization, in conjunction with the United Nations Children's Fund (UNICEF), started the Baby-Friendly Hospital Initiative in 1991. Through it, hospitals and birth centers are identified and commended for adhering to the "Ten Steps to Successful Breastfeeding" considered most important by these two organizations. Hospitals following the Ten Steps provide the best possible support for breastfeeding. Once recognized, the sites are designated as "baby-friendly"—good places to deliver your baby.

Ten Steps to Successful Breastfeeding

Step 1. Have a written breastfeeding policy that is routinely communicated to all heathcare staff.

Step 2. Train all healthcare staff in skills necessary to implement this policy.

Step 3. Inform all pregnant women about the benefits and management of breastfeeding.

Step 4. Help mothers initiate breastfeeding about an hour after birth.

Step 5. Show mothers how to breastfeed and how to maintain lactation, even if they have to be separated from their infants.

Step 6. Give newborn infants no food or drink other than breast milk unless medically indicated.

Step 7. Practice "rooming-in." Allow mothers and infants to remain together 24 hours a day.

Step 8. Encourage breastfeeding on demand.

Step 9. Give no artificial teats or pacifiers (also called *dummies* or *soothers*) to breastfeeding infants.

Step 10. Foster the establishment of breastfeeding support groups and refer mothers to them on discharge from the hospital or clinic.

this information beforehand to make an informed choice. After they decide to breastfeed, they frequently don't get adequate encouragement or support.

To breastfeed successfully, women must have competent, wise guidance. They need empowerment to trust themselves and to strengthen their self-confidence and self-love, because those are the best conditions for rearing a family with a high level of self-esteem. This goal should be our highest common priority.

When moms don't get the support they need, they may have trouble starting a nursing relationship with their baby, as Gina found. Here's her story.

> *Selena was my first child. None of my sisters had breastfed. I was completely inexperienced and really needed support. Most of the nurses in the hospital were nice and wanted to help. They brought Selena to me whenever I wanted them to. But none of them had the slightest idea about breastfeeding. Either they communicated their own doubt or gave me contradictory advice.*

> *Many things went wrong. I still wonder why no one let me try to breastfeed without nipple shields even once. I had to use them from the start because someone said my nipples "weren't appropriate" for breastfeeding. I'm not surprised Selena didn't like sucking on nipple shields. She was tiny, and the large shield in her mouth must have been uncomfortable.*

> *When my milk came in and my breasts got engorged, everyone told me something different—Because the milk didn't flow on its own, I had to use a noisy breast pump. I would sit for at least half an hour each time on an uncomfortable chair without armrests and with no real support for my back. My arms went to sleep, my back hurt, and I felt tense. This started a vicious cycle. I would spend the whole day pumping and feeding the pumped milk by bottle. Selena began not to want anything to do with breastfeeding. She screamed when I tried to put her to my breast. It became a frustrating and exhausting ordeal.*

> *I didn't give up. Despite the early difficulties, I have now breastfed Selena exclusively for six months, thanks to the dedicated help of my friend Liz. Now I realize we could have*

*been spared a lot of trouble if I had gotten supportive,
appropriate, noncontradictory help from the people around me
at the very beginning, if someone had shown me how to put my
baby to my breast correctly and comfortably, if I'd had my baby
with me all the time and if I'd been able to breastfeed often,
without breast shields.*

Successful Breastfeeding

When conditions are right and support is appropriate and caring,
when mother and baby are not separated after birth and can get
acquainted with each other in a natural way, breastfeeding isn't a
problem. This new mom relates her experience after giving birth:

> *My childbirth class prepared me for breastfeeding. My teacher
> treated breastfeeding matter-of-factly. I also observed real-life
> nursing mothers when I visited a breastfeeding support group.*
>
> *Melissa was put to my breast right after birth and brought back
> to me again after she was weighed and checked. I got
> constructive help in putting her to my breast. . . . Back in our
> rooms, we mothers could decide without pressure whether we
> would keep our babies with us around the clock or give them to
> the nurses some of the time—whether our babies would sleep in
> a bassinet by our bedside or snuggled next to us in bed. We
> could say whether we would change the diapers ourselves or
> leave it to the nurses or our partners. Our instructions to the
> staff not to give supplemental feedings were heeded if our babies
> were not with us all the time. I was surrounded by friendly,
> easygoing nurses who were there for me with guidance and
> support. They cheered me on. Fears I might not have enough
> milk for my baby were quickly dispelled by comments like, "I
> have never come across a mother who couldn't breastfeed.
> You'll see."*

Why Mothers Choose to Breastfeed

Mothers choose to breastfeed for different reasons. Here are a few:

> *"Through breastfeeding, I am attached to my child, but not to
> my house. I feel more free and mobile than I would with bottle-*

*feeding. I can nurse almost anywhere. I don't have to worry
about boiled water, formula or sterilized bottles."*

*"If we are invited somewhere, we can stay. I always have
Lori's meal ready—at the right temperature, in the right
quantity and at the right time."*

*"With the money we have saved in the last six months by
breastfeeding, we'll be able to take a trip this summer."*

*"Jonathan and I developed a great bond. When he got a little
older, he would gaze at me with his big brown eyes and pat me
gently while he nursed. It was mutual giving and receiving."*

*"Through breastfeeding, a very intense love developed between
Shari and me."*

But practical and emotional reasons aren't the only reasons women
breastfeed. Many women have their baby's health at heart.

What's in Mother's Milk?

Nature has arranged it so each mother's milk at any given time is
the best food for her baby. *Breast milk is ideally adapted to the baby's
nutritional needs, his growth rate and his immune system.* The baby-
formula industry uses cow's milk to make products, not because it
is the most similar to human milk, but because cow's milk is available in large quantities. It requires relatively little effort or cost to
manufacture.

The most distinct difference between cow's milk and mother's
milk is that cow's milk is suited for cows and the development of
a baby calf. Mother's milk is composed of things suitable for a
human infant. There are many, many identifiable proteins, enzymes,
and other minerals in breast milk that help sustain, protect and
grow the babies who drink it. Breast milk also contains many as-
yet-unknown components.

Infant formula is created to *resemble* mother's milk. But we will see it is a poor substitute for the real thing. What's in mother's milk, and what are its advantages?

Water

Human milk consists mainly of water: All its other ingredients are dissolved in water. Breast milk preserves an ideal, flexible relationship between water and its other ingredients. For example, the first milk the baby gets at a feed is watery and thirst-quenching, while milk toward the end of a feed is creamier and more filling (see Let-Down Reflex, page 43). An exclusively breastfed child doesn't usually need additional fluid, even in hot weather, as long as she is put to the breast sufficiently and her mother takes in sufficient fluids herself. (A mother would have to be seriously dehydrated to affect her milk supply.)

Protein

The main proteins in milk are called *casein* and *lactalbumin*. Casein is a protein that curdles coarsely (it's the basis for yogurt, kefir, cottage cheese and other cheeses); lactalbumin, on the other hand, is a much smoother protein similar to the clear, water-like part of cow's milk that separates from the curd. In cow's milk, the casein-to-lactalbumin ratio is higher than it is in mother's milk. That means cow's-milk-based formula has a lot more coarse, curdling milk protein than mother's milk does. Casein sticks together in the baby's stomach and is much harder to digest than the finer lactalbumin.

Because of this clumping tendency, formula companies dilute, homogenize and add emulsifiers to infant formula. Even so, we observe that bottle-fed babies are more prone to digestive problems such as stomach gas and constipation. Apparently a newborn can only partially digest cow's-milk protein; the remainder is eliminated in the form of large stools.

Because mother's milk is fully absorbed by babies, breastfed babies gain more weight on less breast milk than they would if they were fed the same amount of formula. The large amount of lactalbumin in mother's milk makes it easier to digest, and it empties more quickly from the baby's intestines. For this reason, it is normal for breastfed babies to be hungry sooner than bottle-fed babies; in the beginning, every two to three hours.

Fat

About half the nutritional value of mother's milk lies in its fat content. Fat is especially important to the newborn because it is used to develop new nerve cells.

Mother's milk has many more unsaturated fatty acids than formula does. Fatty acids are particularly indispensable to an infant. They are critical for digestion, protection against infection and possibly intelligence.

Infant formula adds vegetable oil in an effort to duplicate the fatty-acid combinations in mother's milk. This oil cannot make formula the same as the species-specific, healthful milk you produce for your baby.

Carbohydrates

Milk sugar (*lactose*) is present in different amounts in both mother's milk and cow's milk. This carbohydrate is the second-most-important energy source for the baby. The difference in lactose content between breast milk and formula can be made up to some extent by adding lactose and other types of sugar to cow's-milk-based formula. However, some other carbohydrates present in human milk, such as the bifidus factor, are absent in cow's milk and cannot be duplicated in formula.

This beneficial substance is necessary for the growth of lactobacillus bifidus, which helps protect the baby's intestines from disease-producing bacteria (such as certain coli-types and streptococci families). It also protects against infant enteritis (inflammation of the intestines). Medical literature describes epidemics of infant enteritis before the discovery of antibiotics. These cases were only brought under control by feeding the affected babies fresh, untreated mother's milk.

A woman who follows a vegan diet (free of meat, fish, eggs or milk products) needs extra vitamin B-12 to prevent some problems for her baby. Her baby may not metabolize protein properly, for example.

Minerals

Levels of sodium, calcium and magnesium are many times higher in cow's milk than in mother's milk. Infant-formula companies artificially try to reduce these levels, but they cannot duplicate the exact mineral composition present in mother's milk. These minerals may be low in mother's milk, but they are still better absorbed by the breastfed baby than are the same minerals in infant formula.

Vitamins and Iron

During pregnancy, deposits of vitamins A, D, E and K are stored in the mother's body. For a healthy woman who nourishes herself sensibly (see page 87), this supply is often enough to cover most of her baby's entire vitamin requirement during the time she nurses.

> Food with too much iron and no lactoferrin to enable the baby to make use of it prompts illness. It encourages the growth of coli bacteria, which need iron to thrive. Iron in mother's milk is bound with lactoferrin, so it is not available to coli bacteria.

Mother's milk contains relatively little iron, but it does contain the enzyme lactoferrin, which binds itself to iron in the baby's body. Lactoferrin permits the baby to absorb at least half of all iron present in the mother's milk. Without lactoferrin, which is not in cow's milk, a baby absorbs just a fraction of the iron available in his food, even if this food has *added* iron! In the first six to nine months of life, a full-term baby still has the large iron reserve he got from his mother during the pregnancy. The small amount of iron he receives through his mother's milk is enough in this early period.

Antibodies

In the womb, the baby receives antibodies against germs and organisms to which his mother has been exposed. These are called *immunoglobulins*—certain kinds of protein. The time immediately after birth is critical for the baby: The antibodies he receives from his mother during pregnancy are available, but start to disappear. He can't produce his own antibodies yet. His immune system gradually matures in the first year of life. Breastfeeding is ideal for bridging this critical phase. It continues to protect him with his mother's antibodies.

The uterus is a sterile, protected environment. Immediately after delivery, the baby is exposed to countless unfamiliar germs. For this reason, mother's milk in the first few days—*colostrum* or *premilk*—has a particularly high concentration of immunoglobulins, the mother's antibodies. Immunoglobulins travel to the baby's intestinal tract after the first breastfeed and build a protective barrier there against the spread of germs and bacteria. They protect the newborn against all kinds of germs in the mother's environment. Antibodies in mother's milk (to which other proteins, enzymes and certain cells belong) are *not* found in any type of artificial feeding formula.

> Antibodies lose some of their effectiveness when mother's milk is heated moderately, to 133F (56C) and lose significantly more when heated beyond that point. Microwaving breast milk lowers its vitamin C content, destroys some of its protective factors and can potentially burn the baby with "hot pockets."

Immunoglobulins are most concentrated in breast milk in the first few days of breastfeeding. But continuing to breastfeed yields other advantages. One recent research study indicated children who were breastfed exclusively for six months were sick half as often later in life as children who were breastfed less than two months. Other studies have shown breastfeeding protects against a multitude of illnesses—from flu to polio.

Protection against Allergies

In recent years the incidence of allergies has increased significantly. Allergies have become one of the more important medical, and to some extent social, problems we face. Allergic reactions are on the rise at a time when we increasingly alienate ourselves from nature and natural living conditions.

Allergies are hereditary. If one parent (or both) has an allergy—for example, hay fever, a sensitivity to some foods, medicines, dust or cat hair—the child will be allergy-prone too. Eczema, skin problems, stomach pains, colic, vomiting, diarrhea, asthmatic complaints, colds and nervous disturbances such as restlessness, excitability, weakness, pallor—all these can be caused by allergies.

> Common foods that may cause an allergic reaction include wheat, eggs, chicken, rice, yeast, soy, tomatoes, citrus, sugar, vitamin supplements and, above all, cow's milk.

For many infants, the allergy is triggered by cow's-milk protein. Cow's-milk allergies are seven times more prevalent than any other allergies. Half of affected infants exposed to cow's milk show an allergic reaction in the first month of life. In others, the allergy develops over the first six months. Babies may be sensitive to several products or agents that collectively cause an allergic outbreak.

Mother's milk is important in protecting a baby against allergic reactions. Children from allergy-prone families should have colostrum as a first feed. This will "seal" the mucous membrane of the intestinal tract and protect it from unfamiliar protein molecules. *Where the risk of allergy exists, avoid even a single bottle of artificial baby milk for the first six months.*

Many newborns are sensitive to certain foods the mother has eaten. A breastfed child with colic may have this kind of hypersensitivity. In this case, try to find out which foods are affecting your baby. Eliminate them one by one from your diet. If the baby's symptoms improve within three to five days, you probably guessed right. (Under no circumstances eliminate *mother's* milk!) If the baby already reacts to a filtered form of a certain protein (cow's milk, for example), his allergic reaction will be that much stronger upon direct contact with this protein.

Under natural breastfeeding conditions, the breast can make mature mother's milk in just 24 hours.

If you must eliminate several important foods from your diet to conduct your test, consult a nutritionist first. It's helpful to keep a journal for two or three days and record exactly what you eat every day. Also, be aware: Soy-based and "hypoallergenic" baby milks sometimes cause even stronger reactions than regular commercial baby formulas.

Colostrum and Mature Mother's Milk

Colostrum is the thick, yellowish fluid initially produced by the mother during pregnancy and ingested by the breastfeeding baby the first few days following birth. It is particularly rich in protein (see Antibodies, page 11) and contains many vitamins (A, E, K, B-12) and minerals. Because its fat and sugar content is low, colostrum easy for the newborn to digest. Some refer to it as *premilk*. A better term is *newborn milk*. Because of its high

Colostrum: Important Nutrition

Drinking lots and lots of fluid would present a major filtering problem for a newborn's immature kidneys. Nature's perfect answer is colostrum. Colostrum, the first milk produced in the breast, is such a highly concentrated food that even the smallest amount meets the baby's nutritional needs—between 10 and 100 milliliters (ml). The average is 30ml of colostrum produced per day, or about one ounce. Amazing!

1 fluid ounce equals 29.6 milliliters.

immunoglobulin content and other protective factors, colostrum is considered "natural food as well as medicine" (World Health Organization).

Over time, the composition of newborn milk develops into mature, high-calorie mother's milk. How quickly that happens depends on how soon and how often the baby breastfeeds in the first few days. Under natural breastfeeding conditions, the breast can make mature mother's milk in just 24 hours. If breastfeeding opportunities are limited, this process may take longer—three to five days.

Mature mother's milk has more fat and carbohydrate but less protein than colostrum. Though it looks bluish and watery, it has more calories than newborn milk. Normally the fat and carbohydrate content of breast milk increases during the feed; the milk the baby receives at the end of the feed is the most nutritious. It looks creamier, too (see Let-Down Reflex, page 43). The milk's protein content decreases as breastfeeding goes on, so that by about six months of age, the child begins to need additional protein in the form of complementary foods.

As scientifically supported and pursuasive as this discussion is, it's also true we observe the majority of formula-fed children thrive without growth disturbances, deficiency symptoms or dangerous illnesses. That's fortunate. Still, the differences between mother's milk and cow's milk are not insignificant. This is especially apparent with premature or sick infants, whose digestive and immune systems are much more

By about six months of age, the child begins to need additional protein in the form of complementary foods.

sensitive than those of a robust 7-pounder. In these cases, mother's milk can sometimes be lifesaving.

The comparison we've made between mother's milk and adapted artificial feeding should reinforce to every woman that *her milk, in every respect, is the best for her child.* After all, what would her baby select if he could choose for himself?

More Advantages for the Breastfed Baby

Breastfeeding is ideal for a baby, not just because of the virtually perfect composition of mother's milk, but also because it affects his development in significant ways. New advantages to breast-feeding are being discovered all the time. Scientists are just beginning to understand more of what breast milk and breastfeeding provide.

- Breastfed children feed only as much and as often as they are hungry. They cannot be forced to drink, which can happen with a long, hard bottle-nipple they can't refuse. Formula supplies a high-fat, high-sugar diet throughout the feed, which can contribute to overweight. By breastfeeding, babies find their own rhythm and develop a healthy relationship to food. As a result, they are *less likely to develop obesity* in later life.

- Children who are breastfed exclusively from the start, according to Canadian and Finnish studies, are later *less likely to develop diabetes* than those who are fed cow's milk.

- One recent study of 3-month-old children in an iodine-deficient area showed that the *thyroid gland functioned better in fully breastfed children* than in bottle-fed babies who received an iodine supplement. The thyroid gland is important for cell metabolism, growth and maturation of the body, and for regulation of calcium levels.

- *Babies' heart rate, breathing and temperature* are different during breastfeeding than they are during bottle-feeding.

- According to one U.S. study, babies breastfed longer than three months show *a more harmonious, aesthetic development of the teeth, roof of the mouth and facial lines* than babies who were breastfed less than three months or not at all. The jaw movements of a baby sucking at the breast are entirely different than those used in bottle-feeding. The tongue plays a much bigger role. (Incidentally, this also has a regulatory effect on the baby's breathing and thereby on his body tone—the effects are long-term.) That so many children today need to wear braces to correct their bite is certainly due, in part, to bottle-feeding.

⚜ A study conducted in England with premature babies fed mother's milk by tube showed these children exhibited *higher IQs* later. It is thought mother's milk contains countless factors that encourage nervous-system development and the growth and maturation of the brain. This has a *positive effect on psychological development.*

⚜ In one study, breastfed children at six months were found to have *better vision* than bottle-fed children.

⚜ Very few fully breastfed babies are among those two to three children per thousand who die of sudden infant death (SIDS) in the early months of life. Sleeping on the stomach, viral or bacterial infections, allergies, passive smoking and respiratory problems are associated with these mystifying deaths. An infant might develop respiratory problems as a result of breathing toxic gases (which can be caused by ammonia in the urine developed after formula feeding, among other things), according to a 1993 report published in the International Journal of Epidemiology.

⚜ One German medical journal maintains that insufficient skin-to-skin contact or separation of mother and child also may influence the incidence of SIDS. My experiments with Middendorf Breathwork® (see page 40) also appear to confirm this idea. I have found the physical nearness of another person has a definite stimulating and harmonizing effect on the depth and rhythm of breathing. Breastfeeding is an antidote for all these factors.

Healthful for Mother, Too

> *When I put my son to the breast for the first time, I suddenly felt like I was still in the middle of giving birth. My uterus contracted so strongly I had to rely on the breathing techniques I'd practiced for the birth to get through the contractions.*

The same hormone that causes contraction of the uterus during the birth, oxytocin, is released during breastfeeding. Oxytocin helps the uterus contract and return to its normal shape after birth. Hence, early and regular breastfeeding is the best and most natural protection against hemorrhaging and infection in the postpartum period.

There are also long-term health benefits for women beyond the nursing period. Research has shown mothers who nursed often and for a long time have a much lower incidence of breast cancer and ovarian cancer than women who have not breastfed or who have not given birth at all. Also, the latest information on breastfeeding and osteoporosis (brittle bones) suggests the calcium loss breastfeeding women experience is temporary: Calcium levels *increase* once breastfeeding stops.

When Is It Better Not to Breastfeed?

In the past, Rh-incompatibility, newborn jaundice, Cesarean delivery, cleft lip or palate, inverted nipples and even breast infections were all considered reasons not to nurse. Today we know breastfeeding is possible in all these cases and even with hepatitis B (with some limitations). We realize even tiny, premature babies, who were once thought to be unable to drink from the breast, can do so. Mother's milk is even more crucial for them than it is for mature babies.

Very rarely, babies have to be fed with a mother's-milk substitute because of *galactosemia*—an inability to digest lactose. There may also be situations in which breastfeeding is contraindicated on the mother's side. These situations may include

- when she needs to take medication that is absolutely contraindicated for the baby
- if she has AIDS (see page 97)
- mental illness or other serious illnesses that weakens mother so much she cannot care for her baby
- current drug use or drug-treatment therapy, such as methadone, that could get into the breast milk

If more than two years have passed since a woman has had successful treatment for tuberculosis, it is generally OK to breastfeed.

All medical and psychological reasoning speaks in favor of breastfeeding. This makes some mothers feel they *have* to breastfeed—otherwise they won't be an "ideal mother." Pressuring ourselves this way can backfire. It can lead to tension in the relationship with our child. That greatly burdens breastfeeding. Children have sensitive "antennas." They can sense their mom's reluctance very well, and they will respond with reluctance of their own. Sometimes they even go on strike! Perhaps you decided to try breastfeeding despite genuine ambivalence about it. If so, difficulties and an inner resistance may crop up.

At that point, you might ask yourself:

- ❀ What messages were passed to me about breastfeeding?

- ❀ How influenced am I by the people in my environment who want to talk me out of breastfeeding or who may even ridicule me?

- ❀ Am I torn between my child and my partner, who may be openly jealous?

- ❀ Does the closeness, the intimate contact with my baby during nursing confuse me and create a conflict for me? As a result, do I have trouble letting myself simply enjoy my child?

- ❀ Is it difficult for me to "give myself" to my baby as a source of food and comfort? Where could that reluctance come from?

- ❀ Am I afraid my baby is taking something away from me, is "draining" me?

Or:

- ❀ Do your breasts hurt so much that you become tense during breastfeeding? Has this reaction burdened your mutual relationship too much and for too long?

- ❀ Has your baby possibly become used to a bottle and now finds it easier to drink from a bottle than from the breast (maybe throwing a fit whenever you try to feed him)? If so, has this undermined your self-confidence?

You may only have to deal with a few "technical" breastfeeding problems. Or you may be bothered by emotional problems primarily, which frequently turn into technical problems. You can find help to overcome these problems—from a La Leche League Leader, by attending a support group or by talking to a counselor or therapist if you suspect the problem is more deeply rooted. This book and other wonderful resources (see appendices) can help, too.

In some cases, a woman may offer her baby better mothering if she *isn't* breastfeeding. Don't demand something of yourself that overtaxes you (and your child). To decide, look deep inside yourself—look at your vulnerabilities and strengths, assess your present situation with a clear mind and an honest heart. If the circumstances are too difficult to overcome, it may be better for you to feed your baby lovingly by bottle. If that restores peace and harmony, then it will be better for you to bottle-feed than to breastfeed halfheartedly with anguish to both of you.

Since I've stopped breastfeeding after weeks of struggling, I've been able to have an anxiety-free, loving relationship with my child for the first time.

Make a well-considered decision, and then stand by it. Above all, free yourself from unrealistic expectations and guilty feelings that create new problems. As important as breastfeeding is, the quality of your relationship with your child, and his relationship to you, is even *more* important.

Physical Contact and Breastfeeding

I still get goose bumps when I think back to nursing my baby—the touch of that soft little mouth, which filled my whole body with warmth and love . . . the satisfaction of seeing my child thrive and knowing my body gave him everything he needed to grow.

The physical intimacy of nursing can dissolve barriers that almost always exist between people. It brings you and your baby much, much closer. Gradually you get to know each other. This growing familiarity fosters the mutual enjoyment of your breastfeeding relationship. You and your child need each other physically and emotionally. Just as your baby depends on you for nourishment, so do you depend on your baby to empty your breasts so they won't become engorged and painful. You are deeply connected to your baby through your body and your hormones. Nursing is a silent dialogue between the two of you—a relatively equal relationship between otherwise unequal partners.

Even in the first weeks of life, babies look intensely at their mothers while nursing. Their gaze is an important part of their "language" and helps us adults establish an intimate relationship with them. Observing them, we notice babies are much more capable of intense eye contact than many *adults* are! Opening ourselves to their gaze can be a real challenge for an inhibited person. It is our children's gift that they help us perceive the world around us with fresh eyes. With their guidance and modeling, we can learn to experience human contact in a new way.

Newborns and small children need our physical closeness, our tenderness, our touch. We can "talk" to them through our hands long before they are able to understand our words. This does not mean just patting them. Touching a human being while being fully "present" in our hands harmonizes the natural flow of breath in our bodies and can be healing and soothing in itself. We can learn nurturing touch by experimenting on ourselves (see exercise on page 52).

A child needs to be held and carried. He needs our sure, unwavering touch to feel safe and develop trust in the world. Breastfeeding is, without a doubt, a very intimate experience, and that is part of nature's plan. For children, it is certainly the best foundation for developing healthy love relationships in later life and for giving of oneself to life in general.

Perhaps because many of us did not experience healthy, natural closeness early in life, we find more taboos surrounding physical contact in our culture than in most parts of the world. Touch and closeness set off great anxiety in many people. But all of us, children as well as adults, have a biological need for physical closeness and touch. Without it, we atrophy emotionally.

Touch can enliven us, break down emotional blocks and help maintain or establish physical, emotional and spiritual balance. It also balances our hormonal system. Even resistance to infections and other illnesses, far beyond babyhood, seems to be enhanced by early-childhood skin stimulation.

In his observations of children in an orphanage in the 1940s, psychologist René Spitz verified the effects of insufficient social contact: Children who experienced little social contact were much weaker and were more prone to die of normally nonthreatening childhood illnesses. Those who did thrive were all charming in some way that motivated their nurses to pay more attention to them.

Nurses in progressive hospitals have heeded the insight that social and physical contact is important to general health and well-being. They are starting to carry babies who are hospitalized for long periods in baby carriers close to their bodies while doing their work. Parents are encouraged to carry their babies also. Premature, breastfed babies who are carried gain weight faster compared to supplemented babies and tend to go home sooner.

Breastfeeding is, without a doubt, a very intimate experience, and that is part of nature's plan. . . . All of us, children as well as adults, have a biological need for physical closeness and touch. Without it, we atrophy emotionally.

With breastfeeding, intensive body contact happens in a natural way. The baby feels Mommy's skin and takes in her scent. The baby also hears Mom's heartbeat, a steady sound she associates with being in the womb. Hearing the heartbeat seems to have a calming effect. Many mothers notice their babies do better on the left side and prefer to hold them near the heart. Some babies even refuse to nurse on the right breast.

The first year of a baby's life is, in a way, an extension of the pregnancy and a transitional time for the child. She has left the coziness and warmth of the womb but stays connected to Mom a little while longer through breastfeeding before detaching at her own pace.

Fear of Spoiling

A common belief about child rearing was this (and still is, to some extent): A child has to learn life is hard—the earlier, the better! A mother is not supposed to respond to her child's whims; that might spoil him. A smack on the bottom at birth, babies crying for hours in the newborn nursery—that was routine everywhere until a few years ago. And at home, if the child woke up crying, it was "best to close the door and let him cry it out a few times— he'll learn eventually." Some parents told themselves, "After all, we turned out OK, and we were treated the same way."

Every father and every mother has to decide if this is how he or she wants to rear his or her child. It may be true we were treated this way ourselves and still managed to become halfway-decent human beings. But perhaps many of us can still sense the pain caused by too much frustration and loneliness during childhood. Or we may still recall the deep bliss Mommy's closeness, warmth and consolation meant back then.

It is *not true* you can spoil your child with too much love. Genuine, unconditional love, generously and freely offered, gives a child a sense of security and trust in the world. He will actually become independent more quickly and easily later. He will learn to love, to be considerate of others and to give. He learns by example. Many parents confirm the sometimes "high investment" they made during the first years of their child's life paid off if only because the children were so easy to handle later on. The parents themselves could derive much more joy from their children than some others who did not "invest" as much at the outset.

> If you love your baby and it hurts to see him suffer, if you really want to understand his "language" and perceive his needs when he cries, then give your baby all the closeness, love and attention you believe he needs. Don't let anyone make you feel insecure about your decision. Be guided by your inner voice and your natural instincts.

Most little "tyrants"—the spoiled children we hear so much about—have quite a different life and love history. If they receive too little attention, body contact and response to their crying in the first few months of life, they may develop an ambivalent relationship to human contact. These babies may not like to be carried, but they may protest if they are put down. They may not know what to do with themselves, become fussy and dissatisfied. As they get older and better able to express themselves, these little ones get on their parents' nerves. Then parents try to spoil them retroactively. At best they do this by giving their children more love and closeness, but more often they only supply material things, such as toys, candy, clothing and money. These are poor substitutes for love.

On the other hand, not everyone finds the balance between loving and smothering easily. Trying *too hard* to be a perfect parent can lead to a lot of stress and tension. Then it's easy to overreact and overstimulate a baby instead of offering him a natural love and closeness. A little distance at times may be more appropriate than the constant closeness of an overanxious mother or father.

A relationship with a child is an intense form of human contact. Prepare yourself for the fact you will not always have *only* loving feelings! The same difficulties you incur in relationships with other people are also likely to pop up in your relationship with your child. But normally you have neither the possibility nor the desire to separate if you don't get along. You *have* to find a way to live with each other.

The following account of one couple, whose first child was born in China, may help you reflect on the fear in our society of spoiling children, and offer you encouragement:

> If we allowed Helen to cry in her bed for even a moment, our "ayi" (mother's helper) was nearly beside herself with indignation. Our neighbors and friends also believed a baby should not be allowed to cry; it would be cruel. Repeatedly we observed how the Chinese responded very positively to all their babies' wishes. Here it would be called "spoiling" a child. When a baby is hungry, he will naturally eat; so the child determines when he is breastfed. If he cries for other reasons, he is comforted and carried around. Most babies are routinely rocked to sleep in the arms of a caregiver. If the baby cries at night, there are no complaints; more likely, the neighbors ask what's wrong and offer to help.

> Turning one of our four rooms into a nursery caused astonishment, even indignation. "Why does such a small child need a room of her own?" visitors would ask. They felt sorry for this small helpless person who, hardly born, was left to herself. Chinese babies are almost never left alone.

*The most fundamental difference in caring for children [there]
lies in the attitude toward the child and less in individual childrearing methods or other details. Children are taken seriously in
China. Adults are usually just as polite to them as they are to
each other, and don't use a different tone with them—neither
patronizing nor harsh. You seldom see shy children. Children
are often entrusted with difficult tasks, and it is amazing what
they accomplish.*

*But children also have rights. For instance, they have the right
to an explanation of why something is required of them. They
have the right to disagree. Children are expected to behave in a
disciplined way, but on the other hand, they are not subjected to
raw authoritarianism. I've always been surprised at the
patience with which parents discuss differences of opinion with
their children, when it would have been so much easier to issue
a command.*

Old Ways Are Changing

Despite continuing resistance against breastfeeding in many areas,
the pendulum has undoubtedly started to swing back in favor of
breastfeeding. In the past, healthcare providers caring for mothers
pre- or postpartum seldom were trained in breastfeeding matters.
They had few sources of information available to help them. As a
result, they were often at a loss themselves when faced with breastfeeding problems. Now professionals have wonderful resources,
such as Ruth Lawrence's *Breastfeeding: A Guide for the Medical
Profession* (1994) and Jan Riordan's and Kathleen Auerbach's
Breastfeeding and Human Lactation (1993). Workshops for professionals are available, too.

Increasing awareness and training opportunities are slowly
bringing about higher breastfeeding standards in hospitals.
Breastfeeding is becoming a matter of course for more women. The
staff in many hospitals are much better trained now; for example,
in techniques for getting a baby to the breast, in solving sucking
and nipple-confusion problems, and in knowing supportive measures that help mothers. Often International Board-Certified
Lactation Consultants (IBCLC) are hired to teach and assist new
mothers. Women who want to nurse can get help; by phone, from
support groups or even on the Internet from other mothers who
have breastfed successfully.

Since 1978, the U.S. government has strongly encouraged and supported breastfeeding practices. The government has had the help of multidisciplinary task forces, a national committee for the promotion of breastfeeding, the formation of The Healthy Mothers, Healthy Babies Coalition and the federal WIC (Women, Infants and Children) program. The government goal by the year 2000 is for half of all mothers to breastfeed their babies until they are 5 to 6 months old. Health Canada has launched a nationwide "Breastfeeding Friendly" campaign to promote breastfeeding as socially acceptable and to help create "breastfeeding friendly" public places in communities across Canada.

The professional associations of all the major healthcare providers, such as the American Academy of Pediatrics, are committed to putting more effort into breastfeeding education in their curricula. At the University of Rochester School of Medicine and Dentistry, its federally funded Lactation Study Center provides information to healthcare professionals through a telephone hotline. In Canada, a number of hospitals across the country offer breastfeeding clinics or education programs to women with babies.

Private initiatives have started as well: The National Alliance for Breastfeeding Advocacy represents breastfeeding at a policy-making level. The Best Start Program promotes breastfeeding through well-designed campaigns. Wellstart International, with a clinically trained staff and a telephone helpline for brief inquiries and consultations, provides services to breastfeeding families, and lactation-management education programs for healthcare professionals. Pertinent addresses are in Appendix 1.

The American Academy of Pediatrics recommends breastfeeding for the first 12 months of a baby's life at least.

2

Getting Ready
to Breastfeed

T he first weeks with a little baby are strenuous, despite your joy
and happiness. You have to adapt to her rhythm, her needs,
and so many new, unfamiliar details. If you go into labor feeling tired, you are likely to burn out quickly during the first weeks of
your baby's life. Taking extra time for yourself during pregnancy is not
a luxury!

Stockpile Your Energy

Shift to a slower pace *before* the baby is born. Allow ample time for
rest, sleep and leisure (listening to soothing music, taking a walk,
enjoying nature)—for simply *being*. Build a store of tranquility,
peace and strength within you. Your preparation will have a positive effect on your relationship with your baby and on your let-
down reflex. A serene outlook during pregnancy may well have
positive effects on you and the baby in your womb.

Build a Support Network

Reliable information and solid support are key factors for women
who desire a natural, uninhibited breastfeeding experiece. For
some women, attending a childbirth-education class or a prenatal breastfeeding class supplies these important supports. You might

prefer to attend an informal breastfeeding support group instead, where you can learn by observing experienced mothers. These options are probably all available in your community; ask your healthcare practitioner for leads. Any of them will give you practical, detailed instruction about putting a baby to the breast.

But support can come from a number of different organizations and people who support breastfeeding mothers. Choose the places and the professionals who can best help *you*.

Who Mothers the Mother? Finding a Doula

Mothers used to be cared for by their extended family. But families are much smaller and less connected now. Many mothers feel isolated and overwhelmed, even abandoned, after they have a baby. You, your baby and your partner can always use additional help around the home as you get to know each other.

In most countries, women in the community commonly help mothers during the first days after the baby's birth. Their job is to "mother the mother," supporting her and looking after her needs so she can give her baby the kind of love and care she is receiving herself. The mother's primary job in those first days is to devote herself to establishing a relationship with her child, to adjust and be available to the baby.

Today, a new professional has emerged who is dedicated to mothering mothers before, during and after birth. They call themselves *doulas*, a Greek word that means *of service*. Perhaps you can find a doula, even for a short time, who can facilitate your relationship with your child in the first days. It's important, because getting acquainted in a relaxed way with your baby will help your milk flow.

Doulas are available throughout North America. You can find information about doulas on the Internet at various parenting sites or by contacting DONA (Doulas of North America) at www.dona.com, or by calling a 24-hour information line to leave a message: (206) 324-5440 (see page 258). You can also contact the Association of Labor Assistants and Childbirth Educators for referrals at 1(888) 22-ALACE.

About La Leche League

The original La Leche League (LLL) group was founded in the mid-1950s, when seven women talking together at a picnic realized they could support each other's efforts at a time when the social climate was hostile toward breastfeeding.

The seven Founding Mothers, as they became known, read and collected all the relevant scientific material about breastfeeding they could find. Soon they became experts. Living in a puritanical environment, they wanted to avoid the word "breast," so they gave their group the somewhat poetic name *La Leche League*, using the Spanish word for *milk*. At the time, they had no idea their work would have such an impact and that some 40 years later, more than 32,000 LLL leaders would follow in their footsteps in 66 countries around the world.

Breastfeeding Support Groups

It's a good idea to visit a breastfeeding support group while you are still pregnant. You will be welcome. Breastfeeding role models weren't always available when we were growing up. At a breast-feeding group, women see how other women actually breastfeed, naturally and matter-of-factly. They hear about difficulties that were overcome and develop confidence they will manage, too. Many mothers relax knowing they can phone the group leader or another experienced breastfeeding mother at any time if they run into difficulties.

> *If I hadn't gone to a La Leche League meeting before the birth and seen that other women had problems with breastfeeding too and they managed . . . I probably would have given up after a week!*

The Tenth Step in the WHO Statement on Successful Breastfeeding (see page 5) says: "Foster the establishment of breastfeeding sup-port groups and refer mothers to them on discharge from the hospital or clinic." The United States has almost 3,000 active La Leche League (LLL) groups and Canada has almost 300. Other informal groups for breastfeeding mothers exist in both countries as well (see page 257).

La Leche League's recommendations rest on the research of a qualified, scientific advisory board and the experience of many, many mothers. Today, with the American Academy of Pediatrics and the American College of Obstetrics and Gynecology, La Leche League co-sponsors annual seminars on breastfeeding topics for physicians. They also conduct seminars for lactation specialists.

Every month, LLL-trained leaders—mothers who have themselves breastfed and are knowledgeable about breastfeeding—run open meetings for pregnant and breastfeeding mothers where women can learn, mother to mother. Babies and older children are welcome. Watching other mothers and sharing experiences strengthens many women's confidence in their ability to breastfeed and helps them overcome any hurdles they face.

Perhaps these support groups are really just a wonderful substitute for the extended family.

La Leche League has also created pamphlets on just about all topics of interest to the nursing mother, as well as the excellent books, *The Womanly Art of Breastfeeding* (1997) and *The Breastfeeding Answer Book* (1997). Brochures are available through local LLL chapters. Books are available in your local library or bookstore.

In addition to La Leche League, other informal, community-based breastfeeding support groups are available to women who nurse. Public-health clinics and WIC offices frequently run these groups in the United States. Classes are often free of charge; some eligibility requirements may apply. New-mother support groups that include breastfeeding help and information are organized throughout Canada.

These groups provide help that goes far beyond breastfeeding support. By sharing information, mothers (and fathers) learn a natural kind of parenting from one another. Being part of these groups can help raise consciousness about what is healthy and right for new generations of mothers. Enriching friendships develop, experiences are shared, and the older babies present enjoy the company of their peers. Perhaps these groups are really just a wonderful substitute for the extended family. No wonder attendance has continued to grow for more than 40 years!

Learn about nearby breastfeeding group meetings from your childbirth educator, through the white pages, the library, the local paper or the Internet. Or call 1-800-LA LECHE in the United States. In Canada, contact the Infant Feeding Action Coalition

(INFACT) at (416) 595-9819. Nothing replaces direct, personal contact; but when it isn't possible, parents can exchange ideas, information and advice on the Internet, from reading stories about other people's breastfeeding experiences to participating in online LLL meetings. Yes, friendships and support can come from the 'net! (See page 257.)

Lactation Consultants: Help in Special Situations

The United States trained the first lactation consultants in 1985. Consultants were certified through an examination sponsored by the International Board of Lactation Consultant Examiners (IBLCE). Today more than 5000 certified lactation consultants (IBCLC) work around the world. They come from medical and social-service professions; they work in hospitals and in private practice. Consultants serve as routine, postpartum support persons and as on-call specialists for emergency problems. Some are La Leche League leaders. They offer professional help with breastfeeding, especially if disease or some other special health condition is involved. More and more hospitals hire lactation consultants for staff positions. Professional help is also available privately in cases for which even the leader of a breastfeeding group can't help (see page 257 for addresses).

Getting Your Breasts Ready

To prepare for breastfeeding, you will want to prepare your body physically.

Keep Nipples Supple

Avoid substances that dry out your nipples during pregnancy and breastfeeding. Pimple-like bumps surrounding the areola release an oily substance that helps moisten and clean the nipples. Avoid soaping your nipples, because you may wash away this substance in the process. Clean nipples by rinsing them with clear water. Cold water promotes circulation in addition. Spraying your breasts with a massage-type showerhead daily is helpful—once you have gotten used to the cold water!

Follow by massaging your breasts with a mild lanolin cream, such as Lansinoh® for Breastfeeding Mothers, or with a natural oil, such as vitamin E (wheat germ) oil or a rejuvenating massage oil (see page 171). These precautions help keep skin around the breast supple and moisturized and may help prevent stretch marks. Once your baby is born, you can moisturize your nipples with nature's ready-made cream: colostrum and breast milk.

Make Nipples Less Sensitive

Breasts and nipples were made to be perfect for breastfeeding. Yet they have become extra-sensitive because they are normally packed away and protected in a bra. Women who don't wear bras usually have much more "tolerant" nipples because clothing rubs against them all the time.

However, breasts become heavy during pregnancy, and most women feel better with bra support. If you cut out a circular hole in the middle of each cup, your breasts will be supported but the nipples will be in contact with the clothing. (You can save yourself the expense of replacing bras with ever-larger cups if you switch to a nursing bra in the latter part of your pregnancy.) Women who experience rib changes and fat growth will need a comfortable, well-made maternity bra.

Carefully exposing your breasts to sunlight—perhaps in a sunny room—will also help make your breasts less sensitive.

Get Your Partner's Help

There is a simple, natural and pleasurable way to prepare your breasts for breastfeeding: Ask your partner for help. For many women, caressing of the breasts and kissing of the nipples is already an exciting and regular part of love play. Many women who enjoy having their breasts stimulated by their partner report they have few problems with breastfeeding or nipple soreness.

Note: *If you are having premature contractions (beyond the common Braxton-Hicks false labor) or are at risk for premature birth, avoid nipple stimulation.* The hormone that is released during nipple stimulation is the same hormone that triggers contractions. Watch for possible effects like this.

"Awaken" Your Breasts

Some women hesitate to touch their breasts. Depending on messages you received in childhood about this part of your body, you may have consciously or unconsciously "stayed away from" your breasts. You may treat them as if they are not quite part of your body.

Increased awareness of your breasts is helpful when breast-feeding starts. Pregnancy presents a good opportunity to become more familiar and comfortable with them. The following method, which I call *awakening your breasts*, is gentle and works very well for this purpose.

Turn your entire attention to your hands as described on page 52. "Awaken" your hands; let them become sensitive. Then lay them gently and nurturingly on one breast like this: Lay one hand above the breast and one hand below. Relax your shoulders (support your arm on a chair rest if you need to). Focus your inner awareness completely on your hands (particularly the centers of your palms) and on the breast they are touching.

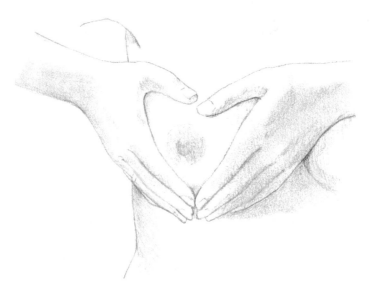

Breast massage using both hands.

The hands will "speak" to the breast, and the breast may "respond." If you give yourself enough time and stay focused on what you are doing, your breast may respond with warm or prickling sensations. It will feel as though it is coming alive—a desirable effect for breastfeeding. Now remove your hands and compare this breast with the other before you turn your attention to that one. Repeat the same steps on the second breast.

You might stimulate your breasts even more by gently and calmly making small, rhythmic, circular motions with your sensitive, attentive hand. *Don't* do this mechanically; meditate on the communication of touch going on between your hands and your breast. At the top of your breasts, it may be more comfortable to make these motions with the palms and base of your hand, while your fingertips may work better for stroking the sides and underside of your breasts.

Begin by making small circles at the base of the breast near the rib cage. Focus on one spot for a few circles, and then move on, spiraling toward the nipple. These motions move the skin and stretch underlying tissue, promoting circulation and supplying the cells with oxygen. You can also massage your breast from the base to the nipple with simple, slow and firm-but-gentle movements of both hands.

You can massage through clothing or directly on the skin. On the skin, use oil or cream, or dampen the breast with warm water. Ask yourself: *How does this feel? Can I enjoy this touch? Has my breathing become deeper and more peaceful?*

Inverted or Flat Nipples

> With my first two children, I was told I would not be able to breastfeed because of inverted nipples—nipples that sank into the breast instead of sticking out. During my third pregnancy I learned inverted nipples are not necessarily a barrier to breastfeeding if you allow a few weeks to prepare and train them. Now, with my third child, breastfeeding is going great.

Inverted or flat nipples are either congenital (present at birth) or develop during puberty. They may occur because of adhesions that shorten the milk ducts and pull the nipple inward (called *tied nipples*). Inverted or flat nipples can cause psychological problems and pose cleaning difficulties. If left untreated, they hinder breastfeeding if the baby can't grasp the nipple properly. If you suspect you might have this problem with your nipples, perform this easy test: Gently compress the edge of your areola with your thumb and index finger. A regular nipple stays erect; a flat nipple retracts. About one-third of all women have retracted or flat nipples.

A true inverted nipple is unmistakable. It "hides" in the breast or inverts if pressure is applied to it. If you think your nipples might be inverted, talk to your healthcare professional about it at a prenatal check-up, or check it with your La Leche League Leader at a meeting. Sometimes an experienced, well-latched-on baby can help pull out an inverted nipple, but it is wise to plan ahead and train the nipples for breastfeeding ahead of time, during pregnancy.

Nipple Shapes

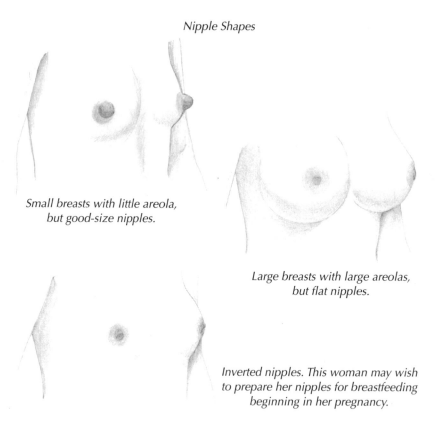

*Small breasts with little areola,
but good-size nipples.*

*Large breasts with large areolas,
but flat nipples.*

*Inverted nipples. This woman may wish
to prepare her nipples for breastfeeding
beginning in her pregnancy.*

> My nipple is the original folding model. For the most part it
> turns inward. If I press to the left and right of the areola, it
> jumps out. It was definitely worth the effort of preparing my
> nipples so I could finally breastfeed my child.

Breast shells (see Sources, page 262), also called *breast shields* or *milk cups*, can help prepare inverted or flat nipples for breastfeeding.

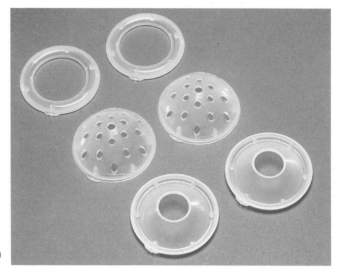

Hobbit™
Breastshells
(breast shields)

Breast shells are two dome-shaped, clear, hard, lightweight plastic shells, approximately 4 inches in diameter that screw together, one on top of the other. The inner shell, which is put over the breast, has a circular hole the nipple pokes through. The outer shell goes on top to fit over the nipple but allows air to circulate around it. Due to the steady pressure they place on the areola, breast shells help nipples "stand up." The nipples are "trained" to emerge.

From the fourth to the seventh month of pregnancy you can wear the shells inconspicuously. Wear a cup size large enough to accommodate the shells, yet snug enough to hold it in place. You can wear the shell a few hours a day at first, gradually increasing the time you spend wearing it.

Recently another simple and effective method has been developed to correct inverted nipples: the Niplette™ (illustration on next page; source, see page 262). This device stretches the adhered areas in the breast near the nipples with continuous, gentle suction. It can *permanently* correct inverted or flat nipples. The Niplette consists of a transparent nipple mold—in the approximate shape and size of a nipple—connected to a small tube. A valve on the other end of this tube is attached to a small suction pump. The

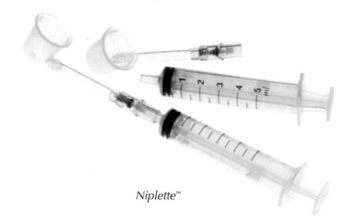

Niplette™

nipple mold is placed over the inverted nipple. With the help of the suction pump, air pressure is reduced in the little mold, drawing the nipple into it. You regulate the pressure.

Depending on your condition, you might use the Niplette for anywhere from three to twelve weeks, worn continuously for eight hours each day. This is easy to manage if you wear loose clothing during the day and don't sleep on your stomach at night. If both nipples are involved, it is recommended to use two Niplettes (a twin set). By the end of treatment, the nipples usually stand out enough to fill the mold. Then you only need to use the Niplette occasionally to correct the possible tendency in the beginning for the nipples to revert. Start this preparation as early as possible in the pregnancy, because the Niplette may not be used in the third trimester. It cannot be used for permanent correction while nursing because the leakage of milk will break the suction; however, the Niplette may be used to pop out the nipple to help baby latch on. You may also use a Niplette at any time before a pregnancy.

Often, if a mother has nipples that seem "questionable" for breastfeeding, she will be advised to place silicone or latex *nipple shields* over her own nipples for each breastfeeding—frequently without ever having tried it without the shields. While they do work for some women, nipple shields can greatly hinder breastfeeding or even spoil it.

> *Putting the baby to breast using nipple shields was a pain. I was always afraid I would forget the nipple shield when I was away from home and be in a real fix. Now we have managed without*

> *them, I really enjoy breastfeeding. It feels good, too—the touch*
> *of Sandra's mouth feels like a caress.*

But breastfeeding with nipple shields is still preferable to not breast-feeding at all.

> *Breastfeeding is nicer without the shields, of course. But when I*
> *had to choose—wean or breastfeed with shields—I opted for the*
> *latter. It was the best solution for both of us.*

Use nipple shields only when you have no other recourse. Nipple shields can cause problems for a variety of reasons: With them, the baby's tongue can't draw the nipple to the back of the throat, the breast isn't stimulated by skin contact, the let-down reflex is disturbed and the baby may become nipple-confused. In addition, the amount of milk a baby can take from the breast is reduced, depending on the type of nipple shield, from 22 to 58%. It is possible to start the feed with the nipple shield in place and then remove it after the milk is flowing.

Be sure the shields are made of the thinnest possible material, such as ultra-thin latex, so they will disturb you and the baby as lit-tle as possible. You can wean a baby from a latex nipple shield by cutting a hole in the tip, gradually increasing its size until the baby drinks directly from the breast. *Note:* This strategy won't work with silicone nipples because cutting them creates sharp edges.

Holistic Preparation for Breastfeeding

Now we have seen how to prepare your breasts for nursing. But I believe emotional, spiritual and social preparation is every bit as important. Perhaps it is even *more* important, because many breast-feeding problems are caused by emotional imbalance, stress, inse-curity or turmoil.

Gaining Confidence, Feeling Secure, Developing Strength

Too often women do not receive adequate support for breastfeed-ing. They are likely to be exposed to contradictory advice, too. For these reasons, it helps to be well informed about breastfeeding from the start, so no one can shake your confidence easily.

Positive thinking affects our body and our feelings. Remembering that *mothers throughout history have been able to breastfeed their babies* can help you develop trust in your own ability. If you deeply believe you can overcome all difficulties, this thought will empower and encourage you when problems do arise.

> *Without encouragement, I would have given up breastfeeding after three weeks. [I was] completely nerve-racked. You helped me feel secure in the awareness that breastfeeding is something totally natural, that no child operates according to plan (which is expected too often in the hospital) and that I could overcome any problem. Sonya's needs, for now, are my number-one priority.*

> *Your book contributed significantly to the calmness and clarity with which I could express my wishes in the hospital. In addition to all the valuable information, most of all I got the message, "I will be successful at breastfeeding if I want to be. With patience and love, it will work. It will be simple if I adjust myself first to the needs of this little being. She will tell me what she needs!"*

Realistic Expectations

The media like to portray beaming mothers with smiling babies. So motherhood is always sheer delight, right? Of course not! Yes, becoming a mother is one of the most amazing transition periods of our lives. The old is gone forever, and something completely new and still unfamiliar is coming into being.

However, for many, the transition to parenthood feels like an emotional roller coaster: one day up on Cloud Nine, the next day down in the dumps. Feelings of infinite bliss and inexpressible joy can alternate with feelings of anxiety, insecurity, exhaustion and of being overwhelmed by it all. *All these emotions are normal.* To some extent our feelings are determined by our hormonal state. We go up and down with our hormone levels. Some problems with breastfeeding may come from excessively high expectations and an exaggerated sense of failure when we do not meet the unrealistic demands we set for ourselves. Pressure to succeed is detrimental to breastfeeding.

Pressure to succeed is detrimental to breastfeeding.

To offset this tendency, you might let yourself be guided by the following messages:

- It is normal for my feelings to fluctuate.
- I do not have to have very strong motherly feelings right away.
- *It's OK* if my child seems like a stranger at first, especially if the bonding process at birth was inhibited for some reason (for example, medication).
- Bonding and love are allowed to grow gradually. I can allow myself time to get used to my baby, and give my baby time to get used to me.
- I do not have to have everything under control. *It is OK* to let everyday obligations slip for something that is a higher priority now.
- I can accept help from other people graciously. Rest is no luxury!

Harmonizing Body, Mind and Spirit

Our physical body is the "home" of thoughts and feelings, just as our brain is. We retain all kinds of past experiences in our body. Some are negative: Injuries, distortions, deficits in our personal history, stress, unfriendly and inappropriate attitudes and behaviors directed toward us—all inhibit our emotions and our power. We may have become "closed" to people or experience—or to parts of ourselves. Our bodies may have become deadened in some areas, and our breath flow inhibited, sometimes reduced to a bare minimum.

Babies are influenced by and react to how their parents feel, which all of us express through our body and our breath. If you are comfortable with your body and feel in harmony with your surroundings, your baby will benefit. If you are not, it makes a lot of sense to turn lovingly to your own body, during pregnancy at the latest, and try to increase that sense of harmony. I suggest trying some of the holistic exercises and practices in this book (see page 49). Pregnancy holds great potential for personal growth, change and transformation, another good reason to consider experimenting with harmonizing exercises now.

We would all do well to take our cue from babies themselves. Babies express themselves largely through their bodies at first. The more *you* are in touch with your own body, the more you can tune into and develop sensitivity and empathy for your baby. When *you* experience your own body and movements as pleasurable, it will be easy for you to allow your child to enjoy his body and his movements with happy awareness too, in a natural, comfortable way.

Many forms of holistic therapies or practices work through the body to bring harmony to mind, emotions and spirit. In addition to those mentioned in chapter 9, you may find Feldenkrais®, Trager Bodywork®, acupuncture, foot reflexology, yoga for pregnancy, belly dance for pregnant women, expressive dance, dance therapy, movement therapy or others offered in your area. Because babies are sensitive to our breath and experience us through it, Middendorf Breathwork®—or any other work that helps harmonize and free breath flow—can be especially valuable. Some of the exercises in this book (for example, on page 49) are derived from Middendorf Breathwork, in which I am trained. Breathwork practices are not about learning breathing techniques; rather, they are about helping us get back to our own natural breath essence, which has a deep, self-healing power and can help dissolve tensions at a deep level.

One emphasis of Middendorf Breathwork is touch, which can help bring breath movement to whatever area is touched. As you experiment with giving yourself nurturing touch, you also prepare for nurturing your baby. In a long-term research study I participated in, I became aware of the tremendous importance of the *quality* of touch for the development of the baby's sense of physical self and his basic sense of trust. Even during pregnancy, you can learn to "awaken" and sensitize your hands, and you will be ready to provide the kind of nurturing touch a baby thrives on (see page 52).

You might nurture and be nurtured by exchanging an intuitive partner massage with your mate. Obtain a book with detailed instructions, or be guided by intuition. Aromatherapy, discussed in greater detail on page 170, can also help you harmonize body, mind and spirit.

What Happens When You Breastfeed?

E very woman has milk in her breasts after the birth of her baby. With few exceptions, every woman could actually breastfeed. Yet sometimes women who want to breastfeed seem unable to do so. Our ability to breastfeed has not degenerated, so why does this happen? Breastfeeding trouble has to do with some fairly concrete, correctable matters:

- insecurity
- lack of trust in ourselves
- lack of positive support
- lack of an understanding of how breastfeeding works

Knowing more about your body and how it works will certainly help you approach breastfeeding with trust and confidence.

Changes during Pregnancy

Most women get the first hint they are pregnant from changes in their breasts. Breasts become harder and fuller; the nipples become more sensitive to touch. Due to increased blood flow, the veins become more prominent and are clearly visible under the skin. The areola becomes larger and darker, and the sebaceous glands in it become more prominent and secrete oil. (The oil keeps the areola supple and protects it during breastfeeding.) Pregnant women find they will need larger bras no later than the fifth month—and often an even larger size by the ninth month. You may get stretch marks, even if you apply cream to your breasts regularly.

From the sixth week of pregnancy, hormones are produced in the placenta of the mammary tissue. You can visualize all this tissue as a "shrub" with 15 to 20 "branches" that come out of the nipple area (areola). When you were an adolescent, only small "shoots" sprouted. Stimulated by the hormones of pregnancy, "branches" (milk ducts) now develop. Smaller branches (*ductules*) sprout from the main branches and are covered with tree-like "fruit" (milk-producing alveoli).

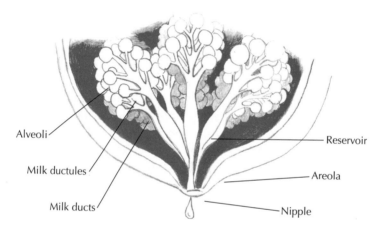

Alveoli

Milk ductules

Milk ducts

Reservoir

Areola

Nipple

The lactating breast

In the second half of pregnancy, prolactin—the milk-producing hormone—is released into the body. It stimulates the alveoli to produce small amounts of milk. The size of the breast is not significant. When the placenta is expelled after birth, the hormones that have maintained the pregnancy drop suddenly, allowing prolactin to flow freely. From this point on, the baby's sucking determines how much milk will be produced.

How the Body Produces Milk

When the baby sucks at the breast, he stimulates nerve endings in the nipple and areola. That signals the brain to produce prolactin. Prolactin encourages the alveoli to secrete milk. At first the baby drinks the milk that has flowed between meals from the alveoli to the main mammary ducts. These ducts broaden at the lower end under the areola, and milk collects into reservoirs (also called *lactiferous sinuses*).

With time, these 15 to 25 reservoirs stretch a bit and can hold more milk. An "overdose" of prolactin at birth can cause a temporary overproduction of milk at first. Fortunately, pain and engorgement can be prevented with early and frequent breastfeeding. Gradually supply adapts to demand.

The baby usually doesn't empty the breast entirely. Normally she drinks about 80% of what's available; the remaining 20% is reserved for times of great thirst. *At six weeks and again at twelve weeks, children often have growth spurts.* Then they *do* empty the breast completely—a signal to the body to produce the usual amount *plus* a 20% reserve. The production of milk during a feeding is caused by prolactin stimulation and by sucking pressure. One hour after feeding, 40% of the total amount is available again and can be called upon as needed.

> Prolactin levels change throughout the day and the milk supply varies considerably. Prolactin levels are highest early in the morning.

The Let-Down Reflex

When the baby breastfeeds, first she drinks the milk that has collected in the milk ducts and reservoirs since the last feeding (the foremilk). The foremilk might be called *the thirst-quenching appetizer*. This milk is fairly watery and low in fat.

Some oxytocin is released when the mother turns her thoughts to breastfeeding. While the child sucks, through the touch of her mouth, more oxytocin and prolactin are released in the mother's body. Oxytocin causes the alveoli, stimulated to make fresh, fat-rich milk by the prolactin, to contract and pump milk into the smaller branches. Milk is pushed through the milk ducts

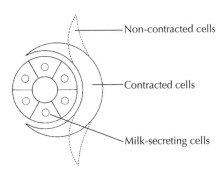

Non-contracted cells

Contracted cells

Milk-secreting cells

The let-down reflex makes cells contract around the alveoli, which forces milk out through the milk ducts into the reservoirs.

into the reservoirs and becomes available to the sucking baby. Sometimes the baby's sucking is so strong the milk gushes out of the nipple, and the baby is overwhelmed by the abundance.

Fat-rich milk, called *hindmilk*, is the baby's main meal. It has significantly more fat and calories than the foremilk. Now the baby can drink all she wants.

A baby should remain at the breast until her sucking has slowed and she seems satisfied. When she is put to the other breast, the foremilk and hindmilk have mixed. The let-down reflex—also called the *milk-ejection reflex*—works simultaneously in both breasts. The baby gets "dessert" most easily from the second breast.

The let-down reflex is necessary for the baby to get enough milk and enough calories. Without it, hindmilk is not available. Now you can understand why it is so important to let your child stay on the breast. The hardest work for the baby is sucking until the let-down reflex occurs. After that he can consume a high-quality meal with relatively little effort. Baby may signal he is full by spitting out Mom's nipple!

The hardest work for the baby is sucking until the let-down reflex occurs. After that he can consume a high-quality meal with relatively little effort.

If babies are taken off the breast too soon—for instance, because the mother or hospital staff are worried about nipple problems—they will still be hungry after breastfeeding, and also the breast will remain full. This can cause problems. The following signs may mean a baby is getting too much foremilk and not enough hindmilk. Baby

- ❧ passes a greenish, liquid stool (This can also mean the baby has an infection.)
- ❧ is fussy at the breast and between meals (Or it may mean he has gas.)
- ❧ does not show a steady increase in weight over time, averaging 100g a week (about 3-1/2 ounces).

Breastfeeding women may experience the let-down reflex as a tingling in the breast (like tiny needle pricks) or as a warm feeling that streams throughout the body. Milk flows freely from 30 seconds to three full minutes after the baby starts sucking, and it may take longer with some newborns. At the beginning of the feed your baby will suck chaotically, in an uncoordinated way. Then, when the let-down reflex occurs, his sucking will slow down and become more rhythmic. His body relaxes. You can actually hear the milk spray into the back of his throat.

Many women experience a smooth let-down from the very first feeding. Others wait weeks before this easily disturbed system functions reliably. Excitement and emotional crises can disturb even a smoothly functioning reflex. Some mothers, though, appear to have a natural talent—their reflex works like clockwork, independent of outside circumstances.

Once breastfeeding is well established, thoughts of the baby or the sight or cry of another baby may cause your milk to flow. (Although it has been many years since I breastfed, I sometimes still feel contractions in my breast when I write or read about breastfeeding).

Should the let-down reflex happen at an inappropriate time, you can stop the milk by pressing your hand against your breast for a moment.

Excitement, anxiety, stress, insecurity, inhibition or lack of self-confidence inhibit the release of oxytocin. Without oxytocin, the alveoli do not contract, and most of the milk waiting in the breast isn't made available to the baby. An inner rejection of breastfeeding, unconscious ambivalence about parenting and other conflicts can have similar effects and may interfere with lactation.

Outside Influences Affecting the Let-Down Reflex

The late Dr. Niles Newton, together with her husband, Dr. Michael Newton, discovered the important connection between the let-down reflex and breastfeeding success. For women who feel vulnerable right after birth, a few disparaging words can mean the difference between continuing or stopping breastfeeding. A negative atmosphere directly affects the let-down reflex.

As the report below shows, other people's comments can greatly influence a woman's ability to breastfeed:

> It was a storybook birth. Lisa found her way to my breast shortly after delivery, stimulating my milk production. I had rooming-in and was well-supported by the nursing staff, who were helpful except for one nurse: "Either you have milk or you don't," she would say. I would not let myself be talked out of what I knew—that if I put my baby to the breast

frequently, I would soon have plenty of milk. It was interesting that the quantity of my milk varied depending on which nurse was around me during feedings.

The babies were weighed periodically before and after feedings. "Not even an ounce," the discouraging nurse commented. "Honey, she took three ounces!" another nurse exclaimed. I could have hugged her. When I got home, I called a La Leche League Leader, who assured me again I would have enough milk within 48 hours as long as I put my baby to my breast every time she was hungry.

A warm shower before breastfeeding really helped me relax. The first two days Lisa seemed to need to suck constantly. We spent the day on the couch while Martin fed me snacks and huge quantities of fluid. Whenever I doubted whether our tiny daughter got enough and whether I really didn't need to weigh her, a call to La Leche League reassured me.

Fortunately, awareness continues to grow. When people are aware of how their words and attitudes affect breastfeeding success, they are more likely to encourage women and help instill confidence and self-trust. When early problems present themselves, caregivers can reassure the new mother it may take a while for mom and baby to get to know each other and find a balance. Caregivers can make it clear the milk supply varies at first but there will *definitely* be more milk with each passing day.

Everyone who is close to a mother can have a significant influence on the breastfeeding relationship in some way. A woman's own mother is certainly influential. Grandmother's experience when she breastfed can affect her daughter's experience. She needs to be aware of her special influence and careful not to abuse it. The let-down reflex can also be strongly inhibited when friends

I became aware of the strong influence a counselor's conviction and certitude has in my early days of telephone counseling in the 1970s. As long as my advice was purely theoretical (I personally had had no problems with an insufficient milk supply), my voice showed my uncertainty, and my suggestions sounded half-hearted. As I became more experienced and was able to tell mothers confidently that they would certainly have enough milk if they breastfed often for two days, according to the baby's demand, the success rate rose to nearly 100%.

who have had negative breastfeeding experiences alarm a new mother with stories of breast infections and sore nipples. Worries can turn into self-fulfilling prophecies. *The more informed you are, the less dependent you will be on comments from others.* The more anxious and unsure you are, the more likely it is that others' opinions and comments will throw you off balance.

The Partner's Role

The most important figure for a breastfeeding mother is her partner. He holds the key to her ultimate success or failure. If he has a negative attitude toward nursing, the situation can threaten the breastfeeding relationship. Sometimes men are worried about their partner's "good figure," are disgusted by breast milk, see the breast as "their toy" or are just plain jealous. Even when partners don't express their feelings overtly, women can sense their rejection. This knowledge can affect the let-down reflex so profoundly that breastfeeding becomes a problem in every way. As a breastfeeding counselor, I discovered many problems of "not enough milk" turned out to be relationship problems.

You may be able to prevent a situation like this from developing. Plan to discuss breastfeeding with your partner during the pregnancy. Talk openly about your feelings and anxieties, particularly as they affect your relationship. A partner who is well-informed about breastfeeding and supports your efforts fully is a huge help. Whenever critical comments from others threaten to negatively influence you, he can encourage and strengthen you.

Inhibited Let-Down Reflex

Many breastfeeding problems—sore nipples, engorgement and breast infection—start with a malfunctioning let-down reflex. If the let-down reflex is inhibited, the baby can only drink milk available in the milk ducts and reservoirs. That is one-third of what should be available. The remaining two-thirds—the freshly made milk—is unavailable. The breast gets tight and heavy because so much milk is left in the breast. Pressure increases in the ductal tissue. Milk ducts press against each other and that reduces milk production.

This condition leads to hard, painful breasts, which can hurt during breastfeeding. Pain leads to tension, which inhibits the let-down reflex still more. A vicious cycle begins. Only a few drops of milk flow out of the engorged breasts when the mother breastfeeds or pumps. She gets no relief for her effort.

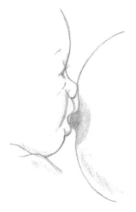

Because the mammary glands
have swollen, the nipples
become difficult to grasp.

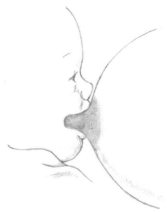

When the breast is softer, the
baby can grasp the nipple and
part of the areola easily.

For her part, the baby has difficulty drinking properly from an engorged breast. She can no longer latch onto the breast and take nipple *and* areola into her mouth. At best, she can grasp the tip of the nipple—but she cannot exert pressure on the milk reservoirs beneath the areola. Added to this, the baby may be held and positioned inappropriately (see page 68 for correct positioning).

Because the swollen breasts are so full, the baby has difficulty breathing and gradually gets frustrated, which makes his mother even more anxious. Hungry and eager, the baby chews and sucks at the front of the nipple. Soon cracks and crevices develop. The nipples hurt even more.

Now germs can get in into the cracks and multiply in the backed-up milk: A breast infection starts. If not recognized and treated in time, a breast infection may lead to mastitis. In rare cases, an abscess results (see Breast Infection, page 113).

Breast infections are extremely uncomfortable and painful. They can make breastfeeding so unpleasant that women may be discouraged to try again with subsequent babies. We must try not to get into this vicious cycle or at least to interrupt it as early as possible. As you will see in chapter 6, such problems are easily prevented.

Triggering and Conditioning the Let-Down Reflex

You can positively condition the let-down reflex through certain actions that will become routine; for example, have a glass of water available at each meal to ensure that your increased need for fluid is met, or place a warm, damp washcloth on your breast before nursing. You could place your hand nurturingly on your breast and be totally present and attentive under your hands for several minutes (see page 52). You could make soft, circling motions along the edge of the breast, or massage your dampened breasts with firm but sensitive touch, moving from the breastbone toward the nipple (see page 32). Expressing a little milk by hand helps milk flow freely and also protects your nipples.

All these measures, carried out regularly at the beginning of breastfeeding, ensure that the let-down reflex functions ever faster and more reliably. At some point, even the thought of your baby will trigger it.

Twenty-Three Ways to Enhance Your Milk Flow

The first days and weeks after birth can be pretty stressful. Everything is so new, so unfamiliar, so different. Before you know it, tension can build up, throw you off balance and inhibit your milk flow. If you can find ways to release these tensions, open yourself up and "give of yourself," then milk will flow freely. Easier said than done! Perhaps you already know your very own ways to relax. But in times of stress, even the simplest possibilities may not come to mind. So here are some ideas.

Whenever you need to center, harmonize, relax, calm or energize yourself, look at this list. Then close your eyes and bring your awareness to the flow of your breath. Just be with your breath. Then open your eyes and let yourself be drawn to the activity that is good and feasible for you right now. Trust your inner knowing to be aware of your needs. Whatever you choose, let it be preceded by the first exercise below—stretching.

You may want to record directions for specific exercises on an audiocassette or let someone with a soothing voice record them for you. Exercises marked with an asterisk (*) can also be done with your baby in your arms.

Enhancing Your Breath Flow

Our breath is affected by and affects all other aspects in us. It is interconnected with heart rate, muscles, nerves, organs, emotions and thoughts, hormones as well as the flow of all liquids in the body, including the flow of milk. Therefore, helping to free our natural breath movement can greatly enhance breastfeeding and reduce stress.

❧ * Stretching is a simple but immensely useful exercise. Make it part of your day. Whenever you feel yourself getting tense, gently and naturally stretch and extend yourself as a cat would. As you stretch, notice how this triggers your breath to flow in all by itself. As you let go of the extension, notice how your breath flows out. Allow a natural, short breath pause, and then allow your body to lead you spontaneously into the next extension. Let breath and movement find each other.

What other parts of your body are calling you? Your extremities aren't the only parts that enjoy a stretch. Your joints—hands, elbows and shoulder joints, your jaw joint, ankle joint and the individual vertebral joints of your spinal column—often need special attention. The back, shoulders and neck are usually especially needy when we are under stress. Stretching parts of your face and even widening the inside of your mouth (watch for its effects on the rest of your body!) might make you feel good. *Be careful not to overextend yourself*, because that makes parts of your body become hard and rigid, which is counterproductive. As a matter of fact, tiny movements can be even more effective than larger ones—and you can do those even with your baby on the breast. Don't let the movements become automatic; instead, be "present" in that part of your body where stretching happens. Bring your entire awareness there.

Most important: After stretching, as after any of the following breath exercises, allow yourself a moment to listen inside your body and "harvest" what you have gained through stretching. Pay attention to how your breath has changed and how you may feel wider and more alive in some parts of you. Does your body signal you to address other needs in other parts of your body? If so, obey those signals.

If you start yawning after this and other movement, do not suppress it. Allow it to rise from your gut and allow your mouth to open wide. Yawning is a natural sign of release and is regenerating. *Maybe now you feel more alive, more relaxed, more calm or spacious inside? Does your breath flow more easily?*

❦ * Shake off stress and exhaustion and stimulate your circulation by bouncing gently on the balls of your feet. Stand with feet parallel, about one foot apart, or as far apart as feels comfortable. Relax your knees and let the weight of your body shift forward a bit, over one foot at first. Begin to gently and rhythmically bounce up and down—raising and lowering your heels softly to the ground. (Important: If you get cramps in your calves, your heels may not be returning to the floor). Shift your weight from one side to the other as you bounce rhythmically. Try to release and let go of tensions in your ankles, knees, hip joints, spinal column, shoulders and neck. Your movements may be large or small, meditative or lively as the spirit moves you. "Shake off" whatever bothers or preoccupies you. Give yourself time to feel what may have changed inside you. Listen inside and ask yourself: *How is my breath now? Do I feel a little lighter? Was I able to shake off some of the burden I feel simply because everything is so unfamiliar?*

❦ While the baby is sleeping, take some time to nurture yourself. The exercise I call "letting yourself be carried" can have a powerful, symbolic effect that extends into other realms of your life. You may want to record the following instructions on tape. With this exercise you can feel the powerful impact of mental messages on your body and therefore on your emotions and your whole being. The change is reflected in the quality of your breath.

1. Lie on your back, with your head resting comfortably on a pillow (do not tilt back your head). Rest your arms alongside your body, palms down. Keep the room warm or cover yourself. If you want to, close your eyes to experience this exercise more intensely. Focus on your breath without altering it. Through your skin, clothing and the blanket, notice your contact to the surface you are lying on. Be aware that you are supported by it.

2. Tell yourself in your mind: "I, (your name), *am letting myself be carried.*" Starting with your feet, focusing first on one foot, wander through your body and take time to experience deeply how in every part of you, you are being carried by whatever you lie on. "*I let my right foot be carried, I let myself be carried in my ankle (even though it may not touch the ground) . . . in my right lower leg, in my knee* (imagine the ground reaching up and gently wrapping around and 'cuddling' your knee) *. . . in my right thigh—I let my entire leg and*

foot be carried." Take a moment to perceive your right leg and foot in comparison to the other side. How does it feel different from the other? Does it perhaps feel bigger—or warmer? Perhaps heavier or lighter? Or . . . ? Then turn your attention to your left foot: *"I let my left foot be carried . . . my ankle . . . my lower leg . . . my knee, my left thigh—the entire left leg and foot. . . ."* How does this side feel? How do both legs feel now in comparison to the rest of your body? Are they balanced again?

3. Continue: *"I let my pelvic area be carried: . . . my sacrum (the broad, bony plate on the lower back) . . . my buttocks . . . the small of my back—the lumbar region (the ground 'cuddles up' to that part of me, too) . . . the middle of my back, my ribs and torso . . . my upper back and shoulder blades . . . the shoulders. I let my right upper arm . . . my elbow . . . my right forearm . . . my right hand be carried (compare arms) —then my left upper arm . . . my elbow . . . my left forearm . . . my left hand. . . . I let my neck be carried by the ground, letting the ground 'cuddle' my neck as well. I let my head be carried and cradled by the ground and the pillow as if cupped by warm, welcoming hands."* Now let yourself experience how your entire body, from head to toe, is being carried by the surface that supports you, surrendering yourself to that experience. *Has your breath changed? Has it deepened in some way? Has your breath become more peaceful? Are you aware of how your breath comes and goes?* Perhaps you notice a brief pause before the next breath—in . . . out . . . pause—an eternal flow of breath. You may feel regenerated now; nerves that were raw may be soothed. When you have had enough, stretch yourself and get up slowly, maintaining your heightened awareness.

Nurturing Touch and Massage

ℰ When you expect the next breastfeeding session to come fairly soon, focus your attention on your breasts. Simply feel them. Perhaps you can imagine your breasts are being caressed by the sun or a gentle breeze. *Can you let yourself enjoy this? Do you feel warmth and some tingling in your breast?*

ℰ * Here is another way of becoming more centered and peaceful inside, through the power of your own *nurturing touch*. By placing one or both hands on a specific area of your body and trying to make intimate contact with the part(s) you touch, you can let your hands and the body area/s you touch "talk to each other." You may soon begin to experience a sort of "body communication." Tension will melt away under your hands, and areas painful from stress can stop hurting as they become better nourished by your breath. You may feel more alive, more energized.

Prepare for this exercise by sitting upright on the edge of a chair or stool with a flat seat. Good posture will help your breath and your life energy flow throughout your body. Feet should be flat on the floor, parallel, with some space between. Let yourself "grow" gently upward, like a flower reaching toward the sun, until you sit up straight without any effort at all . . . with the crown of your head being the highest point. Do not over-stretch; otherwise, your back will become rigid and impair your breathing. (You may also try this while lying down comfortably.) The more you can focus and be present inwardly, the more effective this exercise will be. Once you are familiar with it, you can focus quickly by touching your wrist or shoulder, or by placing your hand in your armpit—whatever "signal" works for you. You can do this even with your baby in your arms. You can calm yourself this way and learn to break a "stress cycle."

1. First "awaken" your hands by massaging or kneading one hand, particularly the palm, with the thumb of the second hand. Do this gently and consciously. With the thumb of one hand, put gentle pressure in the center of the palm of the other hand, or make a spiral motion as if you want to spiral into the depths of your hand. Before you "awaken" the other, become aware of what the "handled" hand feels like.

2. Place both hands to the left and the right of your lower abdomen and "listen" inside yourself, especially with the centers of your attentive hands. Give yourself plenty of time for this. Imagine the areas you touch "cuddle" into your hands, just as a cat would under your touch. You will touch various parts of you, allowing yourself plenty of time. You may feel a "response" from your body, possibly in the form of warmth, a tingling feeling or a sensation that tension there is beginning to melt. Or you may hear gurgling noises as a sign of release and movement in your intestines. You may yawn, or your eyes may water. You may become aware of an ever-so-gentle widening and narrowing underneath your hands—the rhythm of your life-giving breath. Don't *make* this happen, though. Just be, with all your awareness, present in whatever region of your body you touch. Breath will happen on its own.

3. Now place both hands on your sacrum (the flat part of your lower back), cradle and visualize it, cuddle it with your hands. Perhaps the kidney area will "call" you next, an area that often painfully clamors for attention when we are stressed. Let your awakened, sensitized hands linger there a while. Then move up to the lower ribs. . . . Maybe you can also manage to place your hands on the spinal column, touching the lumbar region with the back of one hand and the upper back with the palm of the other hand. You may also want to cradle your neck in the palm of your hand. Nurturing touch on your forehead, your eyes or the rest of your face also feels good. Maybe other parts of your body will yearn for touch (for example, the top of your shoulders, your chest, an armpit, an elbow, a wrist). Maybe you notice a very slight breath movement in the areas you touched, causing a feeling of peaceful wakefulness.

4. In closing, place one hand, palm down, in the middle of the triangle formed by your ribs (the costal arch) and an assumed horizontal line at the height of your navel. That is the center of your body and your being —the source of your life energy and your essence. Place the other hand, with the back of the hand against your body, exactly opposite the other hand in the small of your back. Be aware of the centers of your hand you had stimulated earlier, and position them along the vertebral column, the median line of your body. Then be very centered and aware under your hands. If you do this for a while, it will stimulate your central breath movement (in your middle). From there, the "breath wave" can radiate to other parts of your body. Ask yourself: *Do I feel different inside? What has changed? Do I feel more tranquil or more spacious inside? Do I feel more centered, in touch with my inner being and knowing? How is my breath now? Slower, calmer, deeper perhaps?* You may quickly become aware of how good this nurturing touch feels, and also that overall it really enhances your health and your emotional and physical strength.

A side benefit is that, by applying nurturing touch to yourself, the *quality* of your touch will change, which will benefit your baby and your partner. Your touch will be soothing and calming to your baby. In a university research project I participated in by evaluating videos of parent-child interactions, I became aware of how the quality of touch affects a baby and his relationships.

Of course, you can initiate your partner into this form of touching too. He can do a lot to help you relax. Show him where to place his hand. Imagine that the tensions melt away and dissolve under his hands, or that you entrust yourself to his hand. *Can you feel how the places he touches become more alive, more sensitive? Can you feel the movement of your breath there?*

Maybe your partner would like to sit behind you and hold you and your baby lovingly in his arms while you breastfeed. Let yourself be supported by him. Feel the touch of his body with the entire area of your back. The body contact will do all three of you good, and he will feel included.

⚜ Another exercise that will enliven your body is to have your partner lightly tap your back with the palms of his hands or his fists. He can tap vigorously at the sacrum, more gently in the kidney area, and massage your upper back as strongly as you wish. He may also use his fingertips: Again with relaxed wrists, lightly and rhythmically tap the back (moving from the lower to the upper back) as if light raindrops are falling on it. In concluding, your partner can place one hand on the sacrum, the other hand between the shoulder blades, or place both hands (without pressing hard!) on the top of your shoulders or the shoulder blades to bring you awareness. Ask yourself: *How does my back feel now? How is my breath?*

⚜ Perhaps at this time, when you are giving so much of yourself to others, you would like to let yourself be nurtured a bit through some form of holistic bodywork to help your life energies flow again. This could take the form of therapeutic touch, Reiki, Shiatsu, Middendorf Breathwork or a CranioSacral treatment or a Polarity or CORE massage. This may be especially beneficial if you feel you have emotional blocks that prevent your milk from flowing freely. (In this case, it's a good idea to start holistic bodywork whileyou are still in pregnancy.)

Creative Outlets

⚜ Dance from time to time—alone, just for yourself. Put on music you enjoy. Let yourself be carried by the music and led by your body! Dance your gentleness and your strength, your lightness and your heaviness, your joy and your sadness, your ease and your frustration, your sureness and your doubts, your love and your fears. Become water, fire, air, the earth that carries you, a cloud, a tree moved by the wind, a flower unfolding its beauty—whatever comes to you. Then, standing with your eyes closed, become aware how your body feels now. *Could the power of movement and dance transform you in some way?*

∽ * Humming, singing or sounding tones can lift and lighten your spirit, calm and enliven you. At the same time, it is soothing for your baby.

If you want to try toning in a conscious way, give yourself some quiet time to get started. Even done silently (within yourself) toning can be very powerful, with practice. Different sounds have different effects on your body.

Begin by focusing on your breath. Let it flow in, let it flow out, and wait for it to come in on its own. *Let it happen,* don't *make* it happen. You may want to close your eyes. At first only *imagine* yourself toning; that is, chanting a given tone. As your breath flows in, silently contemplate a tone with it. This could be an "o" (as in so), an "a" (as in sad), an "oo" (as in mood), an "ah" (as in car) or an "mm" (as in mom). Allow whatever tone you choose to flow into you and spread throughout your body. As your breath flows out again, imagine accompanying it with that same tone— silently at first—only as long as your breath lasts naturally. After a few silent tones, tone audibly if you wish, using your voice, but without straining to be particularly loud.

With time, you may observe the different tones "widen" different parts of you; for example, the "oo" creates space in your pelvic area, the "o" widens your center, the "ah" starts in your center and extends through your entire torso. Allow the tone to originate from within the area of your body that feels right. Allow for a short natural pause, after which the breath flows in again on its own with a tone. Accompany the exhalation with a tone again. Try out different volumes and pitches to see what feels best. Toning can become very meditative, centering and freeing. After you finish, listen inside and take note of any changes in your body (especially a sense of more spaciousness and more wakefulness) or in your emotional state (more peacefulness and calm). (Toning can be very helpful during labor too!)

∽ * Meditative music (see Appendix 3, page 275) can harmonize your breathing and have a balancing effect on your body and muscle tone. Peppy music can give you energy and animate you.

Enjoying Nature

∽ * Nature is rejuvenating and uplifting. As conditions permit, get out in the air and the sun as often as possible, but use common sense to protect you and your baby in various weather conditions, of course. Babies thrive on fresh air. Pushed in a baby carriage (in cooler weather wrapped in a lambskin) or near Mom's body in a sling, babies are usually very content.

This may be the only way some colicky babies can be comforted and lulled into sleep. Getting outdoors restores Mom's nerves, too!

Walking and consciously feeling your feet connect with the ground will help you center and calm yourself. Your breath responds to your steps. Walking with awareness puts you in touch with your own natural rhythm. This is important at a time when you have to adapt yourself to the needs of your little baby, because your own natural rhythm goes out of sync.

Walking can be very meditative. By taking long walks, you may be able to come up with answers for some of the issues you have felt uncertain about as a mom. Whenever you go out for a walk, take time to explore a colorful flower, a tender leaf or a strangely shaped cloud, or watch a butterfly, bird or snow falling gently from the sky.

Visualizations

⚛ If you don't have the opportunity to enjoy nature first-hand, use your imagination to "transport" yourself to a place of beauty and tranquility. Center yourself and follow the flow of your breath for a while. Allow an image to arise before your mind's eye. Perhaps you already know this place: a favorite beach, an impressive old tree with sheltering branches, the quiet corner of a city park, a mountain meadow, a rose garden, a bubbling brook— or any pleasant scene that appears before you. Absorb this place with all of your senses: the scent of the flowers, the grass or the pine pitch, the sound of the sea or of leaves rustling in the wind, the taste of salt air, the warm breeze and the sun's rays on your skin. Or you may want to contemplate a photo, a painting of a beautiful vista, a nature scene or a houseplant. Take note of every tiny detail. When you want to return to everyday life, stretch out slowly. You will certainly feel refreshed and strengthened.

A Special Place

⚛ Often in the first few weeks, you may feel tense because of uncertainty, doubt and conflict. You want the very best for your child, but you don't clearly understand his needs and often don't know what is in his best interest. Your child may bring up unresolved feelings and issues. Other people's advice may make you even more confused. *Know that all the answers lie within you.* You need only find ways to access them. If you can become quiet enough—possibly during your baby's naps—you can get in touch with a deeper part of your nature. Then that quiet little voice will speak to you with certainty. The true authority you gain will not only be beneficial now, but will turn into a true gift for your children as you guide them through the years. Here are ways to tap into this precious inner source.

Look for a spot in your home you can turn into your special place—a place that radiates tranquility and well-being to you, a spot where your breath deepens and becomes more peaceful. Decorate it to be cozy and special to you; for example, with pillows, flowers and meaningful objects or symbols. It would be great if you could go there regularly during your baby's nap time, even for a little while, or whenever you need answers to questions. When you enter this place, do so with the awareness it is a special place where you can connect to your inner source. Light a candle if you wish, or use scents to increase your well-being and concentration (see Aromatherapy, page 170). With time, this place will take on a special energy for you. Keep a journal or diary, a pen or pencil, a drawing pad and a good assortment of wax or chalk crayons there. Arrange it so you can sit upright comfortably (maybe lie down, too) and relax.

Now make yourself comfortable. Close your eyes if you want to. Let your breath flow quietly in and out for a while. Feel your breath as it flows in . . . flows out . . . be aware of any pauses before the next breath flows in of its own accord. Your breath may change, becoming more harmonized, as you dedicate your full awareness to it.

Next, after centering on your breathing and becoming still, pick up a pen and start writing down whatever comes to mind. A connection between the hand, the brain and the emotions seems to help us sort out feelings and gain clarity and perspective when we write.

You may want to take this a step further. After concentrating on your breath a while and as you become calmer inside, turn your attention to any issue that bothers you. Let a concise, clear question relating to the issue form. Open your eyes and write it in your journal. Consciously, trustingly put that question into your heart. Become very still. Listen. Transfer the words that come to you into your journal. Do not censor them, even if you have no idea what the words mean. Thank your inner guide, who brought you to these words. As you go back and read what you have written, you may have new insights. Sometimes you will only understand the message a few days or weeks later.

❧ If you are a "visual" person, you may have seen images instead of hearing words—or you may simply prefer the medium of colors. If so, arrange your paper, pencil and crayons or other coloring media in front of you. Close your eyes and place one hand over your heart. Be attentively aware of the movement of breath under your hands. Let a question rise from your heart.

When the question is clear to you, write it at the top of the sheet of paper. Then turn over the paper, pick up one of the colors and let what is inside of you flow onto the paper. Do not attempt to turn out a "nice" picture; just let the colors and forms flow.

When you are done, look at the picture from halfway across the room and let it "speak" to you. Ask yourself what you see, what feelings the painting triggers and what thoughts come to mind. Beneath your question on the back of the sheet, write down the words and impressions that come to you. Don't censor your thoughts. After a moment, read everything over again in context.

Look at your drawing and writing from time to time. You may notice something in it you had not noticed before, or understand something about it in different terms; or perhaps the message will change. You can let new pictures evolve in response to other questions you may have.

Let Water Help You—Hydrotherapy

�֍ Water—the maternal element connected with our feelings—can help us let go of tension. You can let yourself be "carried" by the water in a warm bath to which you have added essential oils. You might complete your bath experience with flickering candlelight. A bath like this can relax body, mind and spirit and is a little like being in the womb. You can mother yourself a little and let yourself be "mothered" by the water.

✖ A warm shower can help wash away burdens. It often works wonders. The warmth promotes circulation and often makes milk spray from your breast. If you don't have time for a shower or a bath, you can submerge your breasts in warm water or lay a warm, damp washcloth on them and enjoy that warmth.

✖ Try an alternating hot-cold shower (hot-cold, hot-cold). This traditional European remedy can simultaneously relax and invigorate you. It works even better when you spray your entire body with a massage-type, hand-held showerhead. Start at the point farthest away from your heart, at the back of your right leg, and swiftly work your way up.

✖ A cold sponge bath will revive you when you are most weary.

✖ Another enjoyable water remedy is an ankle-deep footbath, which you can enjoy between breastfeeds. Did you know the feet have reflex points for all our organs and our entire body? (Manipulating these points creates a response in the associated spots elsewhere in the body.) Put both feet in a small tub filled with body-temperature water, spiced with essential oils or bath oil if you like. Gradually heat the water to about 105F (40.5C) by adding hot water carefully. Soak your feet for about 10 minutes or as long as it feels comfortable. You can put your hands in too. Professional-style "foot spas" with a massaging feature can be purchased at most drug stores. *Can you feel how the cozy warmth allows your body to loosen up and relax?*

You can also let yourself be spoiled by your partner during breastfeeding by having him prepare a footbath for you, with or without an essential oil appropriate for your baby (see above).

Massage

❧ After a footbath, you may want to nurture your feet by massaging them gently. Place one leg across the thigh of the other and begin to massage that foot, remaining focused on what you are doing—kneading, stroking, patting, caressing or just calmly leaving your hand in one place, "listening" inside, making true contact. At the end, encircle your ankle with both hands, with the center of one hand located on the ankle and the thumbs alongside each other. Again, "listen" a moment for a response. Allow ample time for this. Then put your foot back on the floor and become aware of any possible differences between both feet before you tend to the other foot. Ask yourself: *How do my feet feel on the floor now? Do I feel more secure? More grounded? Have my emotions changed? Do I feel more balanced? How is my breath now?*

❧ Perhaps your partner would like to indulge you with an aroma massage while the baby is sleeping. This can help revitalize you during this very demanding time. There are many good books on massage (see page 271).

Natural Remedies

❧ Aromatherapy (see page 170) can contribute to a sense of well-being. The following essential oils can help you nurture yourself and influence your mood positively: sandalwood, honey, jasmine, vanilla, sweet geranium, narcissus, clementine, petit grain, mandarin, may rose and coriander.

Mimosa, Spanish broom, benzoin, tonka bean and cacao lend a particularly homey, warm, cuddly feeling of a nest.

Vanilla, cedar, neroli and melissa counteract anxiety.

Incense, juniper and ysop help you think more clearly.

Mandarin and vanilla essences facilitate bonding with your baby.

For the baby in the first weeks of life, only essence of rose, Roman chamomile or myrtle are appropriate. Other essences would stimulate a baby too much right now. (Also, be aware that some essences are contraindicated during pregnancy—see page 171). The finer the fragrance, the more deeply it works on a spiritual level. Detailed instructions on aromatherapy are found in chapter 9. Sources for essential oils are listed in Appendix 2.

⚘ A homeopathic remedy may be helpful. See page 162.

Reaching Out

The first six weeks are a time of learning for you and your baby—a time of getting used to one another. Don't give up if breastfeeding doesn't work right away. Get help from mothers who are experienced at breastfeeding, such as a La Leche League Leader or a lactation consultant. (Contact your doctor's office or hospital for a referral.) Attend a breastfeeding support group (see page 257). If you can't find one, you might get on the Internet and attend a "virtual" La Leche League meeting held online by a certified LLL Leader. Most of all, keep up your confidence and trust in your body and in Nature's ways—even if the beginning is harder than you thought it would be. Everything will work out!

4

Starting to
Breastfeed

What are the best conditions for learning to breastfeed? Sheila Kitzinger describes them in her book, *The Experience of Childbirth* (1989; page 203):

> *The nearest analogy for favorable conditions for the new mother to learn how to breastfeed is . . . provided by what are commonly considered favorable conditions for love-making: a comfortable warm bed, privacy, a relaxed atmosphere, and a sense of timeless leisure. And just as with intercourse, the first attempts may not bring the delight or satisfaction which was hoped for, so gradually the nursing couple, like the couple making love, learn to understand and respond to each other's needs; for breastfeeding, and indeed the whole of parenthood, is—like any form of loving—a process of discovery.*

During the first 30 minutes of life your baby will rest on your abdomen after the efforts of birth, absorbing his surroundings in a calm, alert state. Gradually he overcomes his initial fears, begins to relax and feels more comfortable. Soon, about 40 to 50 minutes after birth, he will start searching with his little mouth—making sucking motions and smacking noises. His entire little body seems to say: "There must be something here . . . something belongs in this mouth . . ." Infants seem to sniff out their mother's breast and, left to their own devices, often find their way to it quickly. From mother's abdomen they actually crawl to the nipple. When they have finally made it there, with mouth wide open, they latch on so strongly that many a mother cries out in astonishment. Most babies suck strongly and eagerly and seem to make peace with the world only when they know for certain the breast is there. It is best to wait for the baby's own signals and actions of readiness rather than to put him to the breast prematurely. A baby put to the breast right after birth frequently will only lick the nipple instead of sucking it.

The baby finds the breast shortly after birth.

Observations of babies have shown the sucking reflex is strongest 30 to 50 minutes after birth. Then it gradually grows weaker. The sucking reflex only increases in intensity again two or three days later. If the natural rhythm isn't followed, and you try to nurse for the first time before your baby shows readiness or after his initial sucking reflex declines, you may be frustrated by how little interest he shows in the breast.

Some women are baffled when their baby seeks out the breast ("But there isn't any milk yet!"), and then are surprised at how much he or she enjoys being at the breast. This special time helps many mothers gain trust in their ability to breastfeed. With very little disturbance and warm, skin-to-skin contact, mothers and babies can learn about each other.

Of course, sometimes things happen you can't anticipate. The birth may have been long and strenuous for you and your baby.

Observations of babies have shown the sucking reflex is strongest 30 to 50 minutes after birth.

You may have been medicated, and both of you may feel that effect in addition to the general exhaustion of the labor and birth. Your baby may scarcely open his eyes, or he may show no interest in breastfeeding. A little break to recover from it all may be just what both of you need before you can take the next step with breastfeeding. The beginning may be a little harder then, but with patience and trust in yourself, it will work!

Milk "Comes In"

At his first meal from the breast, the baby receives colostrum— the "pre-milk" that is just right for his nutritional needs at that moment. Because it is highly concentrated, colostrum is needed in very small amounts, perfectly suited to the baby's immature kidneys. The small amounts also keep the baby sucking often and long in the beginning, prompting the start of an abundant milk supply. The more natural your birth and breastfeeding conditions and the earlier and more frequently your baby nurses, the sooner colostrum will change to mature, high-calorie mother's milk. Think of it as a supply-and-demand program; your milk supply increases when your baby demands more milk. Feeling comfortable and nurtured in your environment also helps.

Generally milk comes in at any time between the second and sixth day of your baby's life. Many women hardly notice it. Others feel as if they might burst from an overabundance of milk. Swollen breast tissues accompany this condition. Breasts get hard, tight and may hurt. A baby-*unfriendly* hospital, in which babies are placed in a nursery or mother and baby are separated at night, can contribute to greater discomfort and more pain.

Keep in mind engorgement is a temporary phase. You may not be affected at all. For many women, the sensations associated with milk "coming in" disappear within 24 to 48 hours.

On the third day my milk came in—and how! My breasts were as hard as volleyballs. Compounding this, my daughter tended

to sleep for long stretches at that time. When I went to the
nurse looking for help, she handed me an electric pump.
Having informed myself about breastfeeding ahead of time, I
declined in a friendly way and took a shower instead. What a
good idea! As I was massaging my breasts, the milk began to
spray, and the pressure subsided. I spent the next 36 hours
nursing, taking showers and expressing milk.

Put your baby to the breast often to keep the milk flowing. Don't limit the time you spend with your baby. Stay as relaxed as possible. Use ways you may have learned in childbirth classes to deal with any pain. Taking these steps may help reduce engorgement and encourage milk flow. Compresses of cool green cabbage leaves tend to drain the tissues; so do compresses made with cottage cheese. Warm moist compresses put on the breast before breastfeeding can help reduce pain. Ice packs and cold compresses can also soothe between breastfeedings.

You may want to "awaken" your hands and nurturingly touch your breasts as described on page 52 before beginning a breast-feeding session. This may have a "melting" effect and ease any tension you feel. If you can, get in the shower, spray your breasts with warm water and gently massage your wet breasts to encourage milk flow (see page 49). Or submerge your breasts in a sink or basin filled with warm water. That helps milk flow more easily when you put your baby to the breast or express milk (see page 79). Express just enough milk to release the pressure and soften the breast tissue. Pumping more than that may confuse the supply-and-demand principle—you may end up with even more milk. When your breasts become soft again, it *doesn't* mean you lack milk; on the contrary, it means the milk-duct function has regulated itself. Everything is working just the way it is supposed to.

When your breasts become soft again, it doesn't mean you lack milk; on the contrary, it means the milk-duct function has regulated itself. Everything is working just the way it is supposed to.

Most maternity units have managed in the last several years to arrange for babies to stay next to their mothers during their hospital stay. This corresponds to Step 7 in the WHO/UNICEF recommendations (see page 5). However, a few hospitals still do not encourage rooming-in. Even if your hospital doesn't follow rooming-in principles, it must give you free access to the nursery so you can breastfeed, cuddle and bond with your baby whenever you want. If you must be separated from your baby and your breasts engorge, gently express a *little* milk—just enough to reduce the pressure. (See page 79).

Feeding on Demand

Breastfeeding on demand makes sense for several reasons and has many advantages.

- ⚘ A breastfed baby's stomach empties more quickly than that of a formula-fed infant, whose food is harder to digest.
- ⚘ Nature had good sense in organizing frequent feedings in the beginning. Frequent breastfeeding increases mother's milk supply.
- ⚘ Babies who are breastfed frequently benefit from more frequent human contact.
- ⚘ It is easier on the nipples if a newborn sucks more frequently for less time than if she drinks less frequently for longer periods with a stronger suction.

Right after a natural birth, a baby is wide-awake and active. After a couple of hours he usually falls into a long, deep sleep, so his need for nourishment the rest of the first day is not great. After that, newborns may want to feed 10 to 12 times a day, with intervals between feedings fluctuating unpredictably anywhere from 1-1/2 to 5 hours. Eventually the breaks between feedings become longer, possibly with a longer break at night. This may be because as your milk volume increases, so does your baby's ability to hold more food in his stomach. So, forget clocks! Just watch your baby. He will tell you what he needs.

Forget clocks! Just watch your baby. He will tell you what he needs.

While you will produce less than an ounce of milk at first (which is completely normal), in a couple of months, a cup or more of milk may flow out of your breasts at each meal.

Babies usually lose about 5% of their birth weight before they start gaining again. Breastfed babies who are given water or formula in addition to breast milk are likely to lose more weight and start regaining their weight later than fully breastfed infants do. Official growth charts reflect the growth patterns of bottle-fed babies, who are more likely to be overfed.

Every Baby Is Different

Breastfeeding is a learning process. The baby has to learn to drink at the breast, and you have to learn to give her your breast. Although the process of breastfeeding is technically the same with every breastfed baby, in reality every baby is different. Naturally your baby's temperament and uniqueness should be respected and validated from the very beginning.

> *Anya emptied the breast in a few minutes, while Kerry was a real dawdler—slow, leisurely, interested in everything going on around him. The differences in temperament their breastfeeding patterns made apparent in the very beginning can still be observed today.*

Some babies drink timidly, while others suck so strongly it is almost painful for the mother at first. Some babies wolf down their milk so quickly they spit up some of it afterward. Your baby might spread out her meal over a whole hour and take frequent breaks. Or she might play a game with your nipple before she begins to drink in earnest. You have no choice but to learn to accept your child the way she is. Ideally an infant should drink to her own tempo. Eventually she will establish her very own rhythm.

By helping your baby find her own rhythm and allowing her to live by it, you are laying an important foundation for her entire life. Try to learn about your child's rhythm—respect and support her in it. Let your baby lead you, while you remain interested and easy-going about it. You may gently coax your baby, but don't be domineering. Your relationship with this little person will continue long past the breastfeeding period. Try to create a relationship founded on respect and tolerance from the start.

Breastfeeding Basics

All of us owe our thanks to Kittie Frantz, director of the Breastfeeding Infant Clinic at the University of Southern California Medical Center. She made us aware that incorrect positioning is the primary cause of many breastfeeding problems—such as sore nipples, insufficient milk supply, disturbed milk-ejection reflex and a gassy baby. Therefore, putting the baby to the breast correctly can prevent these problems. Here's how.

Get Comfortable

Comfort is important when you breastfeed. Make sure the arm on which the baby is lying is supported, perhaps on the armrest of a chair or couch. You should be able to relax your arm completely. Support your back with pillows. Tension, especially in the shoulders or shoulder blades, interferes with milk flow. If you breastfeed sitting up, put a small footstool under your feet and a pillow on your knees to relieve pressure on your arm. You can buy special nursing pillows, too (see page 263). A rocking chair with broad armrests and a cushion can be ideal for breastfeeding. If you have had an episiotomy, sitting on a child's swimming ring lets you sit and breastfeed more or less pain-free.

Maybe your partner would like to sit behind you. He can cuddle or support your back so you can devote yourself to breastfeeding (you literally have his backing here!). Of course, he has to look out for his own well-being too by having something to lean on himself; otherwise he'll feel uncomfortable and then you will, too.

If you ever breastfeed while standing, plant yourself this way: Set your feet about a foot apart and consciously relax your shoulders. Your partner might cradle your shoulder caps with his hands or place the palms of his hands on your shoulder blades or shoulders. You might want to take just a minute to close your eyes, "listen" to your breath, and become centered and peaceful inside before you breastfeed.

Put Baby to Your Breast

Take your baby in your arms with his front lying horizontally across your body, facing toward you from his head to his feet. In this way his head will lie in the crook of your arm; his lower arm will be at your waist. Let the hand with which you hold your baby safely cup and support his bottom or thigh. Pull your baby close to you so he is in the best position to find your nipple.

Lift your breast with your other hand: Arrange your fingers under your breast, your palm to the side and your thumb above. Rest your fingers *outside* the areola because your baby must be able to grasp quite a bit of it. When you hold your breast this way, you can "tickle" his lower lip with your nipple easily. He will turn toward you and open his mouth wide.

Be patient if you have to tickle for a while. If you press the baby's head firmly against your breast, he will not recognize this as stimulation and will not open his mouth. Or he will get confused and turn toward the pressure on his head. He will also tend to arch away.

Sooner or later your baby will open his mouth wide, like a hungry baby bird. This is the moment to place your nipple, which should be waiting exactly in front of his open mouth, right in the middle, above his tongue. At the same time, pull him in close to you so the tip of his nose touches your breast (he will still be able to breathe) and his knees touch your body. His gums will be able to grasp far behind the nipple to reach the areola. With a good latch, he can reach the milk reservoirs underneath the areola and suck the milk toward the nipple effectively. Your baby will draw your nipple to the back of his mouth, elongating both nipple and areola. If you think he can't breathe freely, pull his bottom closer to you or lift your breast a little with the hand that is supporting it.

Don't press with your finger or thumb on the spot where your baby's nose is. You might pull out the nipple or make it slip so it gets uneven pressure on one side. That can make your nipple sore. Also, you may compress a milk duct this way. Sore nipples can also happen if the baby sucks while his body faces the ceiling and he has to turn his head to the side. (Imagine drinking with *your* head turned completely to the side!) Ear, shoulder and upper arm should form a straight line.

Don't press with your finger or thumb on the spot where your baby's nose is. You might pull out the nipple or make it slip so it gets uneven pressure on one side. That can make your nipple sore. Also, you may compress a milk duct this way.

If your baby gets a bottle from time to time (which requires completely different mouth movements and much less of the baby's initiative), he may only open his mouth wide enough to grasp your nipple when he is back on your breast, instead of the nipple *and* areola. This position easily leads to sore nipples. In addition, many bottle-supplemented babies become nipple-confused and have all the breastfeeding problems that go along with that. If you will return to work outside the home, and your baby needs to receive your milk from a bottle, it's best to wait at least until your milk supply is established and your baby is sucking with ease.

If your breast is too full and your baby has difficulty grasping your nipple, express a little milk in a warm bath or shower before the next feed (see page 82). If he has difficulty getting milk out of your breasts at first, use massage and nurturing touch to help stimulate the let-down reflex. You can also activate the let-down reflex by centering and focusing your total awareness on your breasts (see page 49).

Breastfeeding Positions

You can breastfeed seated, lying down, in a cross-legged "tailor" position or even standing up. The first time you breastfeed, you may be lying on your back. In this position, your baby lies at an angle on your abdomen, with her head above your breast. Support her forehead a little so she can breathe easily. Or, after the baby has crawled to your breast, ask for help to be turned on your side. (The "side" position is also likely at first if you have had a Cesarean section.) In general, your baby will be put to the breast closest to the bed, but breastfeeding also works with the "upper" breast if you can lean forward somewhat. In the side position, your baby lies snuggled close to your body, her mouth level to your nipple, her head on a pillow, your arm or the bed. Make sure your own head is well supported and your baby does not need to turn her head. She may need cushion or pillow support at her back also.

Apart from the more common positions—tummy-to-tummy or seated in a tailor position—you can also breastfeed using the "football hold" (see illustration page 71). This position is so-called because it looks like the way football players run with the ball under their arms. In this position, the baby's body and legs are not cuddled against your abdomen, but are positioned under your arm, along your side and snuggling around you. Let your baby's head rest in your hand and support his back well with your arm. This position is especially recommended when you have sore nipples, to protect a sensitive spot or when the milk ducts are engorged on the outer side of the breast and the lower jaw needs to extract the milk there. The football hold is useful for babies who have trouble latching on and with twins.

> *When I felt a hardened area on my breast above the nipple*
> *once, I placed Kerry so his feet were over my shoulder while*
> *I was lying down. He emptied the affected spot easily with*
> *his lower jaw.*

If you can only quiet your crying baby by carrying him around, you may need to breastfeed while walking, ideally with the baby in a sling. Support from a sling can be a real relief. You may be able to sit down as soon as the baby has latched on.

Putting baby to the breast
(lift breast; other hand
cups baby's bottom)

Football hold

Side position

The Baby at the Breast

In the first days and weeks, the baby's frequent sucking on both breasts helps start the milk flow. Nursing from both breasts helps keep the second breast from becoming overfull at a time when the milk supply is not stabilized. Let your baby suck on one side until you can tell from his sucking that the milk flow has obviously slowed down and the baby is not interested anymore. Trust yourself to understand his signals.

Initially it takes a few minutes for the let-down reflex to function so the nutritious milk can flow freely. Also, at first it takes quite a bit of sucking (15 to 20 minutes) before enough prolactin is released to ensure adequate continued milk production. Wait and see, after a pause for burping or changing his diapers, if he is still interested in the other breast. If so, let him suck

> Children are very different in temperament as well as in their drinking needs and behavior, and these differences should be respected.

as long as he wants to and as long as he is sucking correctly. Don't worry about the time. Let your baby guide you in finding his own rhythm. By following his lead, you can be sure he gets the right balance of foremilk and hindmilk when the milk comes in. With the occasional sleepy and disinterested baby, you may want to take the initiative by switching him for stimulation.

If you have switched breasts at one meal, start the next meal with the breast used last. If you have only nursed on one breast, offer the other at the next meal. A safety pin or ribbon on your bra can help you remember which side comes first. If you breastfeed your baby over a long period, eventually this becomes unnecessary. The baby himself will choose the breast with the most milk in it.

Mothers used to be told to limit each feeding during the first few days to prevent sore nipples. Today we know correct positioning prevents sore nipples better than shortening the breastfeeding time. If your nipples are somewhat sensitive at first, you can always take your baby off the breast when he seems full. You can tell from the absence of sucking and movement in his throat that the milk flow has subsided.

> For the first two months, I was never quite sure whether Dennis was really eating or only suckling on the breast or was maybe even asleep. He took nearly an hour for each feed. Later on, he finished in no time—he emptied a breast in five minutes.

Is Baby Getting Enough Milk?

Maybe you had wonderful support for handling your new baby after the birth. But maybe you received questionable, insufficient

Soothing Your Baby

Some babies who appear fussy and discontented at the breast are getting enough to eat, but they have an unquenchable need to suck that is not fully met while they are feeding. Many mothers respond to this by letting their babies suck at the breast for comfort—but sometimes too much of this can make them fussier! Other mothers feel overburdened by nursing their baby extensively to soothe him, and they resort to a pacifier. (This is a personal choice. However, pacifier use can lead to nipple confusion and other problems.) Sometimes a father enjoys having a way to calm his child by offering his little finger so the baby can suck on it.

or contradictory advice, and now are doubtful, confused and insecure about breastfeeding. That happened to Jennifer:

> *Brian seemed to be hungry all the time. At night he woke up crying several times, and I decided I didn't have enough milk. Suddenly my milk looked so thin and watery and my breasts felt so soft. . . . Breastfeeding didn't work with my friends, either . . . and then there was that nurse who said, "As soon as you get busy at home, your milk supply will drop." I guess that's what's happening.*

To repeat: *It is absolutely normal for a newborn baby to be hungry often in the beginning, because his sucking causes milk to be produced.* Expect your baby to wake up at night for the first few months. Because of their small stomachs and immature digestive systems, most babies wake up at least twice in the night. Do not be in a hurry to get your baby to sleep until morning. In the uterus he received nourishment night and day. It will take time for him not to need those night feedings. Again, let your baby take the lead.

Remember: Mature mother's milk looks more watery than colostrum (page 14), but has everything your baby needs. When your breasts stop overproducing—after production has adapted to your baby's needs—they will feel softer. As long as your baby sucks freely on demand, you will have enough milk.

Some mothers wonder, "How do I know if my baby got enough?" You only need to look at your baby. If your baby seems content, has moist skin, bright eyes and at least five to eight wet diapers a day after the milk comes in (one or two before that), he is getting enough to eat. (If you use disposable diapers, it can be hard to judge wetness. When in doubt, weigh and compare diapers on a kitchen scale to get a feel for the difference.)

In the first months, he will gain on average 4 to 8 ounces (110 to 125g) a week or at least a pound (1/2kg) a month, counting from his lowest weight. Growth curves can be quite variable: One baby gains slowly at first and catches up quickly later; another one gains quickly in the beginning and then maintains that weight for a while. Parents who have information about their own development as babies frequently observe their baby's weight curve is similar to that of one or both of his parents.

Placid babies who have long pauses between feedings and sleep through the night early in life are more likely than active babies to take in too little milk. If you are concerned your baby may become dehydrated, you can tell by a skin test. A sure sign of dehydration would be wrinkly, dull skin without resiliency. If you were to lift the fold of skin on the baby's stomach, it would remain pinched-looking. A baby's skin should not stay indented but return to normal when pressed gently. Another sign of insufficient fluid intake is rings around your baby's eyes. If your baby shows signs of dehydration, see your pediatrician right away. If you're unsure about your baby's weight gain and don't trust yourself to judge, let your nurse practitioner or pediatrician examine him.

Increasing Your Breast Milk

Perhaps you and your baby, for whatever reason, have fallen into a pattern of taking long breaks between feedings. When that happens, you may not receive enough sucking stimulation to encourage good milk production. But don't worry; this is not a problem. As we've seen, breastfeeding is a matter of supply and demand. If you concentrate entirely on your baby's needs for a short time and breastfeed him whenever he is hungry, you will be producing enough milk within 48 hours.

Keep Up Your Fluids!

It doesn't matter what you drink—water, herbal tea, milk-making tea, buttermilk or fruit juice (just watch to see if your baby shows a sensitivity to anything). Get in the habit of consuming healthful foods (see page 87) and stay away from soft drinks. Be careful about coffee and caffeinated tea. The baby "drinks" this with you, and many babies get very restless from it. Do avoid alcohol entirely (see page 95).

When Kerry was seven months old, we took a camping trip along the Atlantic coast. It was terribly hot, which we hadn't expected. Kerry was thirsty constantly. Before we left, he had started taking great interest in solid foods in addition to drinking from the breast, but now he was only interested in the breast. For two days he breastfed almost every hour, day and night, and then there was enough milk for me to exclusively breastfeed him again.

Trust that you can increase your milk supply whenever you want! When you leave the hospital and come home, lie down with your baby in bed, or sit on the couch or a comfortable rocking chair and put your baby to your breast. Make it a habit to drink something yourself whenever your baby feeds. You need fluid to make milk.

Emotionally and rationally prepare yourself to feed your baby frequently. Having your baby at the breast "constantly" for a couple of days may demand a lot of you, but you will be rewarded with a plentiful milk supply.

Growth Spurts

Babies seem to have predictable growth spurts—between the seventh and tenth days, the fourth, sixth and twelfth weeks and at around six months. Suddenly their growing bodies need more food. They suck more frequently, which signals mother's body to make more milk. If you put your baby to the breast as often as he is hungry, you will have enough milk within two days.

Supplementing at this time would disturb the balance of supply and demand and start the weaning process. Insecurity and worry about "having enough breast milk" could inhibit your let-down reflex in addition. Your baby would have more trouble

Removing Your Baby from the Breast

During breastfeeding, the baby's mouth creates a vacuum. If you try to pull your baby off the breast, she stays latched on your nipple. Stretching the nipple can hurt! To break the vacuum painlessly, put a finger between the breast and the corner of your baby's mouth. As soon as air flows into her mouth, she lets go, and you can take her off easily.

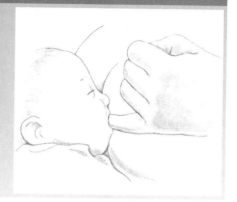

getting high-calorie hindmilk. During these critical days, you may need the support of a breastfeeding group or a mother who has successfully breastfed so you won't be tempted to reach for a formula bottle.

Burping Your Baby

Babies who eat in a leisurely way may not need to burp very often. Babies with eager, strong suction may need to burp a lot. Always check your baby for signs of taking in too much air. Soon you will know his tendencies and how often he will need to be burped.

To burp your baby, lay him against your shoulder and gently pat his back. Put a cloth over the shoulder where he will rest his head, because milk may come up along with the air. You can also lay him on his tummy across your knees and gently massage his back with clockwise circular motions. If your baby falls asleep at the breast, you don't need to wake him to burp him.

Spitting Up

Many parents worry when their babies appear to spit up an entire meal. This can happen with lively children who eat quickly, but don't worry. An old German proverb says, "Babies who spit up, thrive." If your baby gives the impression he is otherwise happy and content, and he continues to feed, gains weight and develops steadily, he probably just swallowed too much air. By six months, he usually will have stopped spitting up for this particular reason.

Other tips:

- ❧ If your baby tends to spit up, pause while you are feeding him so he can burp. (Some babies may resist.)

- ❧ Don't burp him vigorously, and don't move him much.

- ❧ It can help to express a little milk by hand at the beginning of a feed. That prevents the first strong stream of milk from the let-down reflex from overwhelming the baby. By letting off pressure this way, baby is less likely to gulp a lot of air with the milk.

- ❧ Take another look at the directions for favorable positioning.

- ❧ The baby can also swallow a lot of air if he holds the nipple on one side of his mouth.

Babies who constantly regurgitate food may have an immature stomach sphincter. Basically, their bodies cannot completely control and close the valve that keeps food from going back up into their esophagus (throat). Regurgitating for this reason tends to go away at about six months of age because the baby can now sit up for periods of time, instead of mostly being on her back. This lets the valve mature and close.

> If your baby seems to be sick, doesn't gain weight or has a fever, consult your physician right away.

The Breastfed Baby's Stools

In the first few days after birth, blackish-green meconium—the baby's first stool—is eliminated in great quantities. Colostrum has a laxative effect and hastens this process. Bilirubin, responsible for newborn jaundice (see page 129), is excreted in the meconium. Babies usually have a bowel movement at each meal.

Once meconium has passed through the baby's body, her stools will range from lumpy to liquid. Depending on her mother's diet, the stools may be yellow, yellow-green or brown in color. The stool of a breastfed baby has a mild, almost sweet-smelling odor. In the first six weeks, babies fill their diapers at least two to five times a day, often while they are nursing. Babies over six weeks may absorb nutrients so well they may have a substantial stool only once every few days.

If your baby has fewer than two bowel movements a day and does not seem to gain weight, he may not be nursing long enough to get the highly nutritional hindmilk. Consistently green and watery stools are often a sign the baby is getting too much of the lactose-containing foremilk and not enough of the high-calorie hindmilk. If you are worried about his nutrition, check with his doctor or another practitioner experienced with helping and encouraging breastfeeding.

Parents and physicians are sometimes concerned if the stool is too thin. A doctor unfamiliar with breastfeeding may suggest mothers temporarily replace their milk with formula feeds. This can mean the beginning of the end of the breastfeeding relationship, because it disturbs the balance between supply and demand. Breastfed children seldom have diarrhea. La Leche League advises, "If the baby can take anything by mouth, it should be mother's milk."

Even if the baby's stool has some mucus in it, it isn't a problem as long as the baby is otherwise robust and doesn't appear to be ill. Be sure he really isn't getting anything besides mother's milk. Some babies react to fluoride or vitamins with diarrhea or sore bottoms. If your baby is exclusively breastfed, then stool with mucus may be caused by something you ate and your baby reacted to—often, cow's milk. Don't substitute some other food or fluid for breast milk. Instead, try to find out which food (or medicine) is causing the reaction and then avoid it. If the baby's symptoms improve in three days, your guess was right. If your baby can't tolerate raw or whole cow's milk in your diet, see if he can tolerate your consumption of heated or soured-milk products (yogurt, kefir, acidophilus milk). Always discuss your findings or concerns with your practitioner.

It is extremely rare for a baby to require a lactose-free formula in place of breast milk. Generally the reason is a lactose or milk-sugar intolerance. An example would be *galactosemia*, when the baby is born without a liver enzyme that helps metabolize lactose.

> *Worried about my baby's thin stool, I consulted my pediatrician. He said, "Wean! Your baby can't tolerate your milk. Switch to bottle feeding and give him formula." My baby refused the formula and the bottle. I called a La Leche League leader and she advised me to avoid milk products in my diet. She suggested I consult a physician who was experienced with breastfed babies. So I did. My baby was cooperative enough to give this doctor a "demonstration" as soon as I undressed him. "Terrific," he said, "a perfectly normal mother's-milk stool." I was so relieved!*

Hygiene

In the womb, your baby is protected against illnesses you have been exposed to and all the germs you have formed antibodies against. After he is born, he receives additional protection through your breast milk. Your breasts need no special care: Wash your breasts with clear water and avoid soaps. Wash your hands before you breastfeed.

Change a wet bra as soon as possible because germs reproduce quickly in the presence of moisture, and your nipples will become sore. Wear breast pads between feedings to catch leaking milk. Use 100% cotton breast pads because they let the skin breathe and are very comfortable. The cozy softness of cotton promotes the let-down reflex and helps prevent sore nipples. Cloth diapers or cotton washcloths cut into circles work well also.

Wash your hands before you breastfeed.

Removing Milk from Your Breasts

It isn't necessary, or even advisable, to empty your breasts after feedings. This too disturbs the balance between supply and demand. However, if you want or need to remove milk from your breast and your child isn't available—for whatever reason—you can express it by hand or by pump using a hand or electric pump.

Hand Expression

Hand expression may be the easiest way to take small amounts of milk from the breast. Common reasons for pumping are

- ❦ to relieve full breasts when your baby is asleep or not nearby
- ❦ to make the breast softer before your baby latches on
- ❦ to trigger the let-down reflex or to prevent your baby from getting the first strong stream of milk
- ❦ to provide a meal for your baby when you can't be together

Expressing by hand can take some mental preparation. Sensitize your hands by applying a little pressure to the tips of your fingers and thumbs and the center of your palms in a firm yet sensitive way.

Hand Pumping: The Marmet Technique of Manual Expression of Breast Milk

EXPRESSING THE MILK

Draining the Milk Reservoirs

1. POSITION the thumb and first two fingers about 1" to 1-1/2" behind the nipple.

- Use this measurement, which is not necessarily the outer edge of the areola, as a guide. The areola varies in size from one woman to another.

- Place the thumb pad above the nipple and the finger pads below the nipple, forming the letter "C" with the hand, as shown.

- Note that the fingers are positioned so that the milk reservoirs lie beneath them.

- Avoid cupping the breast.

2. PUSH straight into the chest wall.

- Avoid spreading the fingers apart.

- For large breasts, first lift and then push into the chest wall.

Push into chest wall

3. ROLL thumb and fingers forward, as if making thumb and fingerprints at the same time.

- The rolling motion of the thumb and fingers compresses and empties the milk reservoirs without hurting sensitive breast tissue. Roll

- Note the moving position of the thumbnail and fingernails in the illustration. Finish roll

4. REPEAT RHYTHMICALLY to drain the reservoirs.

- Position, push, roll; position, push, roll.

5. ROTATE the thumb and finger position to milk the other reservoirs. Use both hands on each breast. These pictures show hand positions on the right breast.

Right Hand   Left Hand

AVOID THESE MOTIONS

Avoid squeezing the breast. This can cause brusing.

Avoid pulling out the nipple and breast. This can cause tissue damage.

Avoid sliding on the breast. This can cause skin burns.

ASSISTING THE MILK-EJECTION REFLEX

Stimulating the Flow of Milk

1. MASSAGE the milk-producing cells and ducts.

- Start at the top of the breast. Press firmly into the chest wall. Move

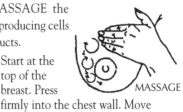

MASSAGE

fingers in a circular motion on one spot on the skin.

- After a few seconds, move the fingers to the next area on the breast.
- Spiral around the breast toward the areola using this massage.
- The motion is similar to that used in a breast examination.

2. STROKE the breast area from the top of the breast to the nipple with a light, tickle-like stroke.

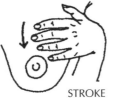

STROKE

- Continue this stroking motion from the chest wall to the nipple around the whole breast.
- This will help with relaxation and will help stimulate the milk-ejection reflex.

3. SHAKE the breast while leaning forward so that gravity will help the milk eject.

SHAKE

PROCEDURE

This procedure should be followed by mothers who are expressing in place of a full feeding and those who need to establish, increase or maintain their milk supply when the baby cannot breastfeed.

- Express each breast until the flow of milk slows down.
- Assist the milk-ejection reflex (massage, stroke, shake) on both breasts. This can be done simultaneously.
- Repeat the whole process of expressing each breast and assisting the milk-ejection reflex once or twice more. The flow of milk usually slows down sooner the second and third time as the reservoirs are drained.

TIMING

The ENTIRE PROCEDURE should take approximately 20 to 30 MINUTES.

- Express each breast 5 to 7 minutes.
- Massage, stroke, shake.
- Express each breast 3 to 5 minutes.
- Massages, stroke, shake.
- Express each breast 2 to 3 minutes.

Note: If the milk supply is established, use the times given only as a guide. Watch the flow of milk and change breasts when the flow gets small.

Note: If little or no milk is present yet, follow these suggested times closely.

Manual Expression of Breast Milk—Marmet Technique, Copyright 1978, revised 1979, 1981 and 1988 Chele Marmet. Used with permission of Chele Marmet and The Lactation Institute, 16430 Ventura Blvd., Suite 303, Encino, CA 91436, USA, (818) 995-1913.

Let one hand gently stroke the other to bring them into your awareness more. Then begin to "awaken" your breast with intensive touch.
A form of body communication takes place: The hand "speaks" to
the breast and the breast "responds," perhaps with warmth or a tingling sensation. Then gently massage your breast with rhythmic,
circling motions. Afterward bend forward and "shake out" your
breasts. You can stimulate your breasts further by spraying them in
a warm shower, soaking them in a warm bath or in a warm-water-
filled basin or by placing warm, moist compresses directly on them.
Now you can begin to express your milk by hand. Handle your breast
with care and gentleness. Refer to the box on page 80, which fully
describes hand expression as developed by Chele Marmet.

Pumping

Sometimes you may prefer to remove your milk using a breast
pump (see instructions on page 141); for example:

- ❀ when you need to express milk regularly because your baby is too weak
  to suck
- ❀ when your baby is in the neonatal intensive care unit (NICU)
- ❀ when you work or are separated from your baby for some other reason
  and you want to increase your milk supply

Pay attention to good hygiene regarding the pump, bottles and
other milk-collecting devices you use, as well as your own hands.
Preparation for pumping is the same as it is for hand expression. Be
sure your nipple is centered in the middle of the pump opening
and that, where available, you use the nipple adapter appropriate
for your breast. Allow yourself time to learn how to pump.

Electric pumps and hand pumps are available. Among the hand
pumps, rubber-bulb pumps are not recommended because they may
injure your breast or nipple, and the milk may become contaminated by bacteria, among other reasons. With cylinder-shaped pumps,
which remove milk by creating a vacuum, you can regulate suction
and speed. You do need both hands for the process, which can be a
drawback. One unique one-hand pump imitates the baby's natural
suck-and-release pattern. This model also offers soft silicone "petals"

covering the funnel. The petals massage the breast during pumping and stimulate the let-down reflex, so the higher-fat hindmilk
becomes available. This pump is effective and suitable for expressing larger quantities of milk in less time without great effort. Mothers
also like the fact it is silent.

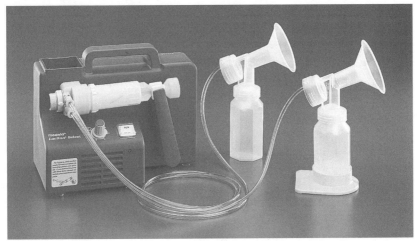

Lactina® Electric pump

Isis® Hand pump

Among the many kinds of electric
pumps available, you'll find one-
handed, purse-sized minis for sale or
rent. If you have to pump frequently
for a longer time, you can rent a larger
electric pump, which is a faster way
of obtaining hindmilk. Try to select
an electric pump that doesn't maintain a constant pressure. It should imitate the suckling cycle of a baby. The
rhythm should be regular and
adjustable to your comfort. For further information on rental and
purchase of breast pumps, check Appendix 2 (page 262).

Many hospitals suggest pumping in cases of sore, flat or inverted
nipples. The milk is then fed to the baby by bottle. This is not
recommended because it can lead to nipple confusion and possible problems when the baby is put to the breast again.

Lactina is a registered trademark of Medela, Inc. Photograph courtesy of Medela, Inc.
Isis is a regestered trademark of Advent America, Inc. Photograph courtesy of Advent America, Inc.

About Supplementing

As a rule, full-term babies get all the nutrition they need if they are allowed to breastfeed on demand. If they get a little less at one meal, they'll ask for the next meal sooner. Even in the hot, dry desert regions of the Southwest, babies manage very well without supplementary fluids, as long as they are allowed to suck at the breast whenever they want. People used to assume breastfed babies would get thirsty without water or glucose supplements. Now we know that isn't true. That worry came from a time when babies were breastfed on a schedule (often with an 8-hour break at night).

We are so used to believing in only what we can measure! Too often we don't trust our intuition or feelings, which *are* reliable. Supplementation is sometimes encouraged "in case the baby isn't satisfied." But supplementing essentially begins the weaning process. Instead, mothers need encouragement to help them learn to trust their ability to give their baby all it needs. One of the highest goals of a maternity unit should be to strengthen a new mother's confidence in this way.

Supplementation may encourage the development of allergies. If a family has a tendency toward allergies, it's best to avoid even a single bottle of formula.

Supplementing from a bottle disturbs a baby's sucking pattern. Sucking a bottle requires a less complex type of sucking (sucking and swallowing movements) than does sucking on the breast (sucking, gumming and swallowing movements). Some babies switch effortlessly between bottle and breast, but for many others, their sucking patterns get hopelessly confused. Babies can get "lazy" at the breast because bottle-feeding takes less effort. If you want to avoid this circumstance, feed a baby who needs supplementary fluid with a small spoon or pipette, or even with a small cup.

Visitors

We all love visitors, but we also know they can burden a new family.

> The day I got home from the hospital, my parents came over.
> The next day my in-laws and the rest of the gang descended on
> us. I'm the kind of person who has to please everyone. I
> worried about my parents, I worried about breastfeeding
> Andrew . . . It just didn't work. Everything was so new. Later

> *I made supper for everyone . . . On the following day, same*
> *story . . . Andrew must have felt the tension, and he probably*
> *didn't get enough milk because I was so uptight. He started*
> *crying and wouldn't stop. It was horrible!*

You need your energy for your baby in the early days. Visitors should come prepared to chip in and help care for you and your family, not the other way around. If you know your visitors will be too much effort, or you can't help feeling responsible for them, kindly and firmly put them off until later.

The Baby Blues

A few days after the arrival of the baby, somewhere around the time their milk comes in, many women feel sad and depressed. Experts disagree about whether this mood comes from the hormonal shift in the body or has an emotional basis. For instance, are you worrying about your responsibility, about not being able to do what is best for your baby, about everything that is so new, or about feelings of failure or rejection if you have breastfeeding problems? A depression-like state is probably a combination of several factors. Good nutrition and adequate fluid intake can help a lot. Natural remedies may be helpful. Aromatherapy may help lift your mood: Put two drops of pure jasmine essence and two drops of orange in a fragrance lamp and let it evaporate. Also check out the Bach Flower essences on page 166.

Separating mother and baby after birth seems to increase depression. I have observed that women who keep their babies with them after the birth experience baby blues to a lesser degree.

> *For nine months I carried my baby in me. I was looking*
> *forward to holding her in my arms, looking at her and stroking*
> *her. And now here I lay, with empty arms and an empty*
> *feeling in my whole body . . . I had really felt "high" right*
> *after the birth, and I replayed the birth experience in my mind*
> *all night long. But when I calmed down, I had a powerful*
> *yearning for my baby who was crying for me, probably—far*
> *away in the nursery.*

Lack of Support

What can you do if you are in a hospital that offers no support for breastfeeding? What do you do when you start to doubt your ability to breastfeed, are confused with too much conflicting advice, or when your milk production doesn't start off well because your rhythms are disturbed?

Try to stay calm and find help! Talking to someone who has had a positive breastfeeding experience can help you find solutions to problems. Even one phone call can work wonders. Arrange for the help of a healthcare provider at home, such as a midwife or nurse, or find a doula. Organize things at home so you can devote yourself entirely to your baby's needs for at least three days. Attend a breastfeeding support group meeting as soon as you can, or at least get in touch with a breastfeeding counselor by phone.

Trust Your Inner Voice

As we have grown more accustomed to getting information from television, radio, magazines and books, we have started to expect answers to come from outside of our own experience—from "experts." However, every human being has deep sources of personal wisdom. Intuitively we know the answers to all our questions. We can truly trust these sources. We only have to become calm and quiet long enough to hear the answers, as this woman observed:

> *I realized it is best to rely on my instincts, which still function with this most basic of womanly acts.*

5

What to Know When You Nurse

Maternal Nutrition

Your need for vitamins, minerals and protein while nursing is even higher than it was during pregnancy. If you developed good eating habits and have nourished yourself in a healthful and balanced way, you will find yourself prepared to eat well during breastfeeding.

As a rule, if anyone gets shortchanged nutritionally at this time, it will be you, not your baby. The quality and quantity of your nutrition has little effect on your milk but greatly influences your own health. Almost all women can produce milk of sufficient quantity and quality to promote the growth and health of their babies—even when their supply of nutrients is limited.

Experts figure a nursing mother needs about 500 extra calories per day to make milk, but many mothers appear to need less. A British study explained the phenomenon this way: Apparently the mother's own energy needs decrease during breastfeeding so her body can divert energy to make milk, so she is not dependent on an extremely high caloric intake. At the end of a pregnancy, most women weigh 4 to 8 pounds more than before—nature's way of providing about 18,000 to 36,000 calories for the breastfeeding period. Over three or four months, these reserves from pregnancy will be used up for milk production. However, do not consciously try to lose weight while you are nursing, because you still need about 2,700 calories per day to sustain your milk production.

You will need 50% more calcium than usual when you breast-feed. Milk products are a good source of calcium, particularly in cheeses such as Cheddar, Swiss, Gouda and Camembert. Green leafy vegetables, sesame seeds, almonds or egg yolk are other good sources of calcium. However, do watch your baby for possible allergic reactions if you consume milk products and breastfeed.

A word of warning: Two recent studies in England have found allergies to peanuts are on the rise. Even small amounts may have dramatic effects on health. Babies seem to become sensitized through their mothers during pregnancy and lactation. These researchers advise pregnant and nursing mothers to avoid peanuts and not to include peanuts or peanut butter in the baby's diet for the first few years of their lives.

The list on page 82 gives you general guidelines for balanced nutrition. The more a food has been processed or "improved," the less rich it is in natural vitamins and nutrients. The closer it is to its natural state, the closer it is to being a whole food.

Try to reduce your intake of additives to a minimum. Effects of the chemical additives in prepared foods on our bodies have not been tested adequately and are largely unknown. Ideally, you and your child should eat organically grown vegetables, fruits and grains because these foods are unlikely to contain pesticides and herbicides. If you use salt, use iodized salt or herbed sea salt. Better yet, experiment! Season your food with herbs and spices you enjoy instead of salt.

Exhaustion, depression, irritability and excessive weight loss may be connected to poor nutrition, especially to a deficiency in B-vitamins. B-vitamins are found mainly in grains and brewer's yeast.

You need 50% more calcium than usual when you breastfeed.

(Brewer's yeast is a nutritional powder you can buy in a healthfood store. Use it in cooking or take it by the spoonful dissolved in water.) Taking B-vitamins will help your milk-ejection reflex.

If you are on a completely vegetarian (vegan) diet, you need to take vitamin B-12 supplements daily. If you do not use vitamin-D-fortified foods and your exposure to the sun or ultraviolet light is limited, a vitamin supplement is recommended. It may be a good

General Nutrition Guidelines

Food Group Requirement	Food	Daily
Protein Foods Plant Protein	Legumes, soybeans, nuts, grains and seeds, sunflower seeds, brewer's yeast and certain vegetable combinations	2 servings (at least one portion of legumes)
Animal Protein	Fish, shellfish, poultry, red meat, eggs, milk, cheese and yogurt	2 servings (2 to 3 ounces; 56 to 84 grams) (vegetarians: See page 90)
Milk and Milk Products	Skim and whole milk, kefir, buttermilk, yogurt, hard cheeses, cottage cheese	5 servings (5 to 7-1/2 ounces; 140 to 210 grams)
Grains (generally rich in B-vitamins)	Whole grain breads, cooked grains, flakes or raw grain cereal from wheat, barley or oats, natural rice millet, corn, wheat germ, wheat bran, whole-grain baked goods, sprouts	6 to 11 servings
Vitamin C-rich Fruits	Citrus, kiwi, strawberries, black currants, avocado, star fruit	1 serving each of C-rich fruits and vegetables (1 to 1-1/2 ounces; 28 to 42 grams)
Vegetables	Beans, peas, potatoes with skins, tomatoes, green and red peppers, broccoli, asparagus, all kinds of cabbage, parsley, chives, uncooked produce, leafy greens, Brussels sprouts	
Yellow, White or Red Fruits or Vegetables (generally rich in vitamin A)	Apricots, mango, peach, cherry, melon, pineapple, papaya, carrots, yellow squash, cauliflower, kohlrabi, asparagus	1 serving
Green, Leafy Vegetables (vitamins A, E, B, K, iron folic acid, magnesium)	Lettuce, spinach, Swiss chard, Belgian endive, dandelions, kale, watercress, alfalfa, fennel	2 servings
Fats (contain vitamin E and essential fatty acids)	unsaturated, unhardened oils (e.g., cold-pressed sunflower oil, olive oil, grapeseed oil), margarine, butter	2 tablespoons

Milk-enhancing Tea

Pour hot water over a mixture of the following herbs:

Stinging nettle   Balm mint, optional
Caraway seeds   Fennel seeds
Anise seeds

Steep 3 minutes. Strain and sip.

Note: These herbs should be available at your healthfood store.

idea to consult a registered dietitian for specific recommendations tailored to your own eating habits.

Women often ask me, "Should I avoid any particular foods when nursing?" Basically, no. But some babies react to seeds (such as sesame), citrus or other acidic fruits. They may develop a rash, for example. Other babies will go "on strike" whenever milk changes flavor because Mom has eaten garlic, cabbage or some other strong-flavored food. If your baby has these reactions or becomes gassy as a result of cabbage, leeks, onions, legumes or particularly cow's milk or grains (especially if you react sensitively to these things yourself), leave these foods out of your diet for now.

What you choose to drink can have an effect also. If you drink something every time you nurse, you will probably take in at least two quarts of fluid a day. Avoid coffee, black tea and even small amounts of alcohol. You may want to try herbal teas or grain drinks, such as Postum®. Three or four cups of milk-enhancing tea may work wonders (see box). If you like to drink fruit juices, you may want to dilute them with water. Especially with citrus juices, watch your baby for possible allergic reactions.

Vegetarian Diets

Many people are concerned about their diet, the environment and other species on Earth. For them, choosing to partially or entirely eliminate meat from their diet addresses these concerns in a positive way. Eating less meat, or no meat, is also an option for a nursing mother. Opting for a vegetarian diet does not mean you have to stop eating well. However, plant protein does not provide

Food-combining Chart

The following foods complement each other. Combine a food from each column as shown to create a complete protein. Frances Moore-Lappé describes protein complementation in detail and offers lots of imaginative recipes in her classic book, *Diet for a Small Planet.*

Rice	+	Legumes (well-cooked)
Rice	+	Brewer's yeast
Corn	+	Legumes
Wheat	+	Legumes
Sesame seeds	+	Beans
Sesame seeds	+	Wheat and soybeans
Beans	+	Rice or polenta, wheat, milk, sesame seeds
Mushrooms	+	Peas or Brussels sprouts, cauliflower, broccoli
Wheat germ	+	Rice or oats, barley
Wheat germ	+	Sesame and rice
Milk	+	All grains and vegetables, nuts, seeds

a complete protein (all eight essential amino acids). To make up for this, you need to be more aware of what you eat, and eat a wide variety of foods. You will need to eat several foods with complementary amino acids together at one meal to make this chain of amino acids complete. (See box above).

Contaminants in Mother's Milk

For years, articles about contaminants in mother's milk have alarmed pregnant and nursing mothers and made them wonder whether they could breastfeed their babies safely. The contaminants referred to are mainly chemical substances such as DDT, PCBs, dieldrin and dioxin. They have been used as insecticides, disinfectant agents for seeds, coolant in power transformers, impregnating agents and plastic softeners by industry. Often, these contaminants found their way into the body through foods we consumed. For example, consider DDT, which was used as an insecticide in the 1940s to the 1960s and later banned. DDT was consumed by animals (such as cows) in the grass they ate. Humans ate DDT in milk or meat, but also absorbed it through the skin and lungs. Once in the human body, it was stored mostly in the fat, with a half-life in the body of 5 or 10 years, provided no new contaminants were consumed in the meantime.

Through their milk, breastfeeding mothers pass the substances they have absorbed to their children. This happens primarily through the breakdown of fat reserves during the time of lactation. Yet the average breastfeeding mother needn't worry. Only a tiny percentage of contaminants present in the mother's body will actually be released into her milk. Not one case has been reported in which environmental contaminants in mother's milk have injured children.

The number of mother's-milk samples with contaminants above permitted levels has decreased steeply in recent years because today's nursing mothers have grown up with much lower exposure levels than mothers of earlier times. Many of these harmful substances have been outlawed. In most cases, levels of pesticides found in human milk today are *much less than those in cow's milk.* (Dioxin and furan are exceptions that do tend to be higher in mother's milk.)

Environmental awareness in the Western world has increased enormously. Many people remember the Three Mile Island and Chernobyl disasters, and the devastation caused to people and environments around these contaminated sites. Even though we can no longer escape the damage we have created to our world, we can protect ourselves, to a certain degree, from them. Environmentalist Elke Proestler, who has done extensive research on pollutants in breast milk, says, "I can't adequately shelter my child from environmental stressors. But I hope that by breastfeeding I can impart so much immunological and psychological strength to my son that this will boost his body in becoming more resistant to physical illnesses." She nursed her own child for eight months, and emphasized the results of her study should not be misused to question breastfeeding.

Through plants, animals ingest particles that have settled on the ground from automotive exhaust fumes, incineration of trash, fires, paper production, and so on. They pass these particles along in the food chain. Humans consume them in dairy products, fish, beef, pork and eggs. We store the particles in our body fat. However, the Environmental Protection Agency (EPA) and the World Health Organization (WHO) *see no health risk to infants.* The many benefits of breastfeeding clearly outweigh possible effects caused by environmental contaminants in human milk.

If you are fairly sure your milk has an exceptionally high level of contaminants because of unusual factors (eating fish from contaminated waters, working or living in or near a polluted environment, contact with certain chemicals, such as pesticides in farming), contact your state or provincial health department. This is the best place to get specific advice when you have questions about contaminants in your milk. Your doctor can send a sample of your milk to a private lab to be tested. Be aware that contaminant levels vary greatly over the course of a day. If you have overall levels considerably above those known to be safe, talk with your doctor.

Before making any decisions, find out whether you live near a contaminated area. If you do, the water, soil and air around you may also be affected. Everyone may be in contact with contaminants in this case.

To protect your health and your children's health, avoid or reduce your consumption of high-fat meats, fatty organ meats or high-fat dairy products. Studies have shown vegetarians have measurably lower levels of the contaminants in their fat deposits or in mother's milk than do people on mixed diets. In general, animals such as beef cattle consume large quantities of plant food that could be full of contaminants (pesticides). If you were to eat meat from an animal that had ingested contaminants, you would be exposed to the high dosages of contaminants the animal has stored in its fat. Although plants can and do get exposed to contaminants, you would have to eat large amounts to approach the quantity of contaminants in meat.

You also will expose your family to a lower level of contaminants by growing fruits and vegetables yourself, or by buying certified organically grown fruits and vegetables untreated by pesticides. Peel or thoroughly wash produce you buy before eating it.

In and around the house, limit the use of certain chemicals—cleaning products, paints, insulation materials, paintbrush solvents and pesticides. Breathing the air in rooms treated with PCP wood preservers is more dangerous than many orally ingested contaminants—their poisons evaporate fully only after 20 or more years. Use biologically sound materials whenever possible.

Smoking, Caffeine, Alcohol and Drugs

If you smoke, your baby smokes right along with you! What's more, the milk of smokers contains contaminants such as lead and cadmium.

Get Help to Stop Smoking

For everyone's sake, it's best if you stop smoking entirely. Talk with your physician or contact an organization, such as the American Heart Association, that can put you in touch with a stop-smoking support group or provide you with a program to help you quit. Prepare yourself emotionally before you smoke your last cigarette—and then do it! Many successful quitters pick a personally significant day, such as the nearest holiday or a family birthday, to be their first smoke-free day.

You'll never find better motivation to quit than protecting the health of your baby, so this could very well be the time your efforts pay off! But you *will* need support to be successful. Tell all your friends and loved ones you have quit, that you are a *non-smoker* now. Some of them will not be as supportive as you would like them to be. Identify and avoid these people if you feel they might encourage you to smoke again. But most people will applaud your efforts and help you in any way they can. Concentrate on all the health benefits you and your baby will enjoy. And think of how much money you will save!

Smoking during pregnancy can damage your baby. He may suffer from nausea, vomiting, hyperactivity, speech problems or even have a higher risk of cancer later in life. You are well-advised to stop smoking some time before a planned pregnancy and to stay smoke-free after the baby is born.

Passive smoking affects the baby's health before and after birth also. You are exposed to passive smoking if you don't smoke but you work in an environment in which other people smoke, or your partner smokes around you. Tobacco smoke contains harmful heavy metals.

What happens if you can't stop smoking, despite your best intentions? Despite the risks involved, experts believe it is still better for a smoker to nurse her infant rather than bottle-feed her—as long as Mother's cigarette consumption is under 20 a day. Children whose parents smoke are particularly susceptible to respiratory infections. However, breastfed children of mothers who smoke are ill less often than are bottle-fed children of mothers who smoke.

Even 10 cigarettes a day can reduce milk production.

A woman who cannot or will not stop should smoke low-nicotine cigarettes. She should limit her smoking to the times immediately *after* she has breastfed. The half-life of nicotine in the body is 95 minutes.

Caffeine is transferred from your milk to your baby in low concentrations. Your baby's immature liver breaks down caffeine more slowly than an adult liver does. It takes 3-1/2 days for half the caffeine *you* consumed to be eliminated from *your baby's* body. When a baby reacts to caffeine with unusual restlessness, irritability, colic and sleeplessness, it's best to give up this beloved habit—if only for your own self-interest! Cola drinks, black tea, chocolate and many over-the-counter medications contain caffeine. If you "have to have" any of these products, substitute caffeine-free versions for the real thing.

It takes 3-1/2 days for half the caffeine you consumed to be eliminated from your baby's body.

Alcohol is definitely harmful to a breastfed baby. Lower concentrations of alcohol pass to the breast milk, compared to what is in the mother's blood. But a baby's immature liver still can't break down alcohol as quickly as an adult's does.

At one time it was believed small quantities of alcohol weren't harmful and might have a positive effect on the milk-ejection reflex. New research indicates it is better to avoid alcohol completely while you are nursing, because even small amounts (for example, one 6-ounce serving of beer) drunk before breastfeeding can reduce the baby's desire to suck. He will take only about 75% of his usual amount. The baby will suck *more* but get *less*. Try to relax in other ways, such as by doing one of the exercises suggested in chapter 3 (see page 49). These activities can really help. If you want to drink a glass of champagne for a special occasion, drink it right *after* breastfeeding. The benefits of breastfeeding far exceed the risk of an occasional drink every two or three months.

Researchers do not know the complete effects of frequent or occasional **drug use** on mother's milk. However, we know enough about the of drug use to say without hesitation: Avoid *any* contact with drugs! Drugs impair everyone's ability to cope with day-to-day life. Who knows what kind of surprise the suckling baby gets when its mother gets high? One trip to your local hospital's newborn intensive care unit (NICU) should be all the incentive you need to stay off drugs. A look at drug-dependent babies, born from mothers who are also drug-dependent, is a heartbreaking, unforgettable sight.

Swimming and Sauna

You don't have to give up swimming or sauna visits if you are used to them. You can begin swimming again as soon as the post-partum flow has stopped. When you swim, rub cream or salve on your breasts to protect them. The water you swim in should be comfortably warm.

Heat from the sauna may cause you to leak a little milk. Pressing your arms against your breasts will help stop it. Remember to drink a big glass of water or two afterward to bring your fluid balance back to normal.

Breast Cancer

We know that breast cancer is less likely appear in mothers who breastfeed (or have breastfed in the past), but it can happen. If, while breastfeeding—or later, during your monthly self-exam— you find a lump in your breast that doesn't go away, see your doctor immediately. It's helpful if your physician has worked with breastfeeding patients before. He will be able to easily recognize the normal changes associated with the lactating breast.

With an ultrasound test, or in some cases a biopsy, your practitioner may be able to confirm the lump is harmless and relieve your anxiety. You can continue to breastfeed (see Medications, page 99) after a biopsy. However, milk production may be reduced if milk ducts were crossed in the procedure.

If you have had breast cancer and one breast was removed, you can still breastfeed. It is also possible to nurse with a breast that has been operated on.

> Toward the end of the pregnancy, I noticed a lump in my left breast that did not get smaller after the birth or after my milk came in. My doctor removed a tumor from my breast in an out-patient procedure. I had to stay in the hospital for a day because milk ducts were cut during the operation. A lot of milk flowed out of the drainage tubes into a container I carried around for two weeks.

> I breastfed my son undisturbed for two years using both breasts. The breast that had been operated on healed nicely. When my daughter was born, I had no problems nursing her on that side. That breast produced as much milk as the other one.

AIDS

AIDS is an immune-system disease that eventually causes death. It is spread through body fluids. A woman with AIDS or the virus that causes AIDS can spread the disease to her unborn baby. A pregnant woman who suspects she may be HIV-positive should get an HIV test. (HIV stands for *human immunodeficiency virus*. HIV causes AIDS, but unlike AIDS does not show outward symptoms.) In an infected person, the virus is present in all bodily fluid, including breast milk.

Unfortunately, it is still not clear how or when HIV can be transmitted to the baby. Researchers do not understand why the majority of infants of HIV-positive mothers do not become infected. They do not know what protects the baby from an infection in the womb. Because a child apparently can be infected during a vaginal birth, Cesarean deliveries are currently recommended for HIV-positive, pregnant women.

The danger of infecting the baby through mother's milk seems relatively high among mothers who become infected during the time they are breastfeeding and lower in mothers who were infected when the baby was born. The risk of infection for the children probably also depends on the expectant mother's health and immune status. In any case, women who test positive for HIV are currently advised *not* to breastfeed.

Unfortunately, it takes time to find out if a newborn baby is HIV-positive. The most common antibody test works this way: If the mother is HIV-positive, HIV-antibodies will be in her baby's blood after birth, because the mother passes antibodies to her baby through the umbilical cord. These antibodies disappear 6 to 18 months after birth. Only then can doctors determine whether the baby is infected or not. A new test in the United States checks for duplication of HIV-virus fragments in the baby's blood. This test, called the *PCR test*, can be done in most hospital laboratories. The test is most reliable when performed 4 to 6 months after the baby's birth. Ask your doctor if it's available in your area.

If you are HIV-positive and would still like to give your baby breast milk, you have the option of obtaining donor milk from a milk bank. Milk from milk banks is safe because the banks must pasteurize all donor milk. This process destroys bacteria and viruses, including HIV.

AIDS research continues at a rapid pace, providing patients with a constant stream of new information. The best sources of information are the numerous AIDS help organizations and your own local health department.

Supplementary Nipples

Humans normally develop only two nipples along the milk lines that run the length of the body. Occasionally other, less-well developed nipples are seen along this line. Usually they do not develop into milking sites, but there are exceptions. One woman wrote to me about her experience:

> *Around my armpits on both sides, I have duct-type tissue with "nipples" about 1-1/2 inches in size. During my pregnancy, this tissue enlarged so much that my obstetrician thought I might become engorged or get a breast infection in the supplementary "breasts." I didn't let myself get discouraged because my "normal" breasts were all right. Three days after Henry's birth, the milk came in in all four "breasts." It was painful. Milk leaked out of the duct complex down my left arm, which was awkward. Cooling and rubbing the spot with a cream the doctor prescribed helped. After about three weeks, the swelling abated because milk production in that area had not been stimulated. I breastfed Henry for six months, and we had a close relationship.*
>
> *Now that he is weaned, the extra duct-type tissue has faded so much that no one would guess I ever had a problem. I'd like to encourage all women to fulfill their desire to breastfeed, despite any "abnormalities."*

Immunizations

In general, breastfeeding mothers may be immunized. You will not have to wean if you need a vaccination. If you plan to visit another

Caution!

As a rule, use the same caution with medicines during breastfeeding as during pregnancy:

- Take as little medication as possible.
- Be especially careful with combination preparations.
- Do not self-prescribe medication.
- Always seek medical advice.

country, check with your doctor to see if you will need vaccinations before you go.

Breastfeeding babies can get the usual immunizations. The reaction to immunizations is better among fully breastfed infants than artificially fed infants. Protection is more effective.

Medications

Basically, expect the baby to receive some of whatever medication you are taking. Most medications go into the breast milk in more or less high concentrations and do affect the baby. The baby can tolerate some substances without negative side effects, but others are dangerous even in low concentrations.

Nursing mothers should *not* self-prescribe medication—not even those made from natural plant sources, because they too will interact with the body. Check with your doctor. If he or she needs more information, a complete list of medications and their effects on breast milk is published by the AAP (Committee on Drugs of the American Academy of Pediatrics). You doctor may wish to refer to Ruth Lawrence's book, *Breastfeeding: A Guide for the Medical Profession*, (1994) for detailed information.

If you are prescribed medication for your own health, be sure the doctor knows you are breastfeeding. Ask him or her to select a drug that will have the least effect on the baby. The risk factors for mother and baby must be weighed carefully, on an individual basis. If you cannot avoid medication incompatible with breastfeeding, you will have to pump your milk and discard it until you are off the medication, or wean your baby. If you decide to pump temporarily, continue to pump until the medication is out of your system. Consult your physician to find out how long certain medications will remain in your breast milk.

Menstruation and Contraception

In cultures where babies are breastfed automatically, and mother's milk is the primary source of nutrition in the first year of life, the space between babies is between 18 months and 2 years, if no other contraceptive methods are employed. The first period for non-nursing mothers occurs 4 to 6 weeks postpartum. For mothers who breastfeed in a limited way—every 4 hours, no night nursing or supplementation—periods return after 2 or 3 months. For mothers who breastfeed fully, it may take 6 to 18 months, although the period might return as soon as 4 months after birth. Prolactin levels, which are stimulated by breastfeeding, influence the effectiveness of breastfeeding as a contraceptive measure.

The relative effectiveness of breastfeeding as a contraceptive measure is best ensured when

- newborns are put to breast immediately after birth and suck frequently around the clock
- when their mothers use no bottles, pacifiers or nipple shields
- when babies get no supplementary foods in the first 6 months
- when breastfeeding continues into the second year

These factors help suppress hormones that would lead to pregnancy. But be warned: Even something as seemingly minor as taking long breaks between breastfeeds (more than 4 hours) within a space of 24 hours can counteract contraceptive effectiveness!

A more scientific name for this natural approach of contraception is *the Lactation Amenorrhea Method (LAM)*. LAM specifies if you are fully breastfeeding around the clock, without supplementation, your baby is less than 6 months old, and you have had no vaginal bleeding after 56 days postpartum, your chance of becoming pregnant is less than 2%. If you combine this with taking your basal temperature in the morning and observing your cervical mucus secretion, your chances of pregnancy are reduced to less than 1%.

In one detailed study of 130 women in Chile, researchers found the probability of pregnancy was very low at the end of 6 months postpartum in women who were breastfeeding exclusively and had not menstruated (1.8%). For women who nursed exclusively and had a return of menses, the probability was 27.2%. The pregnancy probability rate for mothers who had only partially breastfed was 40.5%.

A good, comprehensive overview of the various forms of birth control, their use, effectiveness, advantages and disadvantages is available in *Our Bodies—Ourselves for the 21st Century*, from the Boston Women's Health Collective (1998). Another excellent book is *All about Sex* from Planned Parenthood of America. If you definitely don't want to get pregnant, it makes sense to take the appropriate measures as soon as your postpartum flow has ended.

If you feel you don't meet the requirements of LAM, you will need to find other forms of forms of contraception. The pill is not appropriate for nursing mothers. While nursing, you can use condoms, spermicidal jellies, vaginal tablets and sprays. Basal-temperature readings and the diaphragm are only moderately effective. Taking your temperature every day is normally a good way to find out if you have ovulated. But you need a regular sleep pattern to get a reliable reading, and that is seldom possible with a newborn in the house.

If you definitely don't want to get pregnant, it makes sense to take the appropriate measures as soon as your postpartum flow has ended.

The diaphragm is a rubber cap used with a spermicidal gel. A diaphragm fits over a woman's cervix—the entry to the uterus—to prevent sperm from reaching an egg and fertilizing it. A health practitioner must fit you for a diaphragm. If you used this form of birth control before your baby was born, you will have to be refitted for a diaphragm, because the cervix changes shape during the birth process.

Using the pill, especially the combination pill, while breastfeeding is not advisable for several reasons. Preparations with estrogen and progestin (sometimes called the *combined pill*) will reduce your milk supply. Nor is it advisable to use the "mini-pill" (the progestin-only pill). Manufacturers claim nursing mothers can use the mini-pill because it doesn't inhibit milk production. However, it changes the unique composition of mother's milk to a lower-quality product. Very little research has been done on the possible

immediate and long-term effects of the estrogen and progestin hormones on the baby. Occasionally breast enlargement in somewhat
older boy babies and some masculinization in girl babies have been
observed. Animal studies, which indicate deviations in sexual dif-
ferentiation and behavior, suggest caution.

Dressing for Breastfeeding

Nursing Bras

It *is* possible to find nursing bras that are both flattering and practical. Look for one in a natural fabric you can open easily (with
one hand) and discreetly. Don't buy a nursing bra immediately
after the milk comes in, because your breasts are swollen at that
time. They will reduce a little in size after a few days. Make sure the
cups are large enough. They should not pinch; breast infections
are more likely when milk ducts are compressed and milk cannot
be emptied out of the ducts. The bottom of the bra that surrounds
your rib cage should not be too tight because it offers poor support and may give you a backache.

After a few weeks, once the breast is back to its normal size,
women with good connective tissue and small breasts sometimes
revert to their usual lightweight, elasticized bras. The cup is
simply pulled under the breast for nursing. Some mothers can go
bra-less again. Still, you may be more comfortable in a supportive
nursing bra.

At the beginning, you will probably want to wear a bra day
and night—to give your heavy breasts support and because your
milk may leak between feeds. Your breasts will get smaller later,
while you are still nursing, and then you will be able to use a smaller
bra. Nursing bras come with breast pads to absorb leaking milk.
Don't use bras with plastic pieces in the cups. The plastic holds
in moisture, which encourages germs and fungi to grow. Breast
pads made of cotton or silk feel best. But you can make comfortable breast pads from washable cotton diapers, which is better for
the pocketbook and the environment.

Clothing

Two-piece outfits are the most practical: slacks or a skirt with a sweater or a blouse. When the baby is hungry, you need only pull up the upper garment slightly to put your baby to breast. People around you usually won't even notice. Many women wear loose shirts or blouses until their breasts fit into their old clothes again some weeks later. A friend of mine wore a loose cotton dress with wide fluttering sleeves while she was nursing. She just pushed aside the sleeves to lay her child discreetly on the breast at the arm opening.

I recommend wearing patterned material because spots from leaking milk aren't as noticeable.

Certain summer clothes (a loose dress with elastic, or clothing that opens in front) offer easy access to the breast but require a little more courage and self-confidence because there's a clearer view of the breast. If you place a shawl or blanket over your shoulder, the baby and your breast, you're less likely to be disturbed or offend anyone. I recommend wearing patterned material because spots from leaking milk aren't as noticeable. Today, nursing mothers have more fashionable clothing options than ever before, especially through mail-order catalogs (see page 263).

6

If You Have
a Problem

Certain circumstances create a good foundation for a positive nursing experience:

- ❀ giving birth in a respectful atmosphere among people who are sensitive to your needs and who will help you react to your baby immediately and instinctively

- ❀ taking time before the birth to focus on breastfeeding with feelings of peace and serenity

- ❀ being in an environment where natural body processes, especially the basic principles of breastfeeding, are respected

- ❀ feeling you are supported after the birth of your baby by experienced caregivers who will help you put your baby to the breast and care for him

But some situations can make you feel so helpless that you want to give up. That doesn't have to happen, because most problems are temporary. Mastering a crisis will help you grow stronger. You really can overcome most problems. This chapter provides help and encouragement for problems that occur most often.

Not Enough Milk

I'm going crazy—my baby cries after every feeding. How do I know if my baby is getting enough?

If your baby's eyes shine, he has healthy skin and at least 6 to 10 wet diapers a day, then he is probably getting enough milk. If he is lively and gains weight steadily, his discomfort may come from something besides hunger. Are you misinterpreting the baby's crying as a hunger signal? (Very quiet babies risk not getting enough milk more often than do those who cry a lot—see page 74.) Are you interpreting the normal changes in your breasts (getting softer) as signs of insufficient milk? There may be several possible explanations for this fear.

Possible Causes

❧ Your milk production is not being stimulated sufficiently because

- You and your baby are separated for long periods of time.
- The hospital does not have a 24-hour rooming-in policy.
- Your baby's hunger has been satisfied with supplementary formula (or glucose water) and he is less eager at the breast.
- Your baby is often given a pacifier to satisfy him, so he demands the breast less often.
- Your baby is too weak to suck at the breast right now.
- Your baby is very sleepy or doesn't announce his need to nurse often enough.

❧ Your let-down reflex is being affected by

- stress, fatigue, insecurity or anxiety
- ambivalent feelings about breastfeeding
- tension in your household (for example, if your partner is opposed to breastfeeding; see also page 179)

❧ Your baby is not correctly positioned at the breast (see instructions for correct positioning, page 70).

❧ Because of a growth spurt, your baby needs more of your milk. You can't satisfy him until your milk supply increases to meet his new demand.

❧ Your daily habits are influencing your milk production or the milk flow:

- Do you rest often enough?

- Are you taking medication, including birth-control pills?

- Do you smoke?

- Do you drink alcohol (see page 95)?

- Are you doing too much or having too many visitors?

- Are you drinking enough fluid (see note on page 75)?

- Are you eating well-balanced, nutritious meals (see page 87)? Although eating well does not generally affect your milk supply, it can positively affect your health and well-being.

> *Now I look at Cameron's crying as a "crisis" he's having and not as a sign I have too little milk. So when he cries a lot in the evening, I accept it. I don't let it drive me crazy. Now things are much better in our family—especially for me! I pick Cameron up, pat him and talk quietly with him. I don't try to settle him down with a pacifier or the breast any more.*

What Can I Do?

❧ Breastfeeding is a matter of supply and demand. The more you nurse, the more milk you will have. If your baby doesn't ask to nurse often enough, you may have to wake him at certain intervals (for example, every two or three hours) for a while to "condition" the baby and your body.

❧ Many babies are especially restless in the late afternoon. This restlessness may have nothing to do with breastfeeding and everything to do with too much activity or some new stimulus. Your baby may be "processing" the many impressions he had during the day (see Colic, page 120).

❧ If you have nursed your baby on both sides, go back and give him the first breast again before ending the session. Do this for a few feedings to increase your milk production.

❧ If you can't stimulate enough milk by the baby's sucking, increase your milk supply by hand expressing or pumping (see page 79).

❧ Sometimes, between the sixth and tenth days, mothers worry they don't have enough milk. There is some reason for this. Leaving the hospital, having total responsibility for the baby at home, maybe having a lot of visitors to the home who want to admire the baby—all these create a stressful situation that coincides with the baby's first growth spurt. It's possible your milk supply is *temporarily* not meeting your baby's needs. *Don't supplement! Instead, breastfeed more often.* In 48 hours your breast milk production *will* increase.

❧ You may be afraid you don't have enough milk when you notice your breasts have gotten smaller and softer again. Don't worry! It means the milk ducts have stabilized. The right amount of milk is being produced.

❧ At 6 and at 12 weeks, babies have growth spurts. Follow the same advice as before: Breastfeed more often, don't supplement, and your milk supply will increase again.

❧ In many cases there is enough milk, but the let-down reflex isn't working. Check out the many helpful suggestions in chapter 2, pages 49-61. Try to find your inner balance through a massage, a warm shower, a footbath, a warm drink, music, a comfortable atmosphere, harmonizing fragrances, breathing and relaxation exercises, or visualization exercises to "nurture" the breast and release the milk flow. Allow yourself times of quiet and contemplation to "turn off."

❧ Find a doula to help during your first days with your baby (see page 27). Spend a day or a weekend in bed and let yourself be nurtured, even spoiled, without feeling guilty.

❧ Arrange for outside help for your household.

❧ Find support from a breastfeeding group or from other nursing mothers in your area. You can even find support over the telephone or on the Internet.

❧ If something worries you, talk with someone you trust—a friend, minister or rabbi, therapist or counselor. "Getting it off your chest" may bring relief.

❧ As soon as your baby gets a bottle, the weaning process begins. Your milk supply will be reduced. Even glucose water spoils the baby's appetite for mother's milk. The fine balance of supply and demand is disturbed. If you have already given one or more bottles and want to reverse the trend, gradually replace the formula feedings, one at a time, with breast milk. If you have decided to continue to offer formula at certain meals and nurse at other feedings, there may be a consequence: Your baby may suck less and less well at the breast as a result.

❧ Be sure you get enough fluid (more than two quarts or liters a day) and eat a balanced diet (rich in calcium, protein and vitamin B-12). Many women can increase their milk supply by drinking milk-enhancing teas (three to six cups a day—see page 90) or by taking a vitamin-B-rich, brewer's-yeast supplement.

About Homeopathy

Homeopathy is based on the idea that "like cures like." It is a way of healing the body using very small doses of an agent that can cause symptoms of the ailment. Seek a consultation with a homeopath or a naturopathic doctor for proper diagnosis. *Naturopaths* are grounded in natural remedies and the interrelationship of a person's body, mind and spirit in healing. *Homeopaths* are specialists in homeopathy. See page 162.

Note: Discuss your interest in homeopathy with your doctor *before* you begin taking any homeopathic remedy. Your own doctor and your baby's doctor should be aware of remedies you are taking or plan to take.

- Above all: *Have faith you can increase your milk production at will.* You can do it!

- You might try a homeopathic remedy under the guidance of a specialist. Let the practitioner know you are breastfeeding. Some homeopathic remedies typically used in this situation are Bryonia C6, Calcium Carbonate C6, Ignatia C6, Pulsatilla C6 and Zincum metallicum C6. (See page 162.)

- You may want to try Bach Flower remedies. Ask yourself what emotional condition might be inhibiting your milk production or flow. A trained therapist may be able to help you choose an effective remedy based on your answer. Plausible remedies for this situation include: Agrimony, Cerato, Clematis, Crab Apple, Elm, Holly, Hornbeam, Impatiens, Larch, Olive, Pine, Rock Water or Star of Bethlehem. (See page 164.)

- Aromatherapy may help. To stimulate milk production, you can make a massage oil with which to gently massage your breast. (See box.) While your baby is still a newborn, do not apply the oil to your breast too close to feeding time, because the fragrance will be too strong for the baby's sensitive nose. Also, avoid rubbing the oil into the nipple and areola.

Milk-stimulating Massage Oil

1/4 cup (50ml) almond oil
1/4 cup (50ml) calendula oil
10 drops star anise oil
2 drops rose oil
5 drops fennel oil
2 drops coriander oil

Combine ingredients in a clean bottle with a tight-fitting lid. Shake well.

About Bach Flower Remedies

Bach Flower remedies are part of the growing field of flower-essence therapy. Certain essences are thought to redirect your energy field to correct a disharmony that may result in emotional disturbance or even illness. *Bach Flower remedies are not an alternative to medicine and cannot cure illness.* They are consistently useful in spiritual, psychological and emotional reconnection. Like many things, effective treatment depends on proper recognition, knowledge and diagnosis. Contact Bach Flower USA (see page 266) for a list of Bach Flower Therapists near you. For a list of common Bach Flower essences used during the breastfeeding period, see page 166.

Note: Discuss your interest in Bach Flower Therapy with your doctor *before* you begin taking any Bach Flower remedy. Your baby's doctor and your own doctor should be aware of remedies you are taking or plan to take.

Full, Uncomfortable Breasts

While most women tend to worry about having too little milk, others have the opposite problem. The feeling you have "too much milk" develops from an initial imbalance between your supply and your baby's demand. Pumping *isn't* the solution to this problem. When you pump, your body assumes your baby needs the milk and produces even more to adapt to the increasing "demand."

What You Can Do

- Give your baby the same breast in any 3-hour period.
- Until your body adjusts, express only enough milk on the other side to ease the tightness in the breast.
- Use an ice pack if the breast hurts. Wrapping ice cubes in a towel makes a nice ice pack. Your body will adjust in a few days. If the breast isn't stimulated for hours, milk production will decrease gradually.
- Drinking sage tea (half a cup, sipped throughout the day) can decrease milk production. (Recipe, page 177.)
- You might try a homeopathic remedy under the guidance of a specialist. Let the practitioner know you are breastfeeding. Homeopathic remedies typically used in this situation are Phytolacca C6 or Pulsatilla C6. (See page 162.)
- You may want to try Bach Flower remedies. Ask yourself what makes your milk flow so generously. A trained therapist may be able to help you choose an effective remedy based on your answer. These essences

Milk-reducing Massage Oil and Compress

Oil

3 oz. thistle oil
10 drops sage essence
5 drops mint essence

Combine ingredients in a clean jar with a tight-fitting lid. Shake well.

Compress

2 drops lemon essence
1 tablespoon honey
1 quart (or liter) water
2 drops sage essence

Dissolve lemon essence in honey. Add honey mixture and sage essence to water and mix well. Dip a clean washcloth into the mixture, wring, and place on the breast as a compress.

may be recommended, depending on your answer: Agrimony, Cerato, Clematis, Crab Apple, Elm, Holly, Hornbeam, Impatiens, Larch, Olive, Pine, Rock Water, Star of Bethlehem. See page 164.

⚜ Aromatherapy. To reduce your milk, gently massage your breast using Milk-reducing Massage Oil. If you have a newborn, use this just *after* you nurse. Cool, damp compresses can also help. For recipes, see box.

Sore Nipples

When you begin to breastfeed, usually in the first 2 to 4 days, you may have nipple discomfort. The soreness seems to be unrelated to the length of time your baby is at the breast or whether you prepared your nipples before birth. Your nipples may remain a little sensitive for a few days after the birth. Fortunately, this problem tends to disappear quickly. Try to find out what may be contributing to your discomfort, and make the necessary changes.

Possible Causes

⚜ Most commonly, the baby is not properly positioned (see page 68).

⚛ The baby isn't taking enough of the areola into her mouth or isn't latching on correctly because

- of the way she is positioned
- the breast is engorged
- the nipple is retracted
- she has nipple confusion because of a pacifier or bottle

⚛ Your nipple is pulled out of shape on one side.

⚛ Your let-down reflex isn't working well.

⚛ Your skin is not supple enough.

⚛ Your skin is sensitive.

⚛ Your baby has a strong suction.

⚛ If time passes, your nipples are still very sore and your areola is tingly or itchy, you could have a thrush infection. If so, your baby will probably have the same infection in his mouth. Both of you will need medical treatment.

What Can I Do?

What you do depends on what caused the problem.

⚛ Pay attention to the way you put your baby to the breast (see page 68):

- Is his head in the curve of your arm, his tummy against yours, and his bottom cupped in your hand?
- Is your nipple lying in the middle of his mouth, or is it pulled to one side?
- Is your baby sucking just the nipple, or is he taking in the areola too?
- Do you press on your breast with your finger, causing the nipple to tip up in the baby's mouth?

⚛ Don't use soap on the nipple or areola. It destroys the natural acidity of your skin, making the entire area less flexible and more brittle and encouraging cracks to develop.

⚛ Don't wipe off the milk. Instead, allow milk and saliva to dry on the skin. Both have a softening, sterilizing effect.

⚛ Contrary to popular belief, women with sore nipples should nurse *more* often, not less. If the baby is put to breast more often, for shorter periods, he will not be starving at the beginning of the feed and will grip the breast with less intensity. When the baby nurses more frequently, he can grasp the nipple together with the areola more easily because the breasts are not as full. Women who breastfeed on demand have sore nipples half as often as women who feed on a 4-hour schedule.

✦ The baby's initial sucking before the milk lets down can be the most uncomfortable part of the breastfeeding process. You can relieve your child of this job by expressing a little milk by hand before the feeding (see page 79). This way, he doesn't need to suck as strongly at the beginning and can latch on to the breast more easily.

✦ Put your baby to the nipple that is *less sore* first. The let-down reflex will make the milk flow to both breasts. When she is moved to the sore breast, your baby won't need to suck as strongly to get the milk.

✦ If your let-down reflex is not working well (see page 43), your baby has to suck hard without getting good results. The strong sucking can hurt your nipples, which can inhibit the milk-ejection reflex further. Then you need something to help you relax! On pages 49-61, you'll find suggestions that might help.

✦ Alternate the positions you use to put the baby to the breast, to change pressure on the nipples.

✦ Some women I know have had good experience using inexpensive plastic tea strainers to heal sore nipples. They cut off the handle and put the strainer over the nipple, inside the bra. The strainer lets air circulate, and the nipple heals in a couple of days. You may also use breast shells with air holes for this purpose (Sources, see page 263).

✦ Use breast pads made from natural fibers (for example, cotton and silk). Plastic liners may aggravate the situation.

✦ Modified, purified, allergen-free lanolin can be left on the nipple during breastfeeding to heal cracks in the nipple. Vitamin A and D cream and vitamin E capsules also speed healing. A midwife I know with decades of experience has found the application of almond oil helps heal sore nipples quickly.

✦ Centrally heated homes have low humidity and this dries out skin more easily. A humidifier can help.

✦ If you start taking preventive or therapeutic measures for your sore nipples soon enough, you probably won't have to interrupt breastfeeding at all.

✦ *Keep in mind that nipple problems are temporary.*

Rose-water Compress

1 lb. (454g) cottage cheese
50ml rose water
1 drop rose oil
1 drop each, sheep yarrow and chamomile-blue essential oils, optional

Combine cooled ingredients and apply to breast.

⚘ If your cracked nipples seep a little blood into the breast milk, don't worry—it doesn't hurt the baby, and you can continue breastfeeding. It looks worse than it is.

⚘ Use nipple shields during feeding *only* as a last resort, never to prevent a problem. Nipple shields cause many problems of their own.

⚘ Homeopathic remedies may aid healing. You might try one under the guidance of a specialist. Let the practitioner know you are breastfeeding. Some homeopathic remedies typically used in this situation are Castor equi C6, Graphies C6, Phytolacca C6. (See page 162.)

⚘ You may want to try Bach Flower remedies. Could there be internal, spiritual reasons for the sore nipples? What might they be? A trained therapist may be able to help you choose an effective remedy based on your answer. Agrimony, Aspen, Beech, Centaury, Crab Apple, Heather, Holly, Larch or Pine might help. (See description list, page 164.)

⚘ Aromatherapy: Rose water inhibits infection and encourages healing. Cool, damp compresses placed on the breasts can be helpful. Try the recipe I like for a rose-water compress appearing in the box above.

Plugged Ducts or Breast Infection

Engorgement, sore nipples, breast infection, abscess—one breast problem can easily lead to another, more difficult problem. It's smart to know how to recognize these problems and learn how to stop them early.

Your breasts can become *engorged* on both sides when the milk comes in, or after a longer-than-usual wait between feedings. Engorgement can be uncomfortable, but is relieved by breastfeeding. A *plugged milk duct* is different. You may gradually develop hard areas in one breast, which hurt when you touch them. Sometimes the entire breast gets involved. Your breast generally will not feel warm, but your temperature may go up to 100.5F (38C).

Germs multiply in milk clogged in the ducts, setting the stage for a breast infection (*mastitis*). You probably have a breast infection if you get a fever of 101F (38.5C) or higher, sometimes accompanied by chills, have little energy and feel flu-like pain in your arms and legs. The breast also changes: Infected areas appear as red patches, and the skin is hot, swollen and very painful to the touch.

If the infection is left untreated, which is rare, the infected areas may form *abscesses*—fluid-filled lumps under the skin. Abscesses need to be drained by a physician. A woman can continue to breastfeed even if she has had an abscess treated surgically. Often the incision is made well away from the nipple, so uncomplicated breastfeeding is still possible.

Possible Causes

- The time between feedings is too long, and the milk ducts have become too full. They press against each other and can't empty.

- Tension, insecurity and pain inhibit the let-down reflex.

- Emotional problems, conflicts, difficulties adjusting to parenting, social pressures and stress, among other things, can inhibit milk flow and cause engorgement.

- External obstacles (such as a tight bra or badly adjusted straps from a baby carrier), press into the breast and prevent milk from flowing in certain spots, plugging ducts.

- A milk-duct opening at the nipple may be plugged with dried milk.

- Bacteria have multiplied in a milk duct because of an infected nipple.

- Your immune system may be taxed for any number of reasons: exhaustion, poor nutrition, medication or a job. You may be overdoing it with too much attention to external responsibilities and too little time for rest.

- The baby doesn't drink well because he has a cold, is teething or is being distracted too much.

Two women who have had breast infections share their experiences:

> . . . *After a while I saw there were emotional reasons for my repeated breast infections. I don't get along with my mother. Every time she announced a visit, my breast got hard and painful. The infections improved quickly with cottage-cheese compresses and bed rest.*

> . . . *Vanessa wasn't feeding well because she had a cold. I didn't make sure my breast was soft again after each feeding. Along with plugged ducts causing engorgement in my breast, I ran a high fever. My doctor prescribed an antibiotic compatible with nursing, and I stayed in bed. I breastfed Vanessa more often than usual, and made sure the affected side was emptied completely. While she was drinking from one breast, I gently massaged the hard spots with my hand and stroked the breast in the direction of the nipple. Before starting, I had put a warm washcloth on the breast. The engorgement cleared up in a day and a half.*

What Can I Do?

If your breast is swollen, painful, red and you have a temperature, you might try some of these remedies. The earlier you intervene, the better!

- ❧ Stay calm! Go to bed with your baby, and ask someone to take care of you for a day or two. If you can't stay in bed, at least take it easy for a couple of days.

- ❧ Keep your breast empty! Breastfeed twice as often as usual—every one or two hours so your breast doesn't get too full.

- ❧ Position your baby so his lower jaw rests on the hard spot. For example, if the right side of the right breast has a hard spot, position your baby so his legs are cuddled along the right side of your body (football hold—see page 70). If the upper side of your breast is swollen and painful, then your baby's legs need to lie above your shoulders (while you lie stretched out on your back). It sounds impossible, but give it a try—it works! You can also massage milk out of the engorged ducts, although nothing is as effective and powerful as the baby's sucking.

❧ Use ice packs between feedings to reduce the pain, and warm compresses just before the feeding to open milk vessels. Apply the warmth directly on the breast. Often milk begins to flow because of the warmth even before the feeding begins. Hot-water bottles are not appropriate because they are heavy—their weight on the breast can inhibit milk flow instead of encourage it.

❧ Apply "nurturing touch" to your breasts and imagine you are dissolving all the tension and engorgement at the painful spot and getting your milk to flow well. Re-read the information on page 52.

❧ How about treating yourself to a warm footbath? Footbaths can reduce feelings of stress in your whole body.

❧ Place a small brown-paper sack filled with warm, slightly mashed baked potatoes in their jackets—or a compress of cool, raw, white cabbage leaves—on the breast outside the areola. These remedies can reduce swelling quickly, often within hours. Replace wilted cabbage leaves with fresh, chilled ones after a couple of hours.

❧ Add essential oils of yarrow, chamomile blue or lavender essence to cottage cheese or honey. Spread the mixture on your breast and cover it with a light cloth to help protect the breast and inhibit infection.

❧ It can help to drink two cups of fenugreek-seed tea (use 1 heaping teaspoon of seed to 1 cup hot water). After sipping the tea, you can re-use the seeds as a compress on the breast.

❧ Avoid wearing tight clothing. Some restrictive clothing can inhibit milk flow in the ducts. If it is not too uncomfortable, try to go without a bra for a few days, or wear one that is a size larger.

❧ If the duct is plugged by dried milk at the nipple opening, bathe the nipple with water to dissolve the milk residue.

❧ Nurse the baby on the affected side first and often to keep the breast as empty as possible.

❧ Counseling breastfeeding mothers over the years has taught me many nursing problems have emotional origins. Maybe you feel overwhelmed or insecure. Perhaps your husband is jealous of the attention your baby is getting (see page 227) and that bothers you. Maybe you have mixed feelings about certain people who've announced a visit. If something is bothering you, admit it to yourself. Then look for someone you can trust and who listens well. Talking with someone can often solve the problem. You and your good health are at stake. Consider whether your body may be telling you that you've tried to do too much.

✤ You might try a homeopathic remedy under the guidance of a specialist. Let the practitioner know you are breastfeeding. Some homeopathic remedies typically used in this situation are: *For engorgement and plugged ducts,* Phytolacca C12, Conium C6 or Nux vomica C6. *For breast infections,* Belladonna C6, Phytolacca C6, Bryonia C6, Hepar sulfur C6, Silicea C6 or Mercurius C6. (See page 162.)

✤ You may want to try Bach Flower remedies. Could there be internal, emotional reasons for the breast infections? A trained therapist may be able to help you choose an effective remedy based on your answer. Commonly used for this situation are: Agrimony, Aspen, Clematis, Elm, Holly, Hornbeam, Impatiens, Larch, Mustard, Oak, Olive, Pine, Red Chestnut, Rock Water, Scleranthus, Vervain, Wild Oat, Wild Rose, Willow. (See page 164.)

✤ You and your practitioner may decide to use antibiotics if other remedies do not affect the swelling or pain, or if a true infection occurs.

Continue breastfeeding. La Leche League studies have shown breast infections can be cured within three days with frequent nursing, bed rest, warm and cold compresses and antibiotics. Women who wean often have pain and infection for quite a while longer.

Practitioners used to think bacteria from the infected breast, which the baby gets through drinking breast milk, might be harmful for him and cause intestinal-tract disturbances. Experience shows this is seldom the case. Most germs are destroyed by the baby's stomach acid.

Differences between Plugged Ducts and Infection

The transition point between plugged ducts and breast infection is flexible. Often what is called a *breast infection* is merely plugged ducts with the beginnings of an infection. Antibiotics are not needed at this stage and shouldn't be used prematurely. Talk to your practitioner to make the right choice for your situation. *If you do develop mastitis, take care of it immediately. It is a dangerous complication that must be treated with antibiotics.* Let the practitioner treating your mastitis know you wish to continue breastfeeding.

Nipple Shape Is a Problem

If you have a nipple shape that is challenging for your baby to grasp while breastfeeding, you can try a number of helpful options.

What Can I Do?

❧ Inverted and flat nipples can be conditioned during pregnancy by wearing breast shells or using a Niplette regularly (see page 35). You have time to change your nipples after your baby is born, also. Breast shells can be used between feedings to encourage your nipples to stay in the correct shape.

❧ Before feeding, stimulate your nipples with cold water so they will stand out. Rub them with the flat of the hand, pull them out, twist them (gently), or use a breast pump. If your partner wants to, he might suck on them for a while.

❧ In many hospitals, a silicon or latex nipple shield—similar to the nipple on a bottle—is recommended to treat flat or sore nipples. Using this device is certainly preferable to not nursing at all. But try it only when nothing else has worked, because it can disturb the baby's sucking pattern. Many babies get so used to the nipple shield that it is difficult to put them directly to the breast again. If you use latex shields, you can snip away at the rim a tiny bit at a time until the baby is sucking directly on the breast. The heavier red-rubber shields reduce the milk obtained by 58% and increase the infant's sucking rate and time spent resting. The thin-type latex shields work better—they reduce the milk by 22% and do not affect the sucking pattern.

In some hospitals, the milk of mothers with nipple problems is pumped from the beginning and fed to the baby by bottle. In the long run, stimulation from the pump is not sufficient to enable a mother to breastfeed fully. Also, the nipple on the bottle disturbs the baby's sucking pattern. As a result, he will have even more trouble getting used to your flat nipples later. Avoid this kind of management if you can. A woman who follows a vegan diet (free of meat, fish, eggs or milk products) needs extra vitamin B-12 to prevent some problems for her baby. Her baby may not metabolize protein properly, for example.

When Kerry was 10 weeks old, he began to reject the breast at certain times. At first he latched on, then let go of the breast and moved his head wildly, searching in a frustrated way for the nipple. After a few days, when his behavior had about driven me crazy, the problem became clear: Kerry was curious and easily distracted. His sister had figured this out. Jealous, she attracted my attention and Kerry's with loud behavior during nursing times.

When that happened, Kerry stopped nursing, but wasn't really full. Even though he had nursed about every four hours before that and my body was used to this, Kerry now got hungry about every two hours. He was no longer greeted by a full breast with a hard nipple. Instead, he found a soft breast and a somewhat sunken-in nipple, which he wasn't used to. This was why he displayed those searching movements—he was looking for "his" nipple.

I accidentally discovered a trick that solved the problem. I put my little finger in Kerry's mouth. As he sucked on it, I drew him onto my breast. Once he began sucking on the breast too, I removed my finger and Kerry could feed without further difficulty.

Breastfeeding on One Side

Many babies prefer the nipple of one breast so strongly, they go on strike and won't feed at all when their mother wants to put them on the other nipple. If this happens to you, don't be too concerned. It *is* possible to breastfeed from just one breast.

After I had tried for days to force my baby to suck on both sides, I resigned myself to the inevitable. At first I pumped the unused side, but the milk there dried up more and more. I looked a little lopsided, but that didn't stop me from breastfeeding my son for a year and a half—with just one breast.

7

If Your Baby
Has a Problem

Hardly anyone can remain unaffected by a baby's cry—and that's the way it should be. A baby doesn't have many ways to communicate with the world around him. His crying is one way to let us know he is unhappy and needs care and attention. His crying summons us to come to the rescue of this little person who can't help himself yet. Babies have all kinds of new impressions to process over the course of a day, and crying can be a way of processing or expressing them.

Colic

Some infants cry a lot; others cry very little. When a baby cries frequently and apparently for "no reason," people automatically think he has colic. The crying changes throughout the day, often gaining intensity in the late afternoon or early evening. Usually this kind of crying ends abruptly when the baby is about three months old. Although colic is often talked about, it is still not precisely understood, even by scientists. Many parents in this situation feel their nerves are stretched to the breaking point.

> I never thought motherhood would be like this. Our baby cried a lot—lots of times we carried him around all night. We took turns so at least one of us could get a few hours' sleep. It was a very difficult time. Suddenly, at three months, it got better:

*Our baby was increasingly content and rewarded us
with his smile.*

Possible Causes

❧ Colic may be due to an allergic reaction or hypersensitivity to foods you are eating.

❧ It is believed colic has something to do with the degree of maturity in the digestive tract. For this reason, boys—who generally mature a little later than girls—are more apt to be colicky.

❧ Babies who suck very eagerly tend to take in a lot of air, which causes trouble when it gets into the stomach. Babies writhe in pain when they have finished eating and cry. By crying, they swallow even more air and make the pain worse.

❧ Poor positioning can increase the risk of colic. Babies swallow more air in certain positions.

❧ Rapid emptying of the stomach, caused by the hormone motilin may lead to colic.

❧ A baby may react to smoking in the immediate environment by developing stomach and intestinal disturbances.

❧ Your baby's constant crying may make you tense. Your tension may increase your baby's distress.

❧ It is possible your baby's crying is a symptom of unprocessed experiences and impressions. She may be trying to process experiences such as the anxiety of people around her or simply her average daily experiences. Some believe a baby who has had a difficult birthing experience may try to process it this way.

❧ Crying can be your baby's reaction to changes such as sleeping in different beds or too much travel. Your baby may also react to some underlying tension or stress in the family.

❧ Depending on your baby's temperament, he may be especially sensitive to overstimulation (such as living on a street with heavy traffic, the television or radio, a lot of visitors), or to the erratic rhythms in the family's daily schedule.

❧ Crying may be the way your baby expresses excess energy. When he cries, he activates a nervous-system mechanism that helps him reduce tension and calm himself.

❧ You may be switching your baby to the second breast too soon, so he is getting too much foremilk and too little hindmilk, he cries because he is dissatisfied.

✿ If crying goes on and on, let a physician check your baby to rule out illness.

What Can I Do?

If your baby seems to have stomach pains

✿ To rule out allergies, eliminate some types of cow's-milk protein, such as whole or nonfat milk, from your diet. Try eating yogurt, kefir or acidophilus milk instead. In a day or two, if your baby feels better, you will have solved the riddle.

✿ Be sure you haven't eaten or drunk something else your baby may not be able to tolerate. The combination of sugar and whole-grain products can cause gas. If you are concerned, omit one food per day and monitor your baby's reaction or improvement.

✿ Burp your baby thoroughly.

✿ If your baby has trouble managing your initial milk flow, express milk beforehand until the milk-ejection reflex occurs. Or interrupt the feed as soon as you feel a tingling in your breast so the initial rush of milk can flow into a diaper or a small cup. This way your baby won't be overwhelmed and swallow too much air with the milk she drinks.

Babies have all kinds of new impressions to absorb over the course of a day, and crying can be a way of processing or expressing them.

✿ Try nursing your baby while you are lying on your back to see if that improves things.

✿ Try carrying your baby in a vertical position.

✿ When your baby is full, maybe he can comfort himself by sucking on your finger while you hold him in your arms. It may help him relieve tension.

✿ A gentle massage of the lower abdomen or around the navel in a clockwise direction (following the intestine) can be helpful for your baby. Use the following essential oils for massaging: 1 drop of Roman chamomile, 1 drop anise, 1 drop fennel, 1 drop carrot-seed oil and one ounce (20 ml) of sesame oil. Shake ingredients thoroughly in a clean jar before using.

✿ Evaporate a few drops of anise, fennel, coriander and Roman chamomile essential oils in an aroma lamp.

✿ A small hot-water bottle wrapped in a towel can help ease your baby's discomfort; so can putting him down to nap on a lambskin rug or a blanket.

❧ Nurturing touch, which you may already have practiced on yourself, can bring your baby relief. First, sensitize your hands with gentle stroking. Then lay your hands, one on top of the other, over the baby's pelvic area. Imagine you are "radiating" warmth into his body under your peaceful touch. The presence of your hands will help bring breath movement to his pelvis area, harmonizing and relaxing it. Touching the baby's abdomen calms him. You may want to silently sound the tone *oo*—loudly or silently—while you do this.

❧ Pressing the baby's thigh gently and rhythmically against her stomach can help her expel excess air.

❧ Keep in mind colic usually ends abruptly when the baby is around three months old. In that short time, you will have survived this crisis and possibly found increased strength and confidence along the way.

> *Terry cried day and night and writhed in pain. He had to be carried around in always-changing positions. His sleep times varied a lot. All that crying, the chronic sleep deprivation and the jealousy of our other children took us right to the edge.*
>
> *My pediatrician tried to find out why Terry was so restless. Drops for gas, abdominal massage, fennel tea and all that didn't bring noticeable relief, but at least I was doing something. Every day, one of our friends would give me new advice, but also made me more nervous: Maybe Terry had a food allergy or an abdominal blockage!*
>
> *I breastfed Terry exclusively. He ate well and grew normally. But his stomach growled when he nursed and shortly afterward the cramping began again. I tried to drop anything that might cause gas from my diet. Terry had a bowel movement only every seven or eight days. After three months Terry's crying got better. We all relaxed. He still had gas, but no more pain.*
>
> *Terry is eight months old now, a happy, contented baby I take with me every place I go. He began solid food at seven months and has had no digestive problems.*
>
> *In retrospect I can say: Try to survive this challenge somehow. It's good to have a physician who takes it seriously and rules out*

certain causes. The most important thing, however, is having an understanding, helpful and supportive husband and father!

When crying seems to be an expression of "undigested" emotional issues

- "Be there" for your baby. Accept her crying and let her know she is not alone. Support her by taking her in your arms or touching her attentively while saying, "I don't know how I can help you. But I'm with you, and I won't leave you alone."

- Body and skin contact and an upright position are the only solution for many crying babies and their parents. Snuggled in a carrier, close to mother, father or some other helpful person and carried around, your baby may be more or less satisfied. Maybe it helps her to feel your body warmth at night. Don't worry about spoiling her! Your baby is not crying to torment you. She cries because of some discomfort, even if the reason isn't clear.

- You can massage your baby's whole body using a massage oil mixed with 1/4 cup (about 50 to 60ml) of almond oil and 1 drop of rose oil (many books give guidelines; see Bibliography). Or give him a foot massage.

- How about giving your baby a relaxing footbath?

- Is your home filled with obvious or not-so-obvious tension? If so, change something about the situation (by talking it out with your partner, making a change in the rhythm of the day, and so on).

When the baby's crying frays your nerves:

In her very good book, *The Crying Baby*, Sheila Kitzinger writes, "Everything you do for yourself to achieve more space also helps the baby to be more satisfied, and measures that help the baby calm down are good for you as well." How can you do something good for yourself? (See also pages 49-61.)

- Accept offers of help, or ask for others' help, *before* you reach the end of your rope. You need to renew your strength from time to time to stay sane. If none of your relatives, neighbors or friends can help, consider hiring a family helper for a few hours or days right now.

- Cuddle a lot with your baby in bed.

- Take frequent walks with your baby.

❧ If you feel tense or aggressive, don't just swallow these feelings. Find a harmless way to let them out. Perhaps you could stomp your feet, punch a pillow or yell it out (away from your baby, of course). You will certainly feel better afterward. An open discussion about what's bothering you with someone you trust might help reduce the tension.

❧ With your partner, discuss how you both can manage to find some time to "refuel." A sensual, intuitive massage does the trick for some couples.

Other ways to soothe and pacify your baby:

❧ Lay your baby lengthwise on a large cloth or blanket. Hold one end of the blanket securely. While your partner or another person holds the other end, rock the baby. Cradles, hammocks and rocking chairs are also appropriate. As a rule, children love rhythmic movement. Many of them calm down when you put them in the car and drive around the neighborhood.

❧ Many babies stop crying spontaneously when they hear their own voices on tape.

❧ After being in the protective shell of their mother's womb, many babies don't feel comfortable with too much space around them. Your baby may enjoy being swaddled in the first weeks. You can wrap your baby snugly in a cotton blanket, or put your baby in a sling or carrier close to your body.

❧ Play soothing music.

❧ Babies between three and six months of age may be restless and cry a lot because their teeth are coming in.

❧ If you suspect you have too little milk (a rare problem), refer to pages 105-109.

❧ I have found this tea is good for sleep problems you or your partner may have: Mix ground ginger, cardamom, cinnamon and liquorice in equal parts. Fill the tip of a knife with the mixture and stir into a cup of hot water; let the powder settle a little and drink a few sips.

❧ Homeopathic remedies may help your baby with her discomfort. Consult your doctor before you begin, and consult a homeopath or naturopathic doctor for your baby's diagnosis. These remedies are commonly used for babies with colic: Colocythis C6, Dioscorea C6, Magnesium caronicum C6 and Carbo vegetabilits C6. (See page 162.)

❧ Bach Flower remedies are part of the growing field of flower-essence therapy. Consult a Bach Flower therapist for diagnosis. (See page 164.)

The following essences may be suggested based on the emotional cause suspected in mother or baby. *Mother:* Cherry Plum, Clematis, Chicory, Crab Apple, Elm, Holly, Hornbeam, Honeysuckle, Mustard, Olive, Pine, Red Chestnut, Rock Water, Rock Rose, Star of Bethlehem, White Chestnut, Willow. *Baby:* Beech, Centaury, Chicory, Crab Apple, Honeysuckle, Hornbeam, Mimulus, Oak, Star of Bethlehem, Sweet Chestnut, Walnut.

✤ Acupressure can also be helpful. See page 226.

Over-Eager Baby

Over-eager eating can cause nipple problems for the mother and make the baby gassy because she takes in too much air.

What Can I Do?

✤ Feed your baby more frequently, so he isn't famished at mealtimes and eats more slowly.

✤ By expressing a little milk, you can start the let-down reflex so your baby gets plenty of milk right away and doesn't have to suck so heavily.

✤ Stopping frequently to burp her is advisable (especially when the milk lets down), but being interrupted while eating doesn't suit every baby.

✤ To avoid one-sided stress on the nipples because of the strong suction, make sure your baby is properly latched on to the breast. Try different nursing positions.

✤ Bach Flower remedies might help. (See page 164.) Consult a Bach Flower therapist to determine which flower essences would be best for you. The following essences are commonly used in this situation. *Mother:* Crab Apple, Mimulus, Rescue Remedy, Rock Water, Seleranthus, Willow. *Baby:* Agrimony, Chicory, Heather, Impatiens, Vine.

Sleepy Baby

As a rule, babies take the nourishment they need. If they aren't entirely full after nursing, they simply eat sooner next time. But in some infants, this self-regulating mechanism does not function properly. This problem may affect babies born prematurely, babies with severe newborn jaundice, babies born with developmental delays, mental or physical challenges, and even some babies whose mothers received medication during labor or birth. Such babies are especially peaceful. Even after the first few days, they sleep for 4 to 6 hours several times a day.

With such long breaks between meals, as restful as they may be for a peace-loving mother, the baby is short-changed, because mother's milk production doesn't get started or decreases dramatically. The baby's weight remains constant or goes down; there may be growth disturbances. It is vital to get help from a lactation consultant or La Leche League's Helpline (see Appendix 1) and your baby's physician, especially if your baby also has too few wet diapers, floppy muscle- and skin tone and seems apathetic.

What Can I Do?

❧ If your baby tends not to let you know what he needs, you will need to help him temporarily by waking him for feeding every 2 or 3 hours (maybe with one longer break at night). Eventually he will get stronger and livelier and establish his own rhythm.

❧ If it is hard to wake your baby, take off some of his clothing and expose part of his body to the air (very warm air will make him sleepy). Or change his diapers. Or take him outside for a little while. Your baby will also wake up if you bend his upper body forward gently from a sitting position (called *doll's-eyes reflex*).

❧ Gently massage your baby's feet.

❧ You may need to use supplementary stimulation to keep up your milk supply; for example, by expressing or pumping from your breast.

❧ Stay in close contact with your baby's practitioner. One of their main jobs in this situation is to check your baby frequently for any developmental delays.

❧ Bach-Flower Therapy might help. Consult a trained practitioner about which flower essences would be best for your emotional and spiritual state. (See page 164.) The following essences may be suggested based on the emotional cause suspected in mother or baby. *Mother:* Chicory, Pin, Red Chestnut, Rock Water, Seleranthus, Vervain, Vine. *Baby:* Centaury, Clematis, Crab Apple (if you have taken any medication), Hornbeam, Star of Bethlehem, Walnut, Water Violet, Wild Rose.

Weak Sucking Reflex

Babies who are premature, stressed from the birth, affected by medication, have severe jaundice or have a physical challenge may not suck strongly enough to stimulate an adequate milk supply over a period of days or weeks. You'll need a lot of time and patience with this baby if you want to breastfeed him. You may need the support of an experienced lactation consultant also.

What Can I Do?

✿ To spare your baby the effort of nursing strenuously at the beginning of a feed, express a little milk by hand to set off the milk-ejection reflex. It usually takes 30 seconds to a minute (see pages 80-81).

✿ Massage your breast after you have dipped it in warm water so milk from the milk ducts flows toward the nipple.

✿ For babies who find it hard to keep the breast in the mouth, use a special hold (the "DanCer" hold, developed by Sarah Coulter Danner and Edward Cerutti): Hold your breast from underneath, with the thumb lying on the outer side, index and middle fingers on the inner side. Help your baby grab hold of the areola and support the baby's chin with your thumb and index finger, so he can enclose your breast in his mouth. You may need to support his sucking motions at first by pressing upward lightly with your hand. (Photos, page 159.)

✿ After the feeding, pump the rest of your milk to stimulate milk production. You can freeze milk obtained this way.

✿ If your baby is very young or weak, and can't suck your nipple yet, you may still want to pump and store your milk. With his practitioner, discuss the possibility of your baby taking your milk by tube into his stomach—called *gavage feeding* or *nasogastric feeding*.

✿ You may have to feed the pumped milk from a cup or feed the baby from a syringe for days or weeks. As soon as your baby is stronger, put him to breast again. If you used infant formula in the meantime, slowly cut back on the amount you feed your baby by bottle as you gradually increase your own milk supply. Many babies make the transition from bottle to breast easily; others need a lot of your patience. You will need to weigh the advantages and disadvantages here.

✿ For a baby with an underdeveloped sucking reflex, suck training can be useful, but it needs to be done by a person trained in the technique. There's more about this in *The Breastfeeding Answer Book* (see Bibliography).

✿ Bach Flower Therapy might be helpful. Consult a Bach Flower therapist (see page 164) to determine which flower essences would be best for your situation. The following essences may be suggested based on the emotional cause suspected in mother or baby. *Mother:* Gentian, Gorse, Mimulus, Star of Bethlehem, Sweet Chestnut, White

Chestnut. *Baby:* Clematis, Hornbeam, Rock Rose, Walnut, White Chestnut, Wild Rose.

Newborn Jaundice

After birth, most of the baby's red blood cells, called *erythrocytes*, disintegrate and become a waste product, called *bilirubin*. This leads to a condition called *newborn jaundice* in about half of all babies. In these babies, the skin and especially the whites of the eyes take on a reddish-yellow color between the third and fifth days of life. According to recent research, bilirubin is thought to have a protective function (antioxidant effect). About one-third of all babies continue to have high bilirubin levels into the third week of life. The latest information says this can be considered normal in healthy, full-term, breastfed infants.

Premature infants, whose livers have not matured, cannot tolerate high bilirubin levels. They need help to break down the bilirubin in their system. Phototherapy does this by exposing the baby to light under a special lamp. The light decomposes bilirubin in the baby's skin. Very often mother and baby are separated during phototherapy. However, some hospitals now offer a special bed on which mother or father can lie with the baby under the "bili-lights." This special bed is called a *bilarium*. In some places, "bili-lights" are available at a pediatrician's office or can be borrowed from the hospital and used at home. With normal neonatal jaundice, breastfeeding can and should continue.

A rare form of jaundice, called *breast-milk jaundice*, starts later in the baby's life and lasts longer. It peaks between the seventh and tenth days or later. Breast-milk jaundice is diagnosed by taking a bilirubin reading 2 hours after a breastfeeding and then discontinuing breastfeeding for 12 hours. If the baby's bilirubin level drops after that, breast-milk jaundice is the likely diagnosis. After a short period off the breast, the baby can usually go back to breastfeeding, once her bilirubin levels come down. During this time, keep up your milk supply by pumping your milk. Unfortunately, you must discard it. Once you put your baby back on the breast, her bilirubin level may increase slightly once more and then should decrease steadily.

If her bilirubin level rises while your baby is off the breast,

breast milk is not the cause of the jaundice. Bilirubin levels in infants can also rise because of blood incompatibility, infection or for other reasons, which require urgent medical treatment.

What Can I Do?

❧ Early breastfeeding can have a positive effect on newborn jaundice. Colostrum speeds up the excretion of bilirubin.

❧ The more breast milk your baby drinks, the better. Mother's milk helps flush bilirubin from the baby's system. (Giving water, dextrose or formula supplements, on the other hand, interferes with milk production and will not lower the bilirubin level.) So, put your baby to the breast more often! Frequent short feedings are preferable to infrequent, longer feedings.

❧ Expose your baby to daylight outdoors, keeping his feet, hands, head and liver warm.

❧ Homeopathic remedies may be useful. Consult your homeopath for treatment. Depending on the symptomatic picture, one of the following may be recommended: Aconitum C6, Chelidonium C6, Aethusa C6, Natrium sulfuricum C6. (See page 162.)

❧ Bach Flower Therapy might be helpful. Consult a Bach Flower therapist (See page 164.) The following essences may be suggested based on the emotional cause suspected in mother or baby. *Mother:* Cherry Plum, Chicory, Crab Apple, Olive, Pine, Red Chestnut, Rock Rose. *Baby:* Crab Apple, Elm, Rescue Remedy, Star of Bethlehem, Walnut.

Pimples

> *I'm worried because my baby's face is suddenly full of pimples.*
> *Have I eaten something my baby can't tolerate?*

I get a lot of calls like this from mothers whose babies are about four weeks old. As a rule, the rash has nothing to do with the mother's diet but instead with a hormonal transition in the baby's own body.

What Can I Do?

❧ Try an almond-oil massage all over your baby's body.

❧ Try bathing your baby with just mild soap and water. Ironically, many babies are sensitive to the perfumes in products made especially for babies. Less is more when it comes to your baby's skin.

Thrush

Thrush is a candida (fungus) infection the baby may have had from birth or acquired later (for example, from other children's toys he puts in his mouth). Thrush is not a serious illness but it can be unpleasant because it is so hard to get rid of. Thrush usually causes white patches inside the baby's mouth. She may get a rash on her bottom, also.

This fungus may also be found in small quantities on healthy skin or mucous membrane. Normally mother's milk has many protective factors against thrush. But sometimes thrush gets the upper hand at times of stress (when resistance is low) or after taking antibiotics (which can temporarily damage intestinal flora, a significant part of the immune system). Women with diabetes are also more vulnerable to fungal infections.

If, some weeks after beginning breastfeeding, you get sore nipples and a burning sensation in your milk ducts, you may have a thrush infection. Your doctor can prescribe medication for it. Frequently the active ingredient is nystatin. You and your baby both have to take the medicine, even if only one of you shows symptoms of thrush. If your breast is also affected from within, your physician will order a systemic treatment in addition to treating your skin with a salve. Be prepared to treat this condition for a while, because the fungus can be very stubborn.

What Can I Do?

- ❧ Further treatment for thrush: Dab mouth and nipples with a cotton ball soaked in a 0.1% solution of Gentian violet (available from the pharmacy). Continue for two weeks.

- ❧ Pay close attention to hygiene, but don't wash too much with soap; too much soap destroys the protective acidic film on the skin.

- ❧ Keep your nipples dry. Fungi love a warm, damp environment. Expose your breasts to fresh air as much as you can.

- ❧ Don't wear bras made from synthetic materials.

- ❧ Avoid putting substances with sugar or honey on the breast; fungi love sugar.

- ❧ Try to maintain a whole-food, healthful, sugar-free and low-starch diet, rich in vitamin B. Avoid yeast products.

❧ Whenever possible, rest to strengthen your resistance.

❧ Homeopathic remedies can be helpful. (See page 162.) Consult your homeopath for treatment. The following may be used, depending on the baby's symptoms: Borax C6, Calcium carbonicum C6.

❧ Bach Flower Therapy might be helpful. Consult a trained therapist for options. (See box, page 164.) The following essences may be suggested based on the emotional cause suspected in mother or baby: Beech, Centaury, Crab Apple, Sweet Chestnut.

Baby Goes on Strike

> *As soon as I tried to put Jacob to the breast, he began to scream. I couldn't force him. The breast threatened him somehow. That made me feel really bad.*

> *During the morning, I kept trying to put him to the breast, but I felt as though I were violating him because he screamed as soon as he realized what was happening. Sometimes he took two or three swallows, but then the screaming started again.*

These situations happen over and over—sometimes with a baby days or weeks old, sometimes with a baby six months old or more. All of a sudden, the baby goes on strike and doesn't want anything to do with the breast. He doesn't take the nipple fully into his mouth, doesn't suck properly, cries when you try to put him to the breast or rejects the milk.

Possible Causes

❧ Your baby has a cold, and he can't breathe because his nose is stopped up.

❧ His gums hurt because he is teething.

❧ Your baby bit you once, and you yelled "ouch" very loudly. That scared him, and now he balks at the breast.

❧ You let your baby cry, it "insulted" him, and he wants you to know it!

❧ Your baby has problems with the shape of your nipple.

❧ The milk spurting out of the nipple causes problems.

- Your milk supply is down.
- The baby has had a bottle and doesn't like the breast any more.
- The baby is worked up, anxious or distracted (for example, on a trip, when you have visitors or because of a jealous sibling).
- You are tense or resist breastfeeding subconsciously, and your baby is reacting to that.
- Your milk tastes different than usual because you ate a certain food (for example, garlic), you have gotten your period, or you exercised just before breastfeeding. Many women have reported their infants were fussy and colicky after breastfeeding for as long as 4 to 6 hours after strenuous exercise.
- The nursing strike is connected to a "breakthrough" for the baby—a transitional phase.
- With older babies: Your baby might want to wean.

> *Milk spurted out of my breast strongly after Jack had sucked just a little. I thought he should drink that so he would be satisfied sooner. That was a mistake. He choked and completely lost any desire to nurse because I think he felt he was being "railroaded."*

If your baby goes on strike, you may feel helpless, surprised, bewildered, disappointed, frustrated, cheated, hurt or rejected. You may worry how you can satisfy your baby's hunger and at the same time you might wonder what to do with all your milk.

What Can I Do?

- If your baby is having difficulty breathing because of a cold, try to clear his nose ahead of time. Mild suction with a bulb syringe is possible. You can also stimulate movement in his airways by putting a humidifier in his room or giving him a footbath.
- If teeth are the problem, see page 245.
- Try to put your baby to the breast while he is half-asleep in the evening and at night. For the most part, these nursing sessions are problem-free and restore an atmosphere of harmony between you. The "battle" during the day can be forgotten.
- Many babies will nurse if you walk around with them.
- If only one side is a problem, continue breastfeeding on the other side.

- ✢ Re-read the sections "Nipple Shape Is a Problem," "Colic" and "Not Enough Milk" if you think one of these may be the reason for the strike.

- ✢ Express your milk by hand until the situation improves so you don't get engorged and your milk production doesn't decrease drastically.

- ✢ If distraction is the problem, arrange for a more peaceful atmosphere for breastfeeding.

> *I realized I had to plan more time for Jacob than I had up to now. He simply needs more time—even today. The times I counted on a quick breastfeeding, it didn't work. I got impatient (it took usually 1-1/2 to 2 hours to feed him). He swallowed a huge amount of air and had trouble getting rid of it. But with air in his tummy, he refused to keep nursing. I had to burp him about four times during each feeding, and that just took time.*

- ✢ Offer expressed milk for a short time in a cup or on a spoon.

- ✢ Change the nursing conditions—breastfeed naked, for skin-to-skin contact, or in the bath.

- ✢ If your baby only strikes during the day, turn day into night by making the room dark.

- ✢ If you suspect your baby is striking because of foods in your diet, experiment to find out what they could be and change your diet accordingly (see page 90).

- ✢ If you are active in sports or exercise, breastfeed beforehand or wait at least 1-1/2 hours before you put the baby to breast. Shower or at least wash your breast after you exercise, then manually express a little milk and discard it.

- ✢ One mother in my neighborhood, Annette, was advised to put her baby to the breast with nipple shields because of the shape of her nipples. As a result, her milk production never got up to full swing. But after several laborious, stressful weeks, Annette overcame her baby Ginny's strike with the help of her lifelong friend, Sylvia. Sylvia, whose milk flowed easily because of her 6-month-old son Mike's strong sucking, put baby Ginny to her breast. Ginny was motivated by the bountiful milk supply and quickly learned what to do. Annette nursed Mike during this time, and his strong sucking stimulated Annette's milk supply. When Ginny began nursing from Annette again, she had no difficulty because now plenty of milk was available. Of course, the cross-nursing method described here is *not* generally recommended in the era of AIDS (see page 97). It can only be considered a *possible* solution within the very closest circle of friends and family.

- ✿ Nipple shields often cause their own problems, but for some women, nursing with nipple shields seems to be the only solution and is preferable to not nursing at all.

- ✿ Try to center yourself and relax while you are nursing (see Relaxation, page 49) and simply accept the momentary difficulties. Singing or humming while you breastfeed can calm you both.

- ✿ Temporarily, you might want to limit nursing to those feeds the baby accepts with no problem (for example, early morning or nighttime). For the other feedings, give your expressed milk with a spoon or in a cup, or (with an older baby) give some solid food. This could go a long way in re-establishing peace between you. After a few days, try the breast in a relaxed way again—without trying to force nursing. Keep in mind the quality of your relationship with your baby is more important than the question of whether you fully breastfeed.

> *The restful morning feeding in bed works well. During the morning I breastfeed as long as there is no difficulty (maybe 2 ounces). Then I give Jacob some vegetables—as much as he wants—and the difficult morning has been salvaged. At noon breastfeeding works again. In the evening, the child I look after is with her mother, and nursing works again. Before I go to sleep, I put Jacob to breast again and at about 5:00 a.m. he goes to the breast right away, without problems.*
>
> *I'm doing what I wanted to avoid—giving supplementary feeding. But I can't manage any other way. I tried it for weeks and it was nerve-wracking. This way, we manage pretty well.*

- ✿ Depending on the situation, homeopathic remedies may be useful. (See page 162.) Consult a homeopath or naturopath. Mercurius C6, Calcium phosphoricum C6 and Calcium carbonicum C6 may be recommended.

- ✿ If you feel that inner problems are the cause, you can try to work these through with some support or with the use of Bach Flower remedies. Consult a trained practitioner. (See page 164.) The following essences may be suggested based on the emotional cause suspected in mother or baby. *Mother:* Chicory, Honeysuckle, Mustard, Pine, Rock Rose, Selenranthus, Star of Bethlehem, Vervain, Walnut, White Chestnut,

Willow, Wild Rose. *Baby:* Beech, Gorse, Holly, Hornbeam, Impatience, Rescue Remedy, Rock Water, Seleranthus, Walnut.

If you are feeling hurt inside because your baby isn't taking your breast, it may help to know you are not alone in feeling this way. Researcher Dorothy Vossen confirmed this hunch in a survey. She explained the situation so plausibly that I would like to quote her:

> *The list of feelings [involved] is reminiscent of a lover's grief. And this is exactly what has happened: A close relationship has been terminated unexpectedly by one partner. This needs to be processed first. One way to do that is to fight for this relationship (and for the most part it can be won, at least in the case of a nursing strike!), or you need to do real grief work. Fortunately, the "partner" baby is still "there," even after weaning, and other forms of closeness (increased cuddling, playing, making music together, carrying, and feeding) can gradually replace the nursing relationship. As soon as these substitute actions have restored a feeling of harmony with her baby, the mother can feel accepted by her child again and overcome her negative feelings.*

By the way, Vossen's survey revealed many women overcame their baby's strike with the help of breastfeeding groups, midwives or other nursing mothers within 9 hours to 13 days. Positive techniques and patience helped! Most babies only went on strike once. Only a few mothers gave up and stopped breastfeeding.

8

Special
Circumstances

Mother's milk is especially valuable for the premature baby. Premature babies are much more vulnerable to serious infections than full-term babies. The multiple antibodies contained in breast milk—especially those contained in colostrum—can be life-saving for them. Nature has arranged for the colostrum of a mother of a premature baby *to have an even greater potential for protection against infection* than the breast milk of a mother giving birth at term. A mother's own untreated milk is preferable to pooled human milk, which loses some of its precious immunological and nutritional properties in pasteurization or sterilization processes.

Born Too Early

The milk of a mother who has delivered prematurely has a different nutritional composition than the milk of a mother who delivered at term. Some of these nutrients differ throughout the first six months after birth. Breast milk is more digestible and absorbable by the premature baby's immature system than formula. It also is easier on his kidneys, which cannot yet manage a great load.

A number of studies also show that the brain development of premature babies greatly benefits from mother's milk. Breastfed children initially display a higher level of intelligence than their bottle-fed counterparts. For babies who weigh more than 1500 grams, mother's milk is perfect as it is, but smaller babies generally need to supplement with certain minerals and protein for optimal growth.

Preterm babies, depending on their gestational age, can weigh anywhere from well above 5 pounds to less than 1 pound. If your baby weighs close to 5 pounds, he may need to be in an isolette for just a few hours, possibly by your bedside. A very tiny baby may have to spend many weeks in the newborn intensive care unit (NICU) or a special-care nursery, a place that may seem strange and alienating at first. No matter what the situation, your baby needs you. Try to join him in spirit, no matter what the physical environment is like.

Kangaroo Care

In hospitals where gentle management of premature babies has been adopted, babies don't have to miss their parents' closeness. Even the tiniest babies weighing 1-1/2 pounds (700 grams) or less can spend several hours a day in direct, skin-to-skin contact with their parents. This is called *kangaroo care*. Leaning back in a reclining chair, mothers or fathers let their babies—covered with a lambskin or a blanket—cuddle right on their chest. If necessary, the babies are supplied with a touch of oxygen from an outside source to help their breathing. *Kangaroo Care: The Best You Can Do to Help Your Preterm Infant* (Ludington-Hoe and Galant 1993) is a good reference. It contains an extensive chapter on breastfeeding the premature baby.

*I have the feeling my baby . . . absorbs my closeness, my love
and my heartbeat with his entire being. Lying on my bare chest,
he takes in all the physiological things as well as my emotions. I
feel a wonderful connection, and I guess my baby does, too.
When Tommy first comes out of the incubator, he seems
bewildered at first. But then it feels like he "lands"—right
where he belongs. We bond immediately. We play with each
other a little—he pushes me with his little feet, and I respond.*

The tiny newborn lying on his mother's or father's chest absorbs his
parent's breathing rhythm. This stimulates and regulates his own
breathing. He is kept warm by their body heat. Closeness like this
can be a great help to parents whose baby has been born early,
before they had a chance to adjust to the idea of birth and parenthood. Anxieties, which increase greatly when parents are separated from their baby, are reduced or eliminated through direct
contact. Guilt feelings disappear when parents can "be there" for
their baby. The parent-child bond, so important for the emotional
and spiritual well-being of both baby and parents, is deepened.
One father said, "I feel so much closer to this child than to any of
our other children."

This way of caring for premature infants is gentle and humane.
Usually babies cared for in this manner can be released to the
familiar care of their parents even at a very low weight, whenever
it is safe to do so, because their parents learned to handle them in
the hospital. It's not the baby's weight that determines his readiness to go home, but rather how mature his bodily systems are.
Regular professional monitoring is still indicated, of course.

Caring for Premature Babies

Research studies are proving that parental touch has an immense
effect on premature babies. This awareness has led to new prema-
ture-care policies, allowing parents unrestricted visitation of babies
in the NICU. If your baby is in the NICU, spend as much time
with him as possible. You will become more confident as you help
care for your little one.

Premature babies gain weight particularly quickly if they are
lying on a lambskin, on a waterbed covered with a lambskin, or—
for the tiniest ones—between two hospital gloves filled with warm
water.

It makes sense to get in touch with self-help groups for parents of premature babies (see page 259) and share experiences with other parents in the same situation. La Leche League has published a 28-page information pamphlet on premature babies, "Breastfeeding Your Premature Baby" (publication number 26).

Breastfeeding the Premature Baby

If your baby is born less than a month short of his expected due date, you may be able to breastfeed fully from the start—with some caring, professional assistance. When your baby has started to gain weight and his system has matured, you may be able to go home together.

Many doctors believe babies who weigh less than 4 pounds (1.8 kg) cannot drink or swallow and are too weak to suck. They believe milk could get into the babies' lungs if they were to drink breast milk. Or they feel drinking on the breast requires more energy than the baby has available. Babies therefore are routinely fed through a tube inserted through their nose to their stomach. Researcher Marina Marcovich's work in a preterm-neonatology clinic in Vienna, Austria, has shown that regardless of weight, premature babies should have an opportunity to breastfeed from the beginning, as soon as they make sucking and smacking motions. She found even 1-1/2-pound (700 grams) babies are capable of drinking from mother's breast. The smallest baby to suck successfully at the breast weighed about 1 pound (460 grams). When a mother sees her premature baby thriving on her milk, she feels good about herself, and her self-confidence and trust in herself are strengthened. Consult your baby's practitioner to see what options would be best for your baby.

If you want to breastfeed your premature baby and are separated from him, or your baby is still too weak to get enough milk from your breast, you will need to pump your milk as soon as possible after birth to stimulate milk production.

Pumping Your Milk

When pumping, consider the following:

❀ As soon as you feel up to it after the delivery, start pumping.

❀ Pumping at least five and up to eight times a day helps boost milk production and keeps it going. Pumping with your baby nearby is probably easier for you, but even a photo of your baby can help your milk flow better.

❀ Wash your hands in hot, soapy water and rinse your breast in clear water before you begin.

❀ Before beginning, place warm compresses on your breast or apply nurturing touch (see page 52).

❀ If you rub your nipples gently while you wash them, the milk-ejection reflex will start more easily.

❀ Every piece of equipment that comes in contact with the milk must be sterilized and can't be touched again.

You'll find instructions for expressing milk by hand on pages 80-81. If you expect the baby to be in the hospital for a long time, you'll have to use an electric pump (see page 82). Most hospitals make electric pumps available. You will probably find it is more convenient, long-term, to rent one. The most effective ones pump both breasts simultaneously. (If you use a one-sided electric pump, it is a good idea to express milk by hand from the other side to get the milk flowing.) Moisten the inner side of the pump with a little water so the breast will slide in more easily. You can help start the milk flow with a light massage. Don't set the pressure too high because you might injure your nipples.

Fill the milk into sterile bottles or plastic bags. Try to use hard-plastic containers because microphages in the milk (cells that protect your baby from infection) stick to glass receptacles. Most hospitals, however, do use glass bottles.

Breast milk for a full-term baby can be stored longer than breast milk for a premature or sick baby. Current recommendations are to use fresh breast milk immediately, or place it in the refrigerator. Refrigerated breast milk lasts up to 48 hours. You can also freeze breast milk in the freezer compartment of the refrigerator for up to 3 months. Breast milk for a full-term baby can be stored safely in a deep freezer at 0F (-18C) for six months or longer, but breast milk for a premature baby should be stored no longer than 3 months in this way.

Freeze milk immediately after pumping. Label each bottle or bag and store appropriately. Do not mix milk from different pump times. After thawing, shake the milk gently, because it tends to separate during freezing. (Note: Vigorous shaking actually destroys some nutrients.)

If you pump more than your baby can drink, freeze the milk you pumped first and feed your baby with the higher-fat hindmilk so she can get a high-calorie meal with the least possible intake of fluid.

Don't put yourself under pressure when you pump, or your milk supply may drop. Give yourself a break and reduce your pumping to 4 or 5 times a day. You can increase your supply when your baby is with you again.

Because the milk from the mother of a premature baby is matched exactly to the needs of her baby, her milk is the very best for him. You can, of course, supplement it with donor milk. Be sure to know the health and HIV status of the donor, or obtain the milk from a certified milk bank.

With everything we know now about the benefits of breast milk, most hospitals are happy for mothers of premature babies to supply their pumped milk. Depending on their maturity and clinical condition, premature babies can be fed at first from a syringe filled with a sugar solution or mother's milk, or they may be fed by cup, bottle or stomach tube, or, if they are lucky, directly from the breast. Feeding methods are mixed as a rule, at least in the beginning. With breastfeeding, how much your baby takes isn't the most important thing—at first he may only get a teaspoon or two. What's most important is the stimulating, protective closeness he gets by being with you.

With breastfeeding, how much your baby takes isn't the most important thing . . . What's most important is the stimulating, protective closeness he gets by being with you.

In this way, you get the feeling of having a "normal" parental relationship with a young—if very small—baby. Your milk production is also enhanced. Spend as much time with your baby as you can and become familiar with his care.

Even when your baby is fed primarily by stomach tube, there are good reasons to add breastfeeding to his routine. Through the baby's sucking motions, the hormone gastrine is released into his system. Gastrine stimulates digestion and helps your baby utilize nutrients better. And, as we know, mother's milk is extremely important for the baby's development and protection against infection.

When giving milk to the baby in a small cup, be careful not to tip it into his mouth. Instead, give your baby the opportunity to sip on his own. If you place the cup at an angle against the lower lip, a small baby will lick the milk with his tongue, like a kitten. Premature babies who have reached the maturity of about 35 weeks slurp the milk and dribble a lot of it. When you breastfeed your little one, hold him so his legs are peeking out at your side from under your arm, or hold him in the opposite arm so your hand can support his head.

If you had only limited contact with your baby, your milk production may not meet his needs for days or weeks after he is released from the hospital, even if you have been pumping constantly. Extended skin contact during the frequent nursing will be good for both of you. Use a nursing supplementer (see illustration on page 150) temporarily while your milk supply is low. La Leche League and Childbirth Graphics have published special brochures on this topic.

After the separation and anxieties about your baby's life and health, it may take you some time to develop maternal feelings. That's normal. Your connection to your baby will develop as you spend time with him and get to know him better.

During these early days, arrange as much relief from household chores and find as much moral support as possible. Even if you can't fully breastfeed, know that every drop of mother's milk you do provide is valuable for your little baby and is worth your effort.

After a Cesarean

You can breastfeed after a Cesarean section, although many mothers will need support for themselves in addition to needing special help caring for the baby. Some hospitals try to help the recovering mom by caring for her baby in the nursery. Unfortunately, this can make breastfeeding more difficult. When mother and baby are both healthy, they belong together as much as possible. Fathers are usually happy to be involved in their baby's care. Perhaps friends or a grandmother could help, too.

If you are having a planned Cesarean, you will probably have an epidural, a type of anesthesia that numbs your lower body while you remain awake. You can experience the birth and hold your baby right away. Your baby's father can be with you for almost the entire birth. After you hold your baby, he will be able to take over while your surgery is completed. He can bathe your baby, talk with her and bond with her.

Put the baby to breast as soon after birth as possible. With a barrier or gate on the side of the bed (to prevent the baby from falling out), you can keep the baby with you and put him to breast without help whenever he wants. You can put him to the other breast, or on your chest for burping, without too much effort by pulling him toward you and turning over together. When you do this, let your breath flow in (don't take a deep breath—let breath happen!) and then turn over together *as you exhale* (this saves your energy). Get a supply of extra pillows to take pressure off the incision and protect it from your baby's squirming. Special breast-feeding pillows work well. Re-read the section on positioning in chapter 4 (page 68).

If your baby is separated from you because of a complication, many of the steps for bringing in and keeping up your milk supply mentioned in chapter 4 apply. One mother describes her unplanned Cesarean experience this way:

> *Everything was completely different from what we expected when I had to have an emergency Cesarean section. Luckily my husband was with me during the procedure. Later he had to tell me all about it, over and over. Because of an infection, Carly was taken to a children's hospital 25 miles away hours after she was born. I had only seen her once, briefly. Now, in addition to the pain and disappointment I felt, I was worried about my baby. I yearned for her, but I was also weak from surgery.*

> *The good experience I'd had nursing our first child and a lot of information about breastfeeding gave me the will to nurse Carly under difficult conditions. As soon as I was a little better, I began pumping colostrum. I pumped every three or four hours, day and night, so I could get my milk flowing as soon as possible. I found out how much milk my daughter needed by talking to her doctors and nurses by telephone.*

> *Once a day, my husband took my milk to the children's hospital and told me how Carly was doing when he returned. Looking*

at pictures of her was very helpful as I was pumping. There were often times when I didn't think I could do this any more. Now I'm happy with the way we managed this situation, and that we all hung on.

When I got out of the hospital on the seventh day, I went first to see my daughter, whom I could finally pick up and hold and put to my breast. I cried, I was so happy. I visited her every day for the next week. I continued to pump at those times when I was away from her. When she came home at last, at 14 days old, I put away the electric pump and breastfed Carly fully from that point. Our relationship grew gradually after that. Through breastfeeding, I was able to work through my guilt and sadness about not experiencing the birth and about the separation. Even now, after almost two years, I need to discuss my feelings now and then with other women who have delivered by Cesarean section.

La Leche League and Childbirth Graphics each have special brochures offering mothers additional help after Cesarean deliveries; La Leche League's is called "Breastfeeding after a Cesarean Birth" (publication number 80).

More Than One Baby!

You've thought about nursing your babies, but wondered if it is really possible to nurse more than one. Yes, it is! When her milk comes in, every woman experiences an overproduction (sometimes more than two quarts a day, according to a recent study). If only one baby needs the milk, the supply tapers off naturally. But if more than one baby needs to be fed, their mother will produce more milk, stimulated by the double (or triple) sucking stimulation and the doubled (or tripled) removal of the milk.

Still, it's not the milk supply that poses the potential problem nursing twins or triplets, but other special factors that may be involved. Many twins and most triplets are born prematurely and often are delivered by Cesarean, with all the difficulties implied by that. Find out how breastfeeding multiples is handled in the hospital before your babies are born. Your hospital may have trained lactation consultants to support you.

When you go home, you leave your hospital support team. Then the real challenge begins!

Most important, *you must have help.* Without it, your plan to breastfeed won't work. You also need to be well-prepared for the challenges ahead, especially in the early days, and you need to be well-organized. It takes a lot of time and energy to care for more than one baby—especially if they are bottle-fed.

Always rest when the babies are sleeping. Rest is not a luxury; it's an absolute necessity for a new mother. Be tolerant about housework; it's definitely a lower priority right now. Ideally, someone else will step in to help for a few days, or take over entirely. Don't hesitate to ask for help if you need it. One mother of triplets learned to ask for help matter-of-factly:

> *It was very helpful when someone took over cooking or helped me by feeding one baby the pumped milk while I was nursing the others. When it got to be too much, I called around to family, friends and neighbors and arranged for some help so I could drink a cup of tea in peace.*

There are lots of ideas for you on this topic in chapter 11. In addition, you may be able to find a charitable or religious organization that will arrange for household help.

Mothers of multiples have to be extremely attentive to high-quality nutrition and additional fluid. Mothers of twins need 60% more calories than usual. Mothers of triplets need more than 3-1/2 quarts (three liters) of fluid daily and are likely to be extremely hungry. Listen to your body and don't ignore the signals it sends.

When it comes right down to it, how does a mother actually breastfeed twins? It helps to surround yourself with pillows to support and relieve your arms and your back. Some mothers prefer to breastfeed their babies one at a time.

One mother of twins woke one baby half an hour before she expected him to wake on his own and put him to breast. She fed *Always rest when the babies are sleeping.* the other one on the other breast as soon as he woke. In the beginning, this woman offered her babies alternate breasts at each feeding because the babies had different appetites, and she wanted to stimulate both breasts equally. After a while she changed sides only

Support for Moms of Multiples

Moral support is just as important as household support. Fortunately a number of support groups are available nationwide (for contact information, see page 259):

- National Organization of Mothers of Twins Clubs
- Mothers of Supertwins at MOST
- Parents of Multiple Births Assn. of Canada

Exchanging information with others reduces any stress and anxiety that you won't be able to manage in the future. And it always helps to swap stories with someone in the same position! These groups are also a good way to find out about safe equipment for multiples.

You'll also find good ideas, guidance and encouragement from books (see Bibliography) and from the special brochures published by La Leche League ("Nursing Two, Is It for You?" publication number 53, and "Breastfeeding Twins," number 52) and other breastfeeding groups.

once a day. A week after *that*, however, she settled on giving each twin "his own" breast so he could regulate milk production to match his needs.

> *My twins slept next to each other in their bed next to ours at night. If one of them woke up, I got him, put him to breast and went back to sleep. When the second baby woke up, I picked him up and laid the other baby gently back in his bed. This saved me a lot of energy. I didn't find breastfeeding twins nearly as difficult as I had expected.*

You can also nurse twins together, which is good because it saves time. It also increases your milk production and is recommended to mothers of multiples for this reason. (Often you don't have any other choice when the babies wake up at the same time!) Twins can be put to breast in the same position as singletons—held in the crook of the arm, with a hand cupped under the baby's bottom. However, you'll need to use both arms and you must be well-supported with pillows (otherwise you will tense up and the milk will not flow as well). The babies' legs may cross over each other, or the babies may lie tummy-to-tummy. You can also hold them under your arm ("football hold"). In the beginning, your babies may be

Feeding twins

able to fit on each of your lower arms while you support the heads
with your hands (open yourself from your underarms and let your
shoulders relax); later on, you'll hold their bodies. Another possibility is positioning the babies parallel to one another, so their
bodies point in the same direction.

One mother talks about breastfeeding her twins:

> *At first, at home, my husband helped me put the babies to the*
> *breast and try out different positions. If both babies were*
> *hungry at the same time, which was usually the case once or*
> *twice a day, I sat in bed, where I had more space than on a*
> *chair and could put a pillow behind my back. For each baby, I*
> *put a pillow left and right on each leg and one pillow for both in*
> *the middle. Then I laid both of them down, and the feeding*
> *could begin. They drank their milk well and quickly. Saving*
> *time this way meant I had more rest in the breaks between*
> *feedings. I burped them, one after the other, when the feeding*
> *was over. Because they usually didn't finish feeding at the same*
> *time, I held one in my arm while the other continued to nurse.*
> *Each baby had only one breast at a feeding—one time the right*
> *one, next time the left one. In the beginning I had more milk in*
> *my right breast, but by switching the babies, they began to*
> *produce the same amount fairly soon.*

*When the babies woke at night and were hungry, I nursed lying
down. This was comfortable and relaxing. Mothers of twins
nurse twice as often as mothers with only one baby. You have
to find a comfortable position!*

Just as with singletons, gradually establish a rhythm with a longer
break at night with twins. One of the babies might sleep through
first, while the other one continues to wake frequently. About
every three weeks there may be "high-hunger days." Usually both
babies will not have this at the same time. If you can deal with it
in a relaxed way, your body will adapt quickly to the increased
need.

Triplets

With triplets, you need to be even better organized. Get well
acquainted with an electric pump, if only because your babies will
certainly come into the world early. You will spend a lot of time
breastfeeding and probably also pumping. In the beginning, someone else will have to help feed one or both of the babies with your
pumped milk.

In time, a rhythm develops that is comfortable for everyone.
Cindy tells about her daily life with triplets during the early days:

*Our two boys, Mark and John, came home two months after
they were born. Our smallest triplet, Irene, had to stay in the
hospital. Then the stress began: In the morning the boys had
their first feeding at about 6 a.m. I breastfed one, and my
husband fed the other one pumped milk from a bottle. Then
they were washed, dressed and went back to sleep. We ate
breakfast and our household helper came about 8 a.m. About
10 a.m., I went to the hospital—30 miles away—to see our
daughter Irene, deliver the pumped milk for the day and
breastfeed her. About 1 p.m. I had to go back because the boys
would be hungry at about 2 p.m. and the household helper left.*

*In the afternoon, I took a walk or went into the backyard with
Mark and John, pumped milk for the next meals and did some
housework. At about 6 p.m. they were fed again and my
husband came home after visiting our daughter in the hospital
after work. We ate the hot dinner the household helper had
made for us that morning. Then I did the wash and my
husband took care of the babies.*

About 10 p.m., the boys got their last meal and were put to bed. I pumped again and fell into bed exhausted. In the first six weeks at home, both of them still breastfed at night, at different times. My husband put them to my breast, and I nursed them more or less in my sleep. By 3-1/2 months, they both slept through the night.

Irene came home four months after she was born and needed a lot of attention because of her fragility and her digestive problems. At that point we put the boys on four meals a day, including solid food. When you have a sick baby, the others have to be in the background sometimes; it didn't hurt them. Now the three children are two years old. Looking back, I wonder how I managed. I guess your strength grows when it has to. And when you have a supportive husband, parents, in-laws, godparents and neighborhood girls who are always ready to help, everything works. Without all that help, the first months would have been really awful for me.

If you attach great importance to breastfeeding your triplets and are having difficulties, you may want to seek the support of other mothers in the same situation or consult a lactation consultant (see page 30). If your milk has decreased since the babies were in the hospital, the following information about relactation can help.

Relactation

If your milk supply has decreased because of illness or separation, or is almost gone because you have begun to wean, you can start breast-feeding again. This process, called *relactation*, requires a lot of motiva-tion and energy, but it is possible.

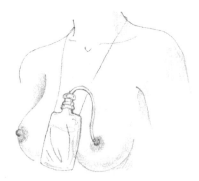

A supplementary feeding can be useful in the beginning. While the baby nurses, he gets milk through a small tube connected to a plastic bottle that hangs around his mother's neck.

Supplementary feeding device

While Alicia was in the hospital, my milk supply decreased rapidly, and by two months she was being bottle-fed. But she had difficulty tolerating formula feeding—she threw up after almost every meal and was constipated all the time. One day a friend told me it was possible to start breastfeeding again, even after interruptions.

Alicia was almost four months old when I visited Ellie, a La Leche League Leader, who encouraged me and explained everything patiently. The day after that, I started breastfeeding again—I mean I tried to start. Because Alicia had been used to the bottle for nearly four months, it was very hard for her to accept the breast again. She kept pushing my breast away with her tongue, looking for her bottle.

I had to find a way to feed her that made us both less unhappy. When I had bottle-fed Alicia, I used a variety of nipples and that helped me now. Eventually we reached a point where Alicia became more tolerant and better able to accept the breast. But it was still very difficult because I had hardly any milk. When Alicia was hungry, I put her to my breast first. Usually she sucked briefly and then demanded the bottle. I switched frequently—breast, bottle, breast, etc.

After about a week she was used to the breast. But I still didn't have enough milk and had to supplement with the bottle. She didn't like the spoon or the pipette or cup and always screamed when I tried to fool her.

After two weeks, Alicia sucked so well on the breast that I didn't have to put the bottle nipple in her mouth first. Now I dripped milk on my nipples while she was nursing. That took a lot of effort, and milk went everywhere in the process.

Then I found out about a breastfeeding aid, which I ordered right away. It was another four weeks before I could fully breastfeed. Gradually Alicia had less and less trouble with her digestion. She didn't throw up any more and she hardly cried. Within a short time she was relaxed and happy. Today she is 13 months old and is still breastfeeding once or twice a day.

Breastfeeding an Adopted Baby

Even women who have never borne a child (those who have had a hysterectomy as well) can nurse an adopted baby. Thousands of women have demonstrated this. But you need considerable perseverance, patience and serenity, a great deal of assertiveness and a strong belief it is possible, because you will have to withstand doubting, incredulous commentary from many other people. This could include your doctor, who may never have heard of it.

Breastfeeding an adopted child works because prolactin release can be stimulated through the baby's sucking or by pumping the breast, even when pregnancy has not preceded it. Conventional medicine is familiar with this phenomenon as a hormonal disturbance called *galactorrhea* (milk flow from the breast not associated with nursing).

The growth of ducts and alveoli to produce milk takes many weeks, during which time the breasts have to be stimulated by sucking or pumping. This onset of lactation can vary from one to six weeks, the average being four weeks after initiation of stimulation. When the infant is actually nursed at the breast and being nourished by supplements, milk may appear within 1 or 2 weeks. Adoptive mothers cannot approximate the level of growth in the breasts that occurs during pregnancy, so adoptive mothers usually produce a milk supply that is smaller and less responsive to demand.

There is no guarantee of success, however. Not every baby who has been bottle-fed is willing to transfer to a breast that may still be unproductive. And not every woman has a high enough frustration threshold to persevere until success is achieved. Sometimes the emotional and physical difficulties are so great that it makes more sense to bottle-feed.

If you want to breastfeed your adopted baby, prepare yourself for it as you would during a pregnancy (see chapter 2). Then start pumping and hand expressing three to five minutes at a time, several times a day. Try to stimulate the milk-ejection reflex. Your partner's strong sucking at the breast is most helpful for this purpose. In this way, you may have enough milk when your baby arrives to breastfeed almost exclusively. But probably you will have to supplement with artificial feeding or donor milk at first. Most mothers do have to continue feeding with a supplement under these circumstances.

Feed your baby as often as he is hungry, but at least every two or three hours during the day and for as long as he is willing to suck. If you are using a nursing supplement, he will get milk from it while he is sucking at your breast and will be encouraged to continue sucking at the still-unproductive breast. You can also drip milk on the breast with a pipette while he is nursing, or give him milk after he has nursed with a cup, a small spoon or a syringe, until he is satisfied. You can reduce the supplementary feeding gradually, every few days, by about 1/3 to 1/2 ounce (10 to 15ml). During your baby's growth spurts (see page 75), you will have to maintain the same amount of the supplementary feeding, or even increase it a little.

If your baby has been bottle-fed initially and has difficulty transferring from bottle to breast, it can be helpful to nurse him in his sleep or to pick him up before he cries. A baby who is not eager to nurse may get the taste for it—and more readily suck at your less productive breast—by nursing from a breastfeeding friend. *Important:* You need to know your friend's HIV status if you try this, because of the danger of AIDS. This caution does not apply to donor milk from a milk bank, because milk banks follow strict protective procedures. These procedures include pasteurization, which destroys the HIV virus.

> *Monday we got the call our son had been born and we could pick him up on Saturday. I was totally unprepared and had only just begun stimulating my breast. Although Michael had been bottle-fed for a whole week, he sucked patiently at my breast for hours while his food flowed very slowly from a tube lying on my breast. We spent 10 weeks like this, and I was very happy. Even though I had not carried this baby in my body, we were able to get very close through the bodily contact of breastfeeding him. It didn't matter to me how much milk I was making. I saw that there was milk and that Michael grew and developed.*
>
> *At 10 weeks, he suddenly developed nursing difficulties, maybe because he didn't want the tube anymore, maybe because my*

*milk-ejection reflex got stronger. Nursing became a different
experience. I attributed it to our special circumstances and
shortly afterward stopped breastfeeding. Today I know his
problems were probably temporary and could have been solved.
Next time I won't give up so quickly.*

If you want to breastfeed an adopted baby, you need a lot of sup‑
port, especially from your partner. You may also want to consult a
lactation consultant. Get in touch with a breastfeeding support
group, which may be able to give you the address of someone
nearby who has nursed an adopted baby. La Leche League offers the
pamphlet, "Nursing Your Adopted Baby" (publication number
55), which may help also.

Above all, don't pressure yourself to produce milk. Just enjoy the
body contact with your baby as one way to get to know this unfa‑
miliar little person better—and accept everything else as a gift.

Single Mothers

Depending on his temperament and daily rhythm, a baby can leave
a couple "wrung out." But a single mother has no partner who can
look after the baby at night or give her an occasional breather by
tending to the baby. She is likely to feel "wrung out" more often and
sooner than a couple. In this case, friends or family can give you
some reinforcement.

*When Suzanne was four weeks old, I was near exhaustion
because she slept very little and kept me busy night and day.
My apartment looked terrible. If Suzanne slept more than an
hour at a time, I was so tired I fell asleep from exhaustion.
Then I received a tremendous gift. Three of my friends
arranged a "housecleaning party" for me. One washed the
mountain of dirty dishes, one vacuumed, and the third
cleaned—while Suzanne lay at my breast. And then they made
a delicious dinner. It was wonderful.*

The majority of women have full custody of their children.
However, depending on your circumstances, your baby's father
might have joint custody or even full custody. If you are unsure

Support for Single Moms

- Consider looking for a communal living arrangement in which children are welcome, where your baby will have other people to interact with. Through the National Organization of Single Mothers or other single-parent groups (see addresses on page 258), you can find people in the same situation who are as interested in exchanges and mutual support as you are.

- Parents without Partners International has more than 400 support groups in the United States and Canada and more than 63,000 members. It also offers several interesting publications.

how to set up visitation or child support, contact people who can help. Social workers at the Division of Social Services or an attorney can generally advise you about economic (child support), legal (establishing fatherhood, inheritance and other matters) and personal problems. Sometimes they may visit you at home and if you are overwhelmed or ill, they may help you find help through a private agency.

If you are in financial need, you may be able to get support from your county welfare department and the WIC program (Women, Infants and Children supplemental program). WIC is a federal service that provides vouchers for food and nutrition counseling. A new mandate by the U.S. federal government also provides lactation support in the hospital and at home for women in the WIC program. Although WIC is thought to be an infant-formula providing service, their actual responsibilities and goals go beyond feeding styles.

In Canada, contact your public health clinic and county support service to find out what is available to you. The Canadian government has instituted a host of family-and-child credit programs you may qualify for.

When You Are Ill

Having the flu or a cold is no reason to stop breastfeeding. By the time you have symptoms, your baby has already become acquainted with the germs. Mother's milk gives babies antibodies to protect them against all sorts of common illnesses. Even when breastfed babies are ill, the illness is usually much milder than it is for formula-fed babies. The germs causing the illness are not transmitted through the milk except with acute Group A streptococcus. Common illnesses are usually transmitted through skin contact and secretions from the nose or mouth, not through breastfeeding.

Home Remedies

Instead of taking strong medication, you may want to use home treatments for a cold; for instance, hot milk and honey, a chamomile bath, a footbath with aromatic oil and the like. If you see your doctor, be sure to tell him that you are nursing and ask him to prescribe medications that are not harmful if they pass into the mother's milk (see page 99).

Special Situations

Some contagious illnesses require a different approach. In the case of active tuberculosis, your milk is still good, but in general nursing is not recommended because you should not be in contact with your baby (pumping is recommended, however). Mother and child are also separated if mother has chickenpox. Breastfeeding isn't possible when Mom has chickenpox, but pumping is still recommended. If mother has hepatitis B, the baby has to be vaccinated before nursing can continue.

Hospital Stays

If you have to go to the hospital and want to continue breastfeeding, find a hospital that will admit your baby with you. The organization Children in Hospitals (see Appendix 1) can help you. Since we have become more aware of the effects of separation in the earliest part of childhood, many hospitals have arranged to hospitalize mother and baby together if one of them is ill. If a separation is unavoidable, you can pump your milk and have your baby visit as often as possible. You will still need several days to balance your milk supply again once you and your baby are together.

Diabetes

Mothers with diabetes can breastfeed with no problem. There are even indications a diabetic condition improves during breast-feeding. Most diabetic, nursing mothers find they can reduce their insulin after a little while. For diabetic women whose pregnancies have been high-risk, breastfeeding can help them regain trust in their own bodies.

Diabetes itself does not pose a problem, but the condition may result in a higher incidence of sore nipples and breast infections. Prevention is the most important consideration. Women who are diabetic may find their milk comes in a little later (five to six days after birth). But the effort is worthwhile. The colostrum will be most beneficial to the baby in preventing hypoglycemia.

Mothers with Ongoing Illness

If you have thyroid problems, consult with a physician experi-enced in treating breastfeeding mothers. If you have an ongoing (chronic) illness, a support group for your specific problem may help you. In developed countries, an AIDS condition usually precludes breastfeeding.

When Your Baby Is Ill

The breastfed baby gets a lot of antibodies against illness through her mother's milk. Breastfed babies are sick less often than artifi-cially fed infants. When they do get sick, the illness is likely to be less severe, and they get well faster. Many doctors don't realize mother's milk is the best treatment for diarrhea.

When a baby gets sick, she may suddenly want to nurse much more frequently. Even if she was already getting solid food, she may reject it now in favor of mother's milk. You can increase your milk production in response to her increased demand. It doesn't take long if you pay close attention to your baby's needs. It is also possible that your sick baby will reject the breast suddenly (see page 132).

If your baby has to be hospitalized, consider admitting your-self too, if you can manage the time and cost. If your baby will have surgery, he does not have to fast a long time beforehand. There are usually no problems if the mother nurses her baby up to two hours before the operation, unless other medical conditions contraindicate it (for example, digestive problems). If you are sep-arated from your baby, pump your milk to keep up your milk sup-ply (see pages 80-83).

The Baby with Disabilities

Many of us have a picture in our head of what our baby will look like when she is born. Coping with the surprise, shock and reality of having a baby with special needs is hard for many parents. In this situation, breastfeeding may help a woman overcome her disap-pointment and possible feelings of insufficiency or guilt. Breast milk also helps the baby experience love, closeness, and support dur-ing an otherwise confusing time.

Your baby may have to be transferred to a special pediatric facility or newborn intensive care unit (NICU). Depending on the severity of the disability—or even because of the baby's passive, undemanding behavior—breastfeeding may demand extra effort on your part. You will need the caring support of a lactation con-sultant or someone else experienced with your situation. If your baby doesn't demand the breast often enough, you will need to take the lead and put him to breast frequently, even when he doesn't ask for it (see page 132). You may have to pump your milk to build up a good supply. Positions that enable you to hold your breast and your baby may work best at first. You'll need physical support to do this, either from pillows or a sling. Because the danger of infection is usually greater for children with disabilities (depending on what it is), mother's milk is a real advantage! The intensive skin contact you provide during nursing also promotes your baby's development.

Being in touch with a self-help group can make a difference (see page 259). In such a group, parents can find out how babies with neurological damage can be breastfed, or how babies with cleft lip or palate can suck on the breast when a plate is fitted. With both cleft lip or palate, breastfeeding is likely to be successful, though not easy. The problem is maintaining a seal between mouth and breast. A mother may have to hold her baby's mouth positioned over her nipple with the help of the

DanCer hold (illustration below). Some women have been able to use a thumb in the cleft to create a seal by holding the breast to the infant's mouth. Some women manage to fill in the gap created by the cleft through their own breast tissue when the baby opens her mouth wide and latches on well.

Professional, knowledgeable help is needed. These children are especially susceptible to middle-ear infections, so mother's milk is especially important to strengthen their immune system. The Medela pamphlet, "Give Us a Little Time," and a brochure from Childbirth Graphics also give practical help for nursing with cleft lip and palate. Childbirth Graphics has pamphlets on nursing children with Down syndrome and nursing those with neurological impairments as well. Many of the special needs that can complicate nursing are covered in La Leche League's *Breastfeeding Answer Book,* or in pamphlets the organization publishes (such as "Breastfeeding a Baby with Down Syndrome," publication number 23). You may want to consult with LLL's Medical Advisory Board or with a lactation consultant in some situations.

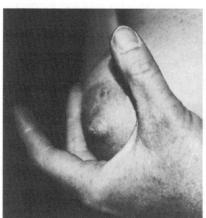 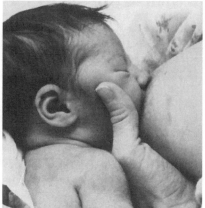

The DanCer Hold: The mother's hand position helps her baby maintain a seal over the nipple.

When a Baby Is Stillborn or Dies

The news a baby is dead strikes like a bolt out of the blue. In one stroke, plans and dreams are destroyed. Life will never be the way it was before. You and your partner may not want to discuss your baby because you believe thinking about what happened will only cause unbearable pain. Better not to see your baby, not to have anything more to do with what happened: "If we don't get to know him, we'll get over it faster."

These thoughts are understandable in the first phase of grief. But what really helps is exactly the opposite. Parents who have seen their baby, held him in their arms for a long time, perhaps bathed him and dressed him, talked with him and given him a name reconcile themselves to the death more easily. They can live in peace with what happened after confronting their grief. It may hurt more at first, but the less you suppress your grief, the sooner and more completely you will heal. Allow yourself enough time for this process and give yourself permission to grieve.

By the 20th week of pregnancy, your body is prepared to feed your baby. Your milk will have come in although you have lost your baby (see Weaning, page 177). At best, you will be surrounded by people who will want to care for you now. Frequently, however, those closest to you feel helpless and withdraw. See if you can find someone to stand by you in these first days and weeks. A local SHARE group can be a big help. Parents in Compassionate Friends or other bereaved parents' groups who have lost a child themselves are happy to support you in this difficult time (see Appendix 1). You might also want to refer to my book, *Help, Comfort and Hope after Losing Your Baby in Pregnancy or the First Year* (see Bibliography).

9

Natural Remedies

S ome situations clearly require conventional medical treatment. But natural ways of healing and natural remedies that have been passed down through the ages also have their place. Phytotherapy, which relies on plants and their active ingredients for healing, is one of our civilization's oldest-known treatment methods. In many European countries, classical, natural methods of healing have been highly respected and used for centuries. In Asia, they have been used for millennia. In North America, interest in alternative ways of healing has begun to soar as their usefulness is being rediscovered, especially within the medical profession. Doctors' books describing these methods, such as Andrew Weil's 8 *Weeks to Optimum Health*, have made the bestseller list. Alternative or integrative medicine is also making its way into medical-school curricula. The U.S. National Institutes of Health even have a division now called the *Office of Alternative Medicine* (OAM).

Many healthcare providers in European hospitals like to use natural healing methods, especially as a complementary measure. They act gently on the system and have relatively few side effects when applied with expertise. Midwives and obstetricians are increasingly likely to seek continuing education in certain natural measures. I'll highlight here some forms of therapy that have been used most commonly in recent years in childbirth preparation, childbirth and postpartum. These entries are cross-referenced elsewhere in connection with certain problems and objectives. See also Appendices 1 and 4.

Homeopathy— Triggering the Body's Self-Healing Powers

The regulatory systems in a healthy body normally work well together and are in balance. Influences *external to* (outside of) your body— for example, a chill or high stress level—or influences from *within*— such as worry, grief or anxiety—can throw a well-adjusted regulatory system out of balance. Your body then develops symptoms, in the form of an infection, nausea or something else. Conventional medicine attempts to eliminate symptoms by destroying what causes them with medicines. For example, to treat an infection, medicine would be used to destroy the bacteria causing the infection.

Homeopathy, a healing method pioneered by Samuel Hahnemann, M.D., 200 years ago, takes a different approach. The objective is to heal *using the agent that caused the problem*. The principle is "like heals like." This agent stimulates the body just enough to begin to *regulate itself* again. Homeopathic remedies are given in the form of tiny globules, drops or tablets in varying potencies listed as the Roman numerals C, LM, or some other combination, and a number such as 6, 30, or 200. Together, the two parts indicate the potency of the remedy.

A distinction is made between two different manifestations of problems: an acute complaint (sudden onset) and a chronic (ongoing) illness. With chronic illnesses, a complete homeopathic history in the form of a comprehensive interview with a trained practitioner is needed. With acute complaints and the type of problems that usually occur during the postpartum period, symptoms need to be accurately defined, including a description of the probable causes, the site of symptoms and the type and modality of the complaints, to arrive at a remedy that may help. If you are new to homeopathy, you will need to consult a trained practitioner. A typical process for diagnosis follows.

1. *Possible cause of the illness:*

> *Example:* Did I get chilled? Or was I suddenly faced with problems with my partner, the baby or disturbing news in the family that caused me to worry?

2. *Exact location of the symptoms:*

> *Example:* Where is the breast infected? What does the infected part look like?

3. *Exact description of the symptoms:*

> *Example:* How does it feel? Stabbing, pounding, pulling? What is the color of the skin: intense, bright red or more bluish? Is the infected area striped? Did the symptom appear suddenly or did it gradually gain intensity?

4. *Modalities:*

> *Example:* How do the symptoms change (such as from resting to being in motion)? Do they appear mostly at night or during the day? Does cooling or the application of gentle heat help?

Many homeopathic remedies are available. Homeopathic remedies are effective only for the specific symptoms and manifestations described. Two people with exactly the same problem (such as too little milk) may need entirely different remedies based on their answers to the questions above. It's like putting together a jigsaw puzzle, except you might use two different sets of puzzle pieces to reach the same final picture. With the help of one of the world's leading homeopathic experts, gynecologist Toni Drähne, M.D., I have compiled a small selection of remedies for the postpartum period. In Germany, Switzerland and Austria, homeopathy is well established, and a selection of the most common remedies can be found in many family medicine chests.

> To find a homeopathic practitioner in your area, check on the Internet or get in touch with American Holistic Health Association (see page 261). Also look in your bookstore, library or in the Bibliography to learn more from books about homeopathy.

If you do not find an exact description, another remedy not listed may apply in your case. Symptoms should noticeably improve with treatment on the same day or at the latest the next day. If they don't, it wasn't the right remedy. Always consult a practitioner who is familiar with homeopathy and breastfeeding before taking anything, or giving *anything* to your baby. For medical conditions, always consult a doctor.

While taking homeopathic remedies, avoid drinking coffee and black tea; this is recommended anyway for anyone who nurses. Stay away from other strong aromas, such as peppermint tea or toothpaste containing a lot of peppermint.

See Appendix 4 for a list of homeopathic remedies that may be useful for certain breastfeeding situations. Use the list as a guide when consulting a homeopath or naturopathic doctor. Consult a practitioner experienced in homeopathy *and* breastfeeding.

Bach Flower Therapy— "Flowers That Heal through the Soul"

Bach Flower remedies are named for London physician Edward Bach, a general practitioner, surgeon, homeopath and bacteriologist. Bach Flower Therapy is related to classical homeopathy and a few anthroposophical methods of healing (see FONMUMA, page 260). Dr. Bach searched for a simple method anyone could use. He identified 38 blossoms that directly affect the human energy system at a vibrational level. Bach Flower remedies are not geared to symptoms, but to underlying problems; that is, to what lies *behind* the symptoms. The remedies address negative spiritual and emotional states that have unbalanced our spirits and which, if the imbalance has gone on for quite a while, may have affected our bodies. Dr. Bach recognized that changing these negative states into more positive ones with the help of the blossoms also caused symptoms to disappear gradually. Normally a combination of several blossoms (between three and six, occasionally many more) is used.

The flowers are divided among seven areas, which correspond to basic emotional states:

1. Fear

2. Uncertainty

3. Lack of interest in the present circumstances

4. Loneliness

5. Oversensitivity to influences and ideas

6. Despondency and despair

7. Over-concern for the welfare of others; co-dependency

Because the method is so simple, you can easily apply it for your own and your family's needs once you have thoroughly familiarized yourself with it through books or perhaps taken a course. The flowers are also appropriate during pregnancy for harmonization and can help mother and baby during labor and after the birth. They are also helpful for a baby when certain states and problems occur. However, if a mother finds certain qualities or behaviors in her baby unbearable, then *she* should take a remedy, not the baby. Where breastfeeding problems are concerned, it is not unusual for both mother and baby to share the same problem (blossom). In addition, other components are involved that are different for each person. If you are interested in using flower essences, educate yourself through books.

The one impediment to choosing flowers yourself is that it isn't easy to recognize and admit to our own "shadow sides"—negative qualities. The heart of the problem, or an important dimension of it, may go unrecognized. If an incorrect blossom is selected, it doesn't matter—it just won't work. But if a crucial blossom is missing from the remedy, its effectiveness is reduced. For a list of experienced practitioners in your area, request an address list from Nelson Bach USA, the official distributor of Bach Flower remedies in North America (address, page 266). Original Bach Flower remedies may be available at some pharmacies or healthfood stores, or by mail order.

Making the Remedy

Using the flowers is simple. Place three drops of concentrate from several selected "stock bottles" in a 30ml (one ounce) pipette bottle. Fill the bottle with water and a drop or two of brandy to conserve it. Place four drops of the diluted liquid on your tongue 4 times a day for up to several weeks, until you feel a positive change. For babies, the dosage is the same as for adults, but make the mixture *without* alcohol and use it up within a week.(Prepare small amounts weekly in sterile pharmaceutical bottles.) Nursing mothers take the drops themselves. The baby may receive drops directly if you let them drip on the areola while nursing.

In acute cases, mothers can take the Bach Flowers by the waterglass method. This applies especially for Rescue Remedy, a combination of five blossoms that can calm and balance you quickly after trauma, accident or extreme upset. Mix 4 drops into a glass of water, and drink in sips until symptoms abate. Then take a few more sips 15, 30 and 60 minutes later. In an emergency, you can also drip the drops *undiluted* from the stock bottle directly on your lips, temple, wrist or elbow. Another form of application is to add about 5 drops to bath water, or place compresses on certain parts of your body. Bach Flower remedies can be used in combination with all other therapies.

The Flower Essences

Following is a list of flower essences, elaborated upon with the help of Dr. Claudia Monte, who has worked with Bach Flower remedies for more than 13 years in her practice, in hospitals and, not least, with her four children. It indicates those flowers (and the corresponding situations) that may be especially applicable for mother and child.

Note: These brief descriptions are not meant to replace thoroughly studying the appropriate literature or consultation with practitioners experienced with Bach Flower Therapy.

Agrimony: For people who conceal inner troubles and uneasiness and act as if everything is "going fine."

Aspen: For people with vague, unknown, unexplainable fears. They may be terrified about a possible pending "disaster," but have no idea what it might be. When children are afraid of being alone or when they sleep restlessly.

Beech: For people critical and unsympathetic toward others (such as their partner); who need more tolerance and understanding for individual differences.

Centaury: For good-natured people, overanxious to please others, having difficulties setting boundaries and saying "no"—who worry they won't be loved otherwise.

Cerato: For people who don't trust their own intuition and ask other people if they are doing the right thing. They doubt the correctness of their own judgment and their decisions; need confirmation from authorities.

Cherry Plum: For people afraid of losing their mind, losing self-control, being out of control; fear of child abuse, fear of a nervous breakdown. Helps with temper tantrums (also in children).

Chestnut Bud: For people who make the same mistakes over and over, who don't really work through and learn from their experiences;

for regularly or periodically recurring symptoms (such as breast infections).

Chicory: For those who are possessive of others and overprotective of their children; when there are problems in mother-child relationship.

Clematis: For those who feel absent, lost in thought, scattered. For babies who are not interested in nursing or their surroundings in general; who have a faraway look on their face. When children are coming down with something.

Crab Apple: The "cleansing flower;" for those who feel there is something not quite clean about them—when mother (or father) has a negative attitude toward milk as a body secretion, rejects sensual feelings of breastfeeding or has aversion to body contact, with resulting sexual problems.

Elm: For otherwise strong people who know their way in life but who temporarily feel overwhelmed by the task at hand: "Where to begin?"

Gentian: For those who are easily discouraged, pessimistic, doubting, skeptical—uncertain due to a lack of faith and trust. For those depressed for known reasons, such as an emergency C-section; when mother and baby are separated.

Gorse: For those suffering chronic illness or who grew up with someone chronically ill; when you feel great hopelessness, are in complete despair, resigned.

Heather: For the "demanding" toddler (also adults)—those who were emotionally deprived in childhood and who now focus on self, feel sorry for themselves, have strong need to put themselves in the limelight; can't be alone for any length of time.

Holly: For those who find it difficult to develop motherly feelings. For siblings and partners who are jealous and envious; may include angry outbursts.

Honeysuckle: For those who find adjustment to parenthood difficult; living in past—regretting what was lost; for parents who may have very weak memories of their own childhood.

Hornbeam: For mothers and babies who are mentally and physically overwhelmed and experience too much stimulation from their environment (this is a common reason for breastfeeding difficulties; it may also cause colic).

Impatience: For those finding it difficult to have patience with self or others and who can't wait out natural developments—who rush other people. Also for fidgety, whiny children for whom things don't happen fast enough, or for children with sleep disturbances.

Larch: For those who do not trust their own abilities—"I can't do it"— who fear failure and tend to be sad and tearful.

Mimulus: For specific, known fears, such as fear of illness or disability. Also for oversensitive children and babies, who cry without apparent reason; may be anxious or clingy.

Mustard: For those suffering attacks of melancholy and fits of gloom —the soul is grieving without apparent reason. This blossom may be helpful to mothers during postpartum depression.

Oak: For dutiful natures, bravely fighting against great adversities; they are completely worn out, but don't complain, don't give up. They are chronically exhausted, ignore a need to rest, are admired by other people.

Olive: For those completely exhausted of body, mind and spirit after a long period of overexertion; they have no more strength. This blossom is almost always appropriate in the postpartum period, especially when there are other children to care for as well.

Pine: For those who are overly conscientious; they easily blame themselves and are prone to self-reproach and feelings of guilt, inadequacy and failure. For people who apologize when they feel exhausted. For those who have initially rejected pregnancy and feel guilty about their feelings. This essence can possibly help address underlying causes of breast infections.

Red Chestnut: For those who are symbiotically attached to their loved ones (they know the needs of others before these articulate them); for those overanxious and overly concerned with loved ones' safety; for those who have worries about their baby's health. When milk leaks if the mother is out without the baby. Help for mother and baby in "cutting the umbilical cord;" for example, during the weaning period.

Rescue Remedy: This is a mixture of five blossom to be taken in the case of trauma, shock, strong upset, accident, surgery, before and after anesthesia, for loss of consciousness (see above).

Rock Rose (or Rescue Remedy): For those in extreme anguish, terror or panic (for example, before the birth) or when the baby is ill—helps stabilize parents so they can better help in an emergency. For children with delicate nerves; at night after a nightmare.

Rock Water: For people who are self-denying, very hard on themselves, who strive for perfection. In case of "baby shock," when previously successful professional women have difficulties adjusting to motherhood. For the mother who has to learn that life with a baby doesn't run according to plan.

Scleranthus: For those who tend to rapid mood swings, for those who "jump" back and forth between two extremes. This blossom is good for problems of ambivalence during pregnancy. For hesitant, emotionally unbalanced children.

Star of Bethlehem: For the aftereffects of emotional, mental and physical trauma (no matter how far in the past) and disruption of and effect on the energy system. Especially for mother and baby after birth, especially an operative birth. This blossom is called "the comforter of the soul."

Sweet Chestnut: For those in despair who have reached their limits; for those who feel they are in an extreme state of emotional and spiritual crisis.

Vervain: For those with fixed principles, which they are convinced of and rarely change. For those who have missionary tendencies and are willing to endure personal sacrifices for their cause; they tend to ignore their own limits.

Vine: For very competent, confident, strong-willed persons, who are hard and uncompromising inside. For those who tend to domineer, who override others' needs.

Walnut: For periods of transition and transformation (for example, pregnancy or weaning); adjustment help after birth.

Water Violet: For proudly reserved, self-reliant, quiet people who solve everything within themselves; distant and aloof. For those who have difficulty making emotional contact with the baby.

White Chestnut: For those whose thoughts spin. May be applicable in the case of breastfeeding problems.

Wild Oat: For those whose energy is spread too thin and who aren't living up to their potential; for those who live in a situation that doesn't "fit" them.

Wild Rose: For those experiencing resignation, apathy; for example, for baby when he has cried for hours; when he has been separated due to hospitalization. For mothers after a miscarriage.

Willow: For those feeling bitter and sorry for themselves. For those who have difficulty accepting the baby as he is.

Work with flower essences is becoming more and more popular in North America and Europe. In California, further intensive studies on flower essences have been conducted since 1978, and 72 flowers—called *the FES Quintessentials*—were identified there. These flower essences are prepared and distributed by Flower Essence Services (see page 266). The mixture and application are the same as with the Bach Flowers. Also refer to the literature (see Bibliography).

Aromatherapy—
Harmonizing and Stabilizing with Essential Oils

Pregnant and laboring women, and mothers postpartum, are subject to particularly extreme bodily changes and mood swings. During these times essential oils may help you regain balance and harmony. Essential oils affect body, mind and emotions alike. They can awaken and strengthen your self-healing powers. In more and more European hospitals, aromatherapy is being used successfully, particularly during labor **(please note those essences contraindicated during pregnancy on page 171).** Aromatherapy can also be a great help to breastfeeding mothers with their babies, because if certain ground rules are followed, they are extremely easy to use.

Pure essential oils, obtained by steam distillation or by cold pressing, can be used as follows:

❖ evaporated in an aroma lamp. Add 5 to 10 drops to the water.

❖ as a supplement to a full or partial bath (such as a footbath). Combine 10 to 15 drops of essential oil with 3 or 4 tablespoons of honey or cream as an emulsifier in a bottle and shake well. Or combine four or five tablespoons of liquid soap with 10 to 15 drops of the oil in a bottle and shake well. Or mix a handful (or two) of sea salt (salt from the Dead Sea is particularly good) with 5 to 10 drops of essential oil and shake well.

Caution!

The following oils (and a few others) should *not* be used during pregnancy because they can cause contractions or are inappropriate for some other reason: aniseed, basil, cinnamon, cinnamon-bark oils, cist rose, camphor, cedar, citronella, clary sage, clove, hyssop, juniper berry, lovage, marjoram, mugwort, myrrh, nutmeg, oregano, parsley, penny-royal, rosemary, sade, saffron, safrole, sage, savory, spearmint, sweet flag, thyme, verbena, vervain.

In the first six weeks of life, only 100% pure rose oil, Roman chamomile or myrtle are appropriate for the baby's sensitive nose.

- ❧ as an aroma massage (as partner massage or self-massage). Add 25 drops of essential oils to 4 ounces (100ml) of basic oil (such as sweet almond, hazelnut, jojoba, aloe) and shake well.

- ❧ as hot or cold compresses. Add 2 to 6 drops (depending on the area of the body) of essential oil (single essence or mixed) to 2 quarts (about 2 liters) of water and 1 teaspoon of honey. Mix well.

Aromatherapy is well tolerated with almost every other therapy. It goes especially well with Bach Flower remedies, but not always with homeopathic remedies.

Wherever appropriate, I have indicated throughout this book what essences might be applied for specific uses and causes. Consult the Resources section or your local library for additional information. Especially recommended is the standard work on aromatherapy, *Complete Aromatherapy Handbook—Essential Oils for Radiant Health* (1990), written by aromatherapist Susanne Fischer-Rizzi, who has been my consultant for this work. Sources for oils are listed in Appendix 2. The oil's effectiveness is tied to its purity (a synthetic won't work); buying oils is a matter of trust. Make sure the label indicates the oils' place of origin.

It would be nice if families could become familiar with folk remedies again.

Acupuncture in Obstetrics

Acupuncture is a traditional Chinese treatment, thousands of years old, which is becoming increasingly well-known in the West. The FDA estimates Americans spend some $500 million annually on acupuncture treatments. A panel of experts convened at the National Institutes of Health in 1997 announced publicly "there is sufficient evidence of acupuncture's value to expand its use into conventional medicine." The panel commented further that "the rate of adverse effects associated with acupuncture is low and often less than side effects associated with conventional treatments."

Acupuncture: A therapy by means of small needle pricks on particular points of the body (acupuncture points) using special, fine, solid acupuncture needles.

Acupressure: A therapy by means of gentle pressure exerted on the acupuncture points.

Moxibustion: A therapy using local warmth (for example, with glowing moxa herb, also called *mugwort*—thus the name) on the acupuncture points. Traditionally only a small number of the body's acupuncture points are appropriate for this sort of local-warmth therapy. It has been used, incidentally, when the baby needs to be repositioned in the case of a breech presentation.

Acupuncture, acupressure and moxibustion (see sidebar, at left) may be used in obstetrical situations. Some obstetrical practitioners are beginning to train in these forms of treatment for use during pregnancy and birth, as well as during postpartum and lactation. During pregnancy, for instance, nausea, toxemia or an unfavorable position of the baby in the womb can be influenced positively by acupuncture. Birth can be eased and sped up. Postpartum acupuncture has been used successfully for the treatment of pain and breastfeeding problems (such as a painful coming-in of the milk, plugged ducts, an emerging breast infection or too little milk).

10

The Nursing Relationship Ends

Over and over in life, we are challenged to let go and take the next step. We grow through these experiences. The desire to grow is part of our programming. Even babies in the womb contribute to the onset of labor and take the initiative to come into the world. Passages between the old and the new are often filled with a mixture of joy and curiosity, coupled with grief over what we leave behind. Still, something inherent in us pushes us on.

The breastfeeding relationship itself is a transitional phase that ends sooner or later. But when? And how? Many people respond intensely to these questions, but they have no easy answers. To recognize your own attitudes and convictions about ending the nursing relationship, you might start by asking yourself these questions:

- ❧ What were my feelings about breastfeeding before my baby was born?

- ❧ Was it my own opinion, or did I adopt other people's values?

- ❧ What philosophy of life are my feelings based on?

- ❧ How have my views changed as a result of living with my baby? What motivated me to change my point of view? Do I know anyone specifically who also shares this view?

✤ Do I really want to wean but just can't? If so, why not?

✤ Or, do I truly want to continue nursing, but have trouble resisting pressure in my surroundings that tell me I shouldn't?

✤ To what extent can I still give freely of myself to my baby for breastfeeding?

✤ How much support do I have to carry out my decision—whatever it may be?

✤ What internal barriers to continuing breastfeeding exist? What external barriers exist?

✤ Have I consciously decided to let my baby wean himself, but subconsciously set a time limit for him?

✤ Where is my baby in his development at the moment? What does he need? What does the breast mean for him? How much does he still need the breast?

✤ Is my baby ready to take new steps?

✤ How do I feel when I think about not nursing anymore? How much do I need my baby? Am *I* ready for a new phase of life with my baby?

✤ Am I relieved when I think about ending breastfeeding? Do I wish it would end, or does the thought of it make me sad, or both?

✤ Can I allow my baby to separate from me?

A need that has been fulfilled leaves us satisfied. In the case of the breastfeeding relationship, the needs of two people are involved at once—and both of their needs are important. But the "right time" for one may not be just right for the other. This is the basic conflict of all our relationships. Situations like these are seldom easy to resolve, but dealing with them helps us mature. If your child wants to nurse beyond a point you have set unconsciously, you may feel impatient and resistant. This is normal; sometimes we can overcome our own limitations, and sometimes we can't.

If, after weighing all factors, you decide it is best for you to end the nursing relationship, then do so with conviction. Be clear about your reasons for the decision. Have confidence in knowing that even days, weeks or months of breastfeeding have been valuable for your baby.

Ending Breastfeeding the Natural Way

Of course, it is ideal when you and your baby decide to end the nursing relationship mutually. If you are willing to nurse your baby until he weans himself, be aware the nursing period may only last nine months, but could also last much, much longer. Heed your child's signals and respect them—even if you yourself don't really want to give up this lovely habit.

> *Kerry weaned himself a day before his first birthday. He had gradually signaled lack of interest in breastfeeding with mealtimes during the day, but his "falling-asleep nursings" were dear to him. One evening he determinedly stopped nursing after a short while, but I had the feeling he was missing something. I got a cup of watered-down juice, which he grabbed from my hand and drank eagerly. After that he seemed satisfied. The next evening, the same thing . . . The evening after that I gave him something to drink out of the cup without putting him to the breast first. He seemed perfectly satisfied and went to sleep right away. When I tried nursing him the following days, he showed no more interest. It even seemed he no longer knew what to do with the breast. My son had weaned himself!*

One mother wrote to me whose baby had become interested in solid food late, but then ate very well and quickly reduced his breastfeedings. He weaned himself at 16 months:

> *Bradley and I had a satisfying, lovely breastfeeding time and found a pleasant stopping-place that seemed right for both of us. Because Bradley learned to eat at his own pace, he still enjoys eating and has a good feel for what and how much he needs.*

Weaning Your Baby

Next to the separation that comes at birth, weaning is the biggest step toward independence for your child in these earliest years. This separation has a significant impact on the development of your child's basic trust. The more gently this transition is made, especially if you want to wean early, the better. Your baby will need increased physical closeness from you to help him over this step. Let the La Leche League motto about weaning guide you: "Gradually . . . and with much love."

Your baby will need increased physical closeness from you to help him over this step.

As long as you don't have to wean immediately because of an emergency of some kind, begin at a time when there are as few other distractions as possible. If your child is sick, was just immunized or is teething, he'll have a hard time handling the additional frustration. At these times, sucking can relax him and promote his self-healing powers. Try not to let weaning coincide with the hot season of the year because more intestinal disturbances occur at this time. The more time you can allow for weaning, the better—for your baby and for you. Don't worry about the physical effects on you or your baby: Your breast milk will be reabsorbed slowly by your body, and your baby's intestinal tract will gradually get used to new food.

If you want to wean and your baby is only a few weeks or months old, start by replacing one breastfeed with a formula-feed, and wait at least a week (even longer is better) until you replace another meal at the breast with a formula feed. If your baby is more than four months old, you can gradually give him solid food instead of a bottle, allowing your milk to supplement his solid-food diet. Gradually, more food and other fluid sources will replace your milk. Some babies adapt easily to the bottle; others don't like having an artificial nipple in their mouths. Use an artificial nipple that is as similar as possible to your own if you transition to formula feeds.

Barbara relates her experience of weaning an older baby:

> For six months I breastfed Marcus exclusively. Then I went back to work, and until he was nine months old I continued to breastfeed him three times a day, along with the solid food he was now taking. I weaned him at a year, and I didn't get the impression he missed the breast very much (maybe the first few days, but that settled down quickly). Because weaning happened in a phase when his motor activity had increased a lot, it wasn't hard for me, either, because Marcus had changed so much. Shortly after weaning I couldn't even imagine how this active, bustling little guy could ever lie still in my arms for 20 minutes.

> Right after I weaned Marcus, it was hard for him to see me in a bikini or without clothes, because he misunderstood it as an opportunity to breastfeed. So I avoided letting him see me this way, and after a week or so he stopped reacting. In addition, I stopped taking him into my bed in the morning (where he had

*always been breastfed). He was eager for his "real" breakfast.
He did show certain withdrawal symptoms he had not shown
before. He put his thumb in his mouth when I changed him,
and he was very eager to be cuddled. For some time afterward
he liked to be carried around in my arms. But after a while
that subsided, too.*

A sudden trip to the hospital by either mother or baby is not necessarily a reason to wean. Set up camp in the hospital together with your baby, if you can. She should not be separated from you during the first year of life; even better, you should not be separated during the first three years.

Of course, sometimes a mother can't avoid having to wean her baby abruptly. She may develop a medical problem, for example. Some babies appear depressed when this happens, and many mothers suffer through their own emotional difficulties, too. Give your baby as much close physical contact as possible to help him over this time.

Medications that suppress lactation have been taken off the market because of dangerous side effects. When you have to wean abruptly, you may want to try homeopathic remedies, such as Phytolacca D1, or consult a homeopath for other options. Aromatic massage and compresses (see page 110) can also help reduce milk flow. Drinking three cups of sage tea a day can support the weaning process by helping to reduce your milk flow. To make sage tea, pour 1 cup of hot water over 1 teaspoon of sage leaves. Let tea steep for 10 to 15 minutes and strain before drinking.

To avoid engorgement and reduce the pain of overfull breasts, express just enough milk to make the pressure go away (don't pump until your breast is empty, or you will stimulate the breast to produce even more milk). Gradually the body reabsorbs milk that hasn't been used. If the breast is swollen, cool it with ice, uncooked cabbage leaves or cold cottage-cheese packs (see page 113).

Your Baby Weans Herself

Sometimes a baby simply rejects the breast, and that's it! Not only can this make a mother very sad but, depending on how frequently she had been breastfeeding, it can be very uncomfortable physically. If your baby is not really of weaning age, try to find out why she doesn't want to nurse (see The Baby Goes on Strike, page 132). If she *is* old enough and this really does mean leaving the breast, respect her decision. Your body needs help to adjust itself to the abrupt change (see above). If you are sad, cry—don't hold back. Tears are a balm for the spirit.

"I Want to Continue Breastfeeding, but I'm Criticized for It"

When one of the two "partners" has had enough of breastfeeding, then the time has come to end the breastfeeding relationship. But as long as you and your baby enjoy nursing, you feel your baby still needs the closeness the breast offers, and you are prepared to give it to him, don't let other people make you feel insecure. If your child feels dependent, that is a fine reason to continue breast-feeding.

Don't believe others who try to tell you the reverse, that your child is dependent upon you *because* he is breastfeeding. That's not true! Tending to a child's needs should not be confused with "overprotection." Overprotection is different, and it can lead to dependency.

> I planned to let my son Dean breastfeed as long as he wanted, about 18 months . . . When that time came, he didn't even consider stopping. In fact, he began to demand the breast more often than ever. I didn't dare tell my friends Dean was still being breastfed and avoided their questions about whether I had weaned. Dean clung to me, and that was a big problem for my husband. Fortunately we could talk about it. Eventually we found a solution. I began to doubt whether my son would ever wean himself and whether this was the right way. I blamed his clinging and his aggressive outbursts just before he turned two on the nursing—until I realized the nonnursing children of friends were behaving similarly at the same age. It helped to have contact with other mothers of nursing toddlers and to get support that way. Dean finally weaned himself at just about three years. In retrospect, I know it was right to meet his needs and give him time to separate himself from me at his own pace.

If you have difficulty withstanding pressure from others, get support from a breastfeeding group and from other nursing mothers.

When Prolonged Breastfeeding Bothers Your Partner

In making any decision, we always have to look at the entire picture, take into account the entire family-relationship constellation. Because a woman who breastfeeds needs her partner's support,
a conflict within the mother-father-child triangle can burden the
breastfeeding relationship and use up a lot of collective energy.

> *Breastfeeding didn't work out with my first child. I was very
> happy to be able to breastfeed my second child and wanted to
> let her decide when she'd had enough. But in my own mind I
> had set a time limit: somewhere between nine and 12 months.
> Lisa's first birthday came, and she wasn't the least bit interested
> in weaning. "Oh well," I thought. Inwardly I was happy,
> because I enjoyed these moments of closeness too.*

> *As time went on, Lisa sucked at my breast with growing
> delight. She was an uncomplicated, happy child, full of self-
> confidence. Although I enjoyed nursing very much, I gradually
> had more difficulty tuning out my doctor's warnings and
> criticism from my friends. But worst of all, my husband
> demanded I stop. To keep peace in the family, I considered
> giving in, despite my own feelings my child still needed me. I
> was torn. Lisa rejected the bottle I wanted to give her and
> demanded her "Mimi," which just about tore my heart out. A
> couple of times I resisted her and felt wicked. The more I
> refused Lisa the breast, the more determined she was to nurse.
> She didn't trust me any more.*

A situation in which everyone in the family is upset may be prevented by discussing feelings before disagreements come to a head.
Some partners are against breastfeeding because of an irrational
anxiety our culture has developed about "spoiling a child." More
often, the partner is simply jealous—jealous he no longer has you
all to himself and that you can feed and comfort your baby with your
breast. During breastfeeding counseling, I have frequently found
relationship difficulties correlate with breastfeeding problems.

Try to be honest and open with each other. After all, breastfeeding can trigger deep, subconscious memories of our earliest
experiences and of the way we were—or were not—nurtured, loved
and validated ourselves. We may be confronted with painful, even

overwhelming, feelings without consciously knowing where they come from or why. Dare to open yourselves deeply and share from the heart. Fathers may find ideas for this talk in chapter 14.

> The relationship between mother and child is extremely important, but a positive relationship between the parents is the basis for the healthy development of any child. That's why it is so important for the relationship to be strong between father and mother.

As a mother, you may ask yourself: Does my partner feel neglected or at a disadvantage regarding our baby? Is he really jealous? What could be the basis for that? How much nurturing, love and closeness did he experience as he grew up? How much did I receive? Am I being "overprotective" of our baby, and his complaints are justified? If the answer is yes, where does this overprotectiveness come from? Could it be an overreaction to deprivation in my own childhood? Do we allow times for only the two of us to be together? If not, how can we create time for our relationship?

Often it is easier to avoid conflict by channeling your energy in a different direction. But in the end this tactic doesn't work. Don't ignore problems; dare to tackle them constructively, with courage. Accept your problems as a chance to improve your relationship. If you can't talk to each other, perhaps you could write letters to one another. When you can't make it alone and the conflict is shaking up your relationship, find help from the outside— from friends you respect and trust, from a self-help group, from a counselor, your pastor or from a qualified marriage counselor.

"I Want to (or Have to) Stop Nursing, but My Baby Doesn't"

Women who were originally prepared to let their baby decide when to wean can get into situations in which they want or need to end the breastfeeding relationship.

> *I breastfed all three children (now seven, five and three years old), each one a little longer, because it was so nice. My daughter Susie, at two years old, nursed five times a day and also at night. Her interest didn't seem to wane. She was a very alert and independent child.*

> *Shortly after her second birthday I had to take antibiotics and had to stop nursing overnight. I was very sad and held Susie on*

my lap. Of course, she felt my sadness right away, became sad herself and wanted to be comforted with the breast. "You can't drink any more; the medicine made Mommy's milk taste bad." She looked at me with big eyes and then said lovingly, "Mama-milk not bad—goood!"

I'd heard of methods South American women use for weaning, and decided to give one a try. I went to the kitchen and mixed a little mustard with a little pepper in a dish and smeared this paste on my breast. Then I took Susie on my lap again and explained to her once more that the medicine had made my milk taste bad. She began to suck and this time she believed me. "Yuck!" She wrinkled her face. She quickly drank a little diluted juice out of a bottle for the first time. We had to repeat this procedure that night and again the next morning, and then she understood: "Medicine makes Mama-milk yuck!"

Of course I was uncomfortable, with my breasts bursting with "yuck" milk. Many people in my breastfeeding group told me my method was too radical. But I felt Susie was old enough at two to understand the situation, especially if I let her sense of taste help her.

She didn't grieve about the milk because it was "sour" now, and I didn't have to fight her. I didn't have to keep my distance from her. I could cuddle her and kiss her, and be Mama, only without breasts. She could sense I was as sad as she was that we had to say good-bye to such a lovely thing—together, not me against her. Two weeks later, when the treatment was finished, I asked her if she wanted to nurse. "Mama-milk yuck!" That hurt a little, but basically I was happy. She was now a little girl and not a baby any more. I was a little worried she'd remember the milk or breastfeeding negatively because of the way we had weaned. But since then, I've been relieved—Susie is three years old, and she is "breastfeeding" her doll because it is "sooo nice."

It's not always easy to wean an enthusiastic older child from the breast. As we've seen, no "recipes" can be suggested because weaning has to do with a relationship between two people. You need to find out what works best for both of you—keeping your child's personality and temperament at heart.

If you want to stop nursing, try reorganizing your daily schedule or make sure the baby's father or some other trusted, familiar
person takes care of him at the times or in the situations in which
he would normally be nursed. Have them offer extra closeness and
cuddling. Try to avoid situations that remind your child of nursing.
Distract him, keep him busy, offer things that capture his interest. Gradually he may think less of nursing and become more interested in other things.

Just as you may have talked to your baby in utero and felt him
respond, so you can enter into "dialogue" with your child now,
when you are both relaxed and happy in a nonnursing situation.
Talk with him from your heart, ask with your heart, listen from
your heart. Perhaps in this way you'll find a solution that hasn't
occurred to you before. Perhaps you can come to a "silent agreement" with each other.

It is difficult to face a direct conflict with your older child. If
you are determined to quit nursing, it will take strength, energy
and clarity of purpose to assert yourself. However, these efforts
must be coupled with love, so you will not appear harsh. If your
child knows your decision is final, but that it comes with kindness
and gentleness, you will have an easier time. Your child will know
where he stands. He won't know that if *you* feel torn in two directions. "It was hardest to stay strong at night," many women report.

If you initiate weaning—willingly or unwillingly—be prepared
to accept your child's strong feelings and allow him to grieve. Be
there for him with compassion and extra nurturing and cuddling.
Dad will need to help, too. If you are clear about your decision
and stand by him sympathetically, with caring and without feelings
of guilt, your child will grow through this experience.

When You Must "Wean" Yourself

If one partner in the nursing relationship is being used or feels
used, then it is time to end breastfeeding. Some mothers have trouble disentangling themselves from nursing. If you think this could
apply to you, ask yourself these questions (in addition to those on
page 173):

❧ Am I using my child as a substitute for a partnership that is
   unsatisfying in some way?

❧ Would it threaten my own inner balance to accept my child's wish to stop nursing and become more independent?

❧ Do I feel prolonged breastfeeding enhances my value? To whom?

❧ Do I measure the quality of my mothering by the length of time I breastfeed?

Breastfeeding can also be a kind of contest mothers carry out at the expense of their children. In this case, breastfeeding is not about what a child wants or needs at all. Games like these interfere with a child's natural development and personal growth.

As wonderful as it is, breastfeeding is not the answer to every childhood need. Make sure your baby has your attention beyond nursing times. Check and re-evaluate your child's changing needs frequently. Adapt to them! The times you spend nursing your baby should blend naturally into times of playing, singing, talking with and reading to your child. *Balance is the key.*

The times you spend nursing your baby should blend naturally into times of playing, singing, talking with and reading to your child. Balance is the key.

What mother has not put her child to breast to quiet him (when she is on the telephone, for instance)? What mother has not given her child a cookie to distract him? Be honest: Do you put your baby to breast from time to time for your own convenience?

When I realized I was pregnant again, I decided first of all to "wean myself." It wasn't easy. First I omitted those nursing times when I had asked my daughter if she wanted to nurse. As unbelievable as it sounds, this reduced nursing by half. I never said she couldn't nurse when she wanted. I just didn't breastfeed her when it was only for my own convenience. I didn't respond to my husband's request to "nurse her for a couple of minutes so we can eat in peace," or to the wishes of my older children to "nurse her so she's out of the way because she is disturbing our game."

But it was an effort. I carried her around a lot, calmed her down, saw she didn't disturb the older children when they were doing their homework or watching their favorite television programs—all times when I had found it more comfortable to breastfeed Monica. I telephoned much less than before and had a hard time for a whole week. I have to emphasize Monica was completely satisfied. She played more with the other children,

> took a more active part in family life and was outside more,
> now she nursed less.

It can be hard to recognize in yourself and admit to over-mothering, of not being able to let go. It requires great honesty and the ability to step back and look at yourself, to know yourself. Think about how much *you* depend on the breastfeeding relationship and whether *you* are prepared to give it up freely whenever your child gives you the signal.

Nursing during the Next Pregnancy

> *I just found out I am pregnant again. I'm still breastfeeding.*
> *What should I do?*

In the early stages of pregnancy nothing much happens to your breast milk. About six weeks after conception, the milk supply begins to decrease and its composition changes. The milk is more like colostrum again and is particularly rich in vitamins, minerals and protein. This is one reason why women in developing countries, where food can be scarce, often breastfeed their children until the arrival of the next baby.

> *Philip weaned himself at 13 months, shortly after I got*
> *pregnant. I don't know if it was because the milk supply was*
> *reduced and he was frustrated by that, or if he didn't like the*
> *change in taste.*

Many babies wean themselves during a new pregnancy; very often the milk doesn't taste right any more. The milk's change in taste is usually due to hormonal changes in the mother's body. But frequently the mother initiates weaning because she finds breastfeeding, especially in the second half of pregnancy, tiring and energy-consuming. Many women complain about sensitive nipples and breast pain.

Tandem Nursing

It is possible to continue nursing a toddler during the next pregnancy. Newborn and toddler are nursed simultaneously. This condition happens frequently enough that it has been given a name: *tandem nursing.*

Taking care of a toddler and a newborn is probably one of the most strenuous tasks a mother can face, regardless of whether both children are breastfeeding or not. Many a mother has breastfed her child during the next pregnancy in the hope he will stop on his own after a short while. Now, however, she notices this child needs her more than ever. She feels he isn't ready to give up the breast yet.

As you consider whether you want to nurse two children at the same time, listen carefully to yourself and respect your feelings, your own boundaries and those of your family. Emotional readiness makes the difference in your ability to *physically* handle this particular challenge. If you decide on tandem-nursing, be prepared for negative feelings toward the older child to crop up from time to time. Other women have had the same problem. Don't reproach yourself for it.

> *It's much easier to nurse Matt and the baby separately. When I am nursing the baby, we form a tight, intimate circle. If Matt wants to nurse at the same time, it feels like an outsider is pushing his way between us. That's why I nurse them at different times now.*

If at any time you feel overwhelmed and aggressive toward your toddler, wean. He'll cope better if you refuse him the breast in a straightforward manner. He'll have a much harder time if he simply feels your general unwillingness and rejection of him.

A Mother Reflects at the End of a Long Nursing Relationship

Rosemary, who gave her daughter, Brie, the time to wean according to her own rhythm and schedule, looks back on the nursing time and the knowledge she gained through it.

> *. . . Nursing had not always been so simple. Tending daycare children since Brie was two weeks old meant nursing her in one arm while bottle-feeding another child in the other arm. We also nursed despite my emergency abdominal surgery and throughout the week-long hospital stay. One winter, she insisted on nursing so much that I did not think I could lift up my shirt one more time. I later realized she had developed a severe rash . . . she was unbearably itchy and seeking comfort the only way*

she knew how. I am glad I had the insight to understand she knew best what she needed. How did I do it? How did I allow this child to continue nursing throughout the many obstacles and the numerous demands on time and energy I had never had before?

For one thing, I learned to trust. With my third baby, I came to trust myself enough to ignore a society that claimed to know my child better than I. I finally stopped listening when people said my child would never grow up unless she were forced to, that I had to be the adult, that I had to "take charge."

I learned to trust Brie mostly by being open and watching her. I watched as she walked and talked and started to use the toilet. I noticed that she would make progress and nurse less, and then almost turn into a baby again, nursing more. I watched her respond when I explained that sometimes she might have to wait to nurse until we got home . . . And later, when she explained she could go camping with her dad and "get by without nursing." I also trusted life. I trusted I would find ways to stay home with her despite the financial hurdles that kept calling me back to the "working world." I knew I had been given everything that was needed to continue nurturing and nursing my precious child. I had no doubt I would grow in my mothering and that together we would overcome the hardships.

Then too, for the first time in my many years of breastfeeding, I was able to see the humor in it all. When people were surprised to learn of our extended nursing, I could admit I never expected to be conversing with a child about "when she thought she might quit." I could giggle and tell them I might have to go off to college with her. I could laugh while trying on bras in a dressing room as my daughter yelled in delight, "That's my nursie!"

In a nutshell, I no longer had to explain my philosophy. I no longer had to enlighten others about dependence and independence and reasons and advantages. Free to simply trudge through this life, doing what I felt just fine, I no longer fought against myself. This has been my first experience with a truly child-led weaning, and I feel satisfied and full. I have done

*a job well, finished it completely, and left nothing hanging. The
lesson I have learned will not only serve me well in the
childrearing years to come, but will last a lifetime.*

Breast Changes after Breastfeeding Ends

Breasts undergo great changes during pregnancy and in the course
of lactation. Many women (especially those who had large breasts
before) fear their breasts will be bigger and heavier as a result of
breastfeeding. This fear is unfounded. Though some mothers'
breasts may become temporarily soft and flabby, they will regain
their firmness a few months after breastfeeding stops.

Immediately after prolonged breastfeeding, the breasts are usually smaller than before, because fat layers were replaced to an
extent by the expansion of the milk ducts. After a while this fat
layer, which gives the breast its shape, redevelops. Many women
with large breasts, however, have observed their breasts remained
smaller after breastfeeding than they were before the pregnancy.

Part 2

Pregnancy, Birth, Breastfeeding and Baby

11

Preparing for Your Baby

P regnancy gives you a few months' time to prepare yourself for the birth of your baby. It gives you time to transition into motherhood. But this time can also give you an opportunity to develop a more centered and leisurely approach to life. Now is the time to learn to be good to yourself, treat yourself with care, find ways to nurture yourself—even small ways—and let yourself be nurtured by others. Later, when your baby demands all your attention, you'll have this ability to center yourself and relax, and it will help when things are temporarily difficult.

The better able you are to "get in touch" with your baby during pregnancy, the more familiar he will probably feel to you when you finally hold him in your arms. Women have a natural advantage over their partners in this because they have felt their child inside of them. You can be a bridge for your partner by telling him what the baby is doing inside you throughout the later period of pregnancy. Both of you need to take time together now to focus on the baby:

✧ What sort of little person is developing deep inside the womb?

✧ Is she a quiet or lively child?

✧ What is his rhythm?

❧ When is she most active?

❧ When does he sleep?

❧ What kind of music does she like? Dislike?

❧ What does he react to in particular?

❧ How might she be feeling right at this moment?

❧ When does he appear to express well-being or displeasure?

❧ What other feelings do I sense?

You may already have experienced the power of attentive touch (see page 32). Now both of you, mother and father, might try placing your hands on your abdomen and see if it is possible have a "talk" with your baby. Or, hold your sensitized hands (see page 32) an inch or two above your abdomen and quietly "feel" your child's presence. Give yourself plenty of time to do this. Does your baby respond eventually?

When the baby is active, try *toning* an *mm, oo, oh, eh* or *ah* sound (for instructions, see page 56). Hum the tone for a while and listen inwardly. Does your baby react? Now try another tone. Do you notice a change in the baby's movements?

You can also ask your baby questions, knowing that on a deep level you have a connection that does not need words. Trust that on some level your baby understands you. Turn inward and listen to the "answers" that come back. You might become more familiar with him or her this way. You'll understand your baby even better when he or she arrives in this world.

A Child Changes Your Life

With your child's arrival, your life will change permanently. Suddenly you and your partner are jointly responsible for a small human being who is dependent on you totally and will need you around the clock. Many parents grow into their new roles matter-of-factly, with no problems. But most need some weeks to adjust themselves to their baby. Don't be surprised if your feelings swing between total delight and deep exhaustion in the first weeks.

Although no one can predict the kind of parenting experience we will have, we can positively prepare ourselves by deciding to share the "parenting load" with our partner from the beginning. Reorganize and change your lives together—with your child's well-being at heart. The following exercises can help.

„ Independent of each other, each partner draws a big circle on a large piece of paper. Within the circle, write down the time commitments filling your life now. Then draw lines between the various activities to show how much time you spend proportionally on each. On a second piece of paper, divide another circle showing the way you imagine your time will be organized after your baby is born. Compare and discuss. Where do you and your partner agree? Differ? How will you compromise to address your different perceptions?

„ A baby demands a lot of time. Rethink your lifestyle and rearrange your priorities now to create the time you will need for your baby. Brainstorm:

- What could I organize differently?
- What could I simplify?
- What could I leave out?
- How could I relieve myself of some work?
- What will I need help with?
- How and where could I get this help?

„ Lack of communication can cause conflicts and disappointments after the birth. Parents may have expectations of one another they don't verbalize. When each side expresses what it wants openly, an exchange of opinions, negotiation, clarifications, compromise and agreement become possible. But first, these expectations have to be made conscious. We live in a time when men and women, mothers and fathers, seek a new understanding of their roles. Devoting some attention to role expectations and role divisions in your family, as banal as this might sound, can help immensely.

„ As a couple, you may want to uncover how each of you sees his or her role in caring for your baby (see example, page 194). You and your partner will each need a piece of blank paper and a pencil. Make a dozen circles on each piece of paper. Label each circle with a job, such as BATHING OUR BABY or FEEDING OUR BABY. Be sure the circles on both sheets of paper reflect the same labels. Now separate for a minute and work alone: Divide each circle to show how the care in each case should be divided between you and your partner as you see it. Will you split some jobs 50/50? Will you be 90% responsible in some areas, such as feeding? Will your partner be mostly responsible in other areas, such as shopping?

Now share your pictorially documented expectations with each other. How do your expectations in these areas compare? Are there some surprises? Do you see a way to compromise when you have different viewpoints?

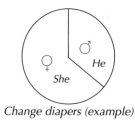

Change diapers (example)

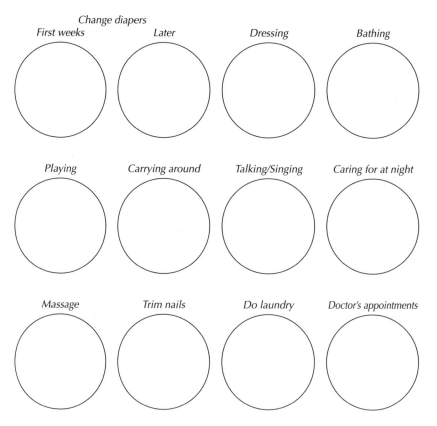

You can do the exercise above with other expectant parents and learn a lot! This is good to do at a childbirth-preparation class. Fathers and mothers can separate into two groups to complete their "circles." Each group may display and discuss the results among themselves, and then rejoin the other group to share their thoughts with the entire class. The exchange of ideas in a group can be fruitful and contribute to a better understanding of each other.

Newborn's Ten Commandments to Parents

Dear Parent,

I come to you a small, immature being with my own style and personality. I am yours for only a short time; enjoy me.

1. Please take time to find out who I am, how I differ from you and how much I can bring to you.

2. Please feed me when I am hungry. I never knew hunger in your uterus, and clocks and time mean little to me.

3. Please hold, cuddle, kiss, touch, stroke and croon to me. I was always held closely in your uterus and was never alone before.

4. Please don't be disappointed when I am not the perfect baby that you expected, nor disappointed with yourselves that you are not the perfect parents.

5. Please don't expect too much from me as your newborn baby, or too much from yourselves as parents. Give us both six weeks as a birthday present—six weeks for me to grow, develop, mature and become more stable and predictable; and six weeks for you to rest and relax and allow your body to get back to normal.

6. Please forgive me if I cry a lot. Bear with me and in a short time, as I mature, I will spend less and less time crying—and more time socializing.

7. Pay watch me carefully and I can tell you those things that soothe, console and please me. I am not a tyrant who was sent to make your life miserable, but the only way I can tell you that I am not happy is with my cry.

8. Please remember I am resilient and can withstand the many natural mistakes you will make with me. As long as you make them with love, you cannot ruin me.

9. Please take care of yourself and eat a balanced diet, rest and exercise so that when we are together you have the health and strength to take care of me.

10. Please take care of your relationship with each other, for what good is family bonding if there is no family to bond to?

Although I may have turned your life upside-down, please realize things will be back to normal before long.

> Thank you,
> *Your loving child*

- Another way to prepare for the arrival of your baby, either as a couple or in a group, is reading together Dr. Donna Ewy's "Newborn's Ten Commandments to Parents," which appears in the box above.

Bringing Baby Home Together

Many of the men who have decided to care for their families by themselves right after the birth are surprised at how much effort it takes.

> *After Laura was born, I stayed home for a week. I never dreamed I would be this busy. I had my hands full with laundry, shopping, taking care of household things. And I spent lots of time holding our daughter, looking in amazement and wonder at this little person who had come into our life. Often I would completely forget about eating, let alone think of cooking something nutritious.*

So much about caring for a baby is unfamiliar at first that everything takes longer than expected. Even diapering your baby requires practice: Until you have developed a certain competency, most of baby's clothing, from undershirt to romper, lands in the washing machine because mother's-milk stool is thin and tends to get on everything.

With all this work, meals in many families get shortchanged. As easy as it may be to rely on fast food for your meals, this habit only aggravates a temporarily unsettled situation. Poor nutrition can cause depression in the postpartum period. Nerves suffer too, especially at a time when a new mother is already under stress because of hormonal shifts and adjustments to motherhood. Eating regular, nutritious meals is important to health and well-being.

Sit with your partner, or perhaps a pregnant friend, and talk about the best ways to eat regularly and healthfully even when life is hectic. Where are the best places to find healthful foods in your community? Healthfood stores, farmer's markets and produce stands are all good choices, but even your local grocery store can be good if you choose foods carefully.

Stock up on whatever can be bought in advance and won't spoil. Frozen vegetables are ideal because they are harvested and flash-frozen before many nutrients are lost, and they cook quickly. Even stocking up

"Organic" is a term that can be used loosely. What qualifies as truly organic is not regulated everywhere. In other words, some produce labeled *organic* and sold at a higher price may not be. With a little research, however, you'll be able to separate the real goods from the imposters fairly easily.

on granola bars for random "hunger emergencies" might be a good idea.

Perhaps you can find restaurants or delicatessens that offer take-out, or even deliver, nutritious meals. Find local sources of organically grown foods (grown without hormones or the use of pesticides), or at least a produce stand, if you live in a more rural area. Shop for produce and organic meat or dairy products on the days they are freshest in your area. If you can't find organic produce to buy, consider growing your own. Nothing beats foods prepared from your own yard or space-saving containers.

If you like to cook, consider preparing casseroles ahead and freezing them in portions. Perhaps a good friend could volunteer to cook a few meals for you during those first days home with your baby. In some areas it is customary for neighbors and friends to bring along a nutritious meal when they visit a new baby. How wonderful it would be if this custom became universal!

Help at Home

In the early days after a birth, a mother needs help—especially if she has other children. We have already spoken about the doula and the support she provides before, during and after birth. In Germany, every mother is cared for by a midwife for the first ten days of the baby's life, longer if there are problems. In the Netherlands, not only does a midwife pay regular home visits, but it is standard for a postpartum helper to provide baby care and housework for 50 hours in the first couple of weeks. Doulas are becoming more common in this country too. If you are interested in finding one, you can get in touch with DONA (Doulas of North America; see page 258), and someone from the organization will assist you.

More and more new dads decide to stay home and tend their families right after the birth. A husband's care at this time can be heartwarming for his partner. A number of companies even have paternity-leave policies. See if this is possible for your partner.

If you are lucky enough to have friends or family nearby, they might enjoy nurturing you and your baby in

Trust yourself to accept outside help when it is offered in a generous, uncomplicated way, when you have a good relationship with the person who offers. Someday you may have the opportunity to do the same good turn to someone else. Life has a way of balancing everything out!

the first days. If you like and trust them, and can be yourself with them, then accept their help without thinking twice. It can be as rewarding for them as it is helpful to you.

Your own mother or mother-in-law might be an appropriate doula who can spend time with you. This is terrific if you have a loving and uncomplicated relationship. But it doesn't always work that way. Ask yourself:

- ❧ Would her presence be a welcome help and give you time to cuddle, nurture and get to know your baby and grow together as a family?

- ❧ Would her love and attention strengthen you and boost your self-confidence?

- ❧ Would she mother you and fulfill your dependency needs in a healthy way?

Or:

- ❧ Could old, unresolved feelings come to the surface?

- ❧ Would the constant need to clarify your relationship take too much energy when you need it for developing a relationship with your child?

- ❧ Would you want to do everything right for her?

- ❧ Are you afraid she would interfere, boss you around and be critical of how you handle things?

- ❧ Could you wind up feeling small and clumsy again in your mother's presence?

My long experience as a breastfeeding counselor has taught me that hidden or open conflicts of this sort can be a catalyst for a breast infection. If you suspect conflicts could arise that you will not be strong enough to handle, don't invite your mother or mother-in-law for a lengthy stay. With love and tact—but also with resolve and without a guilty conscience—offer the amount of contact in these first days that feels right for *you*. Remember, you aren't making a decision "against" anyone, but rather *for* you and your family. In this case, "*harmony* is the best policy"!

You and Your Mother

Pregnancy is frequently a time of changing relationships between mothers and daughters. Daughters develop a new understanding for their mothers. This is often a time of reconciliation. Old conflicts can be buried, injuries forgiven, old wounds healed.

Some mothers find it difficult to let their grown-up children go their own way—even when they are about to become parents. Sometimes, well-meaning advice from a mother who believes she knows best damages rather than bolsters a woman's self-confidence as she explores her own role as a mother. If you intend to have your mother or mother-in-law with you after the birth, consider your relationship and be realistic in your judgment and expectations.

If you intend to have your mother or mother-in-law with you after the birth, consider your relationship and be realistic in your judgment and expectations.

Other Support

Perhaps you can work out some kind of an exchange with neighbors, friends or relatives. A woman in early pregnancy, or someone planning to become pregnant, may be interested in helping you so she can get some experience living with a newborn. It can be helpful for her to get acquainted with a young baby's needs and behavior patterns.

A breastfeeding support group is a good place to meet other pregnant women. Perhaps you can ask your obstetrician or midwife if you can put up a note in her office. Or post a note at a health-food store, in your church or temple bulletin or even in a local supermarket. Why not try a small ad in the local paper? Check out the YWCA and the parenting classes offered in hospitals or community health centers.

You won't hit it off with every woman who contacts you. If you like each other, share your attitudes and expectations openly. But if it doesn't feel right after a little while, have the courage to end the contact—in a friendly and unambiguous way, of course.

Preparing Siblings for the New Baby

Firstborns start off in life with their parents' undivided attention. It's asking a lot of a child to have to share her parents suddenly, especially with a baby who keeps them jumping in the first weeks. Your older child will need your help to cope, but she will also have some wonderful experiences to look forward to with her little brother or sister.

Children have great imaginative powers. With your help, they can feel close to the baby. And the baby can be very real to them even in the womb.

> *Kelly was looking forward to her little brother or sister. We two had a lot of "talks" with the baby. She lifted up my sweater and whispered very softly into my navel. I answered her in a baby voice. She asked it questions about life in Mommy's tummy, and the baby also asked Kelly questions, which she answered patiently: questions about our house, our family, our dog, Grandma and Grandpa, where it would sleep, etc. Kelly sang songs to the baby, told it stories and assured it that it needn't be afraid of being born—life was wonderful, and besides, she would be there to take care of it.*

Children are curious about what goes on in Mommy's tummy. A number of excellent children's books show the baby's growth in the womb in a childlike, fun way—how the baby does somersaults, sucks his thumb, has hiccups and so on. A librarian can suggest titles appropriate for your child's age.

When you set up and decorate the baby's room, you might let yourself be advised by your little "expert." If you are daring enough and live in your own house, you might even enlist your child's help in decorating the walls with his or her paintings.

Making preparations—digging out baby clothing and bedding, setting up the cradle or bassinet and the like—naturally takes longer if you do it with a toddler, but it is great fun and strengthens feelings of belonging and togetherness. The times you spend preparing together are ideal times for talks about how your now-so-very-big child was once small enough to fit into this cradle and these tiny clothes. Children are utterly fascinated to learn they too were once *so* small. They want to know all about their brief pasts.

How about taking your child to visit other women who have just had a baby, so she can get an idea about what her brother or sister might be like? In breastfeeding groups, which I recommend you attend beginning in pregnancy, your child will have the opportunity to see babies of different ages. She'll see tiny babies may sleep or spend a lot of time at the breast in the beginning, but that one can do more and more with them as they grow. For example, you can hold out your finger for the baby to grab, make sounds she can imitate, make faces to amuse him, or laugh together.

Your child can also see how babies drink at the breast. Small children want very much to imitate all they see. You might give your child a doll as his or her own baby. Watch what happens! Boy or girl, your child will probably care for it very well by changing it, carrying it around, rocking it in the cradle and following your example by "breastfeeding" it—if not now, then after your baby is born. These modeling exercises are excellent ways for children to learn nurturing, loving behavior.

Helping your older child learn to love a little brother or sister should be your first priority. But jealousy is also a natural part of any sibling relationship and will be expressed now and then. Sibling rivalry and arguments are a normal phenomenon by which children test the big world in the safety of their small world. They practice assertiveness and giving in, cooperation and compromise through confrontations within the family.

To create the best basis for a good relationship among your children, make sure your child or children can see Mommy and the new baby soon after the birth and as often as possible. The average age difference between children in a family is two to three years. A younger child is more likely to suffer some separation anxiety if she is separated from her mother for a couple of days at a time. She may be upset at the new baby because the baby is the reason Mom left her for what seems to be an endlessly long time.

If mother and baby are in good health, they may want to leave the hospital as soon as possible and go home. This way, the family is together again shortly after the delivery. In Europe, this is called *ambulatory* or *walk-in delivery*. It is less common in North America. Naturally, postnatal home-care is warranted in this situation. In her excellent book for the medical profession, Ruth Lawrence (1994) suggests "the pediatrician should consider employing nurse-practitioners who will make house-calls immediately after [the] birth."

You could also opt to be cared for at home for a few days by a doula or nurse-midwife, but your health insurance may or may not pay for it. Check ahead of time if you want to do this. Some parents decide on a home birth for the sake of their children.

In some hospitals, children may be present for the birth, if that's what the parents want, too. Studies show that such families have very positive experiences, similar to home births. Siblings who are present at birth are less jealous of the baby. Of course, an adult should be present who is there exclusively for the child: someone who is tuned in to her feelings, who can explain the situation to her and hold her in his or her arms if she becomes disquieted and worried at times. Older children should be allowed to move in and out of the room as they see fit. Some hospitals offer classes and videos for kids who want to be present at the birth of their brother or sister to help them prepare for the experience.

Siblings who are present at birth are less jealous of the baby.

Avoid "sending the children away" to Grandma and Grandpa when the new baby arrives because "Mom can't handle everyone yet." At transitional times, such as the birth of a new family member, other changes should be kept to a minimum. Small children depend on the security of a familiar environment and on familiar people, so keep those elements as undisturbed as possible. If medical difficulties make it necessary to send your child away from home, be sure it is to a place your child loves to visit.

Finding a Healthcare Provider You Like

How babies are born and cared for in their formative first years affects them for the rest of their lives; on a larger scale, this affects the course of our culture and our world. After deciding how you want to give birth (see chapter 12) and about the importance of breastfeeding, you'll want to find healthcare providers who think along the same lines you do. After all, you will depend on their support during a critical time in your life.

Discuss with your partner or other pregnant couples what is important to you regarding prenatal and pediatric care. Jot down your wishes. Talk with parents who have been through the same things and who might share your ideas. Make appointments, with several doctors and midwives if need be, and discuss your ideas with them. Afterward, think about how these professionals made you feel. *With whom do I feel compatible? Where can I get the care I want?* Follow your heart in your decision-making.

Making Everyone Comfortable

I would like to mention a few things that enhance the baby's well-being and make life together with a small baby more enjoyable for everyone involved.

Where Will the Baby Sleep?

Many years ago I visited a friend in Canada who had had her first baby just two weeks earlier. It was a typical summer day, hot and humid, and the baby lay lightly dressed in his crib, crying miserably. Although my friend had placed her little son in the middle of a regular-size crib, he had somehow managed to wriggle himself to the farthest corner as usual. At the time I didn't understand anything about children and their needs. Later it became clear to me the baby's abrupt passage from the coziness of the womb to a big crib was too much for him to handle. The baby *needed* boundaries to feel secure and was searching for contact, even though it was with the walls of a bed.

If we were to ask a baby where he wants to sleep those first weeks, he would definitely say he would like most to be cuddled up in bed near Mom and Dad—the place where most children of this world spend their early days. From ethnological observations of mothers and babies in other cultures, we gather this greatly contributes to a child's feeling of trust and security in this new world. (Is it any coincidence these very qualities appear to be so wanting in Western culture today?) Next best, the baby would probably say he would like to lie in a cradle next to Mom. Babies love cradles. Besides being just the right size, a cradle can be rocked. Perhaps a baby finds this soothing because it reminds him of the time when Mom was still his "swaying bed."

Or you may want to consider a bedside co-sleeping arrangement, which will let you keep your baby just an arm's length away from you in bed. Co-sleeping arrangements are beds that attach to the parent's bed. In repeated experiments with adults in my breath workshops, we demonstrated that the breath of another human being nearby stimulates our own breathing, up to a distance of a few feet. I am sure babies thrive better if they sleep at "breath's reach" from us. Who knows, it may even reduce the incidence of crib deaths. However, there are some contraindications to co-sleeping, too—a smoking environment, unhygienic conditions in the bedroom, babies with breathing problems and violent or aggressive behavior in the bedroom are the major ones.

A hooded Moses Basket is another bedding option (see page 264). It makes a sturdy, cozy little "nest" for your infant. A basket as a first bed has one great advantage: It is mobile, so you can tote it along with you. A hanging-basket type with a canopy is also available. You can hang this sort of basket from the ceiling with strong cords and thus turn it into a cradle. It too travels well.

Before you buy any of these products, be sure to check for age and weight limits.

Many mothers have had good experience letting their babies sleep on a cuddly, washable lambskin (see page 264). They find their babies sleep longer and more peacefully on it, and tend to be less fussy. You can take it with you wherever you go and thus ease your baby's fear of falling asleep in a strange environment. Premature infants have been shown to gain weight faster when they sleep on a lambskin. Make sure it is not chemically treated because that could affect your baby's health. A lambskin should smell like a lamb and nothing else!

A rocking chair is a useful gift for an expectant or breastfeeding mother: Rocking and swaying not only calms the baby, but also helps a tense mother relax and become more tranquil.

Driving with Your Baby

When you are traveling with your baby by car, be sure to put him in an infant car seat appropriate for his age and weight. Do this for his safety *every time* you take him out in the car. (Many hospitals won't let you take your baby home unless you have an infant car seat. Some hospitals will lend you an infant car seat if you don't yet have one.) Make sure the car seat is tested, and has good ratings and an official seal of approval for automobiles. Newborn infants should be placed in rear-facing car seats, preferably in the middle of the back seat.

Don't buy used infant car seats. They may have been weakened in a previous accident.

Never place a rear-facing infant seat in the front seat of a car, especially a car with an air bag. And as soon as your infant is old enough to sit in a forward-facing car seat, this too should be placed in the back seat. Air bags save adult lives, but they smother babies.

Baby Carriers, Slings

Baby carriers and slings are a great replacement for baby carriages or strollers. Babies get soothing body contact, and parents have more freedom of movement with their baby:

> *When Anya was five weeks old, we took a rugged hike.*
> *Our trail in a swampy nature preserve came to an abrupt*
> *halt because beavers had built a dam that blocked our path.*
> *Thanks to the sling in which Anya was tucked close to my*
> *body, I had both hands free to pull myself over the obstacles of*
> *tree trunks and branches. Anya looked around with surprise*
> *and interest. When she got hungry later on in our hike, I*
> *breastfed her while walking—our first adventure*
> *for three!*

Look for a carrier that can be used from birth on, one in which your baby can be carried on the front side at first in intimate contact with your body. Make sure the head is well supported. Good carriers can be adapted to the growing baby to accommodate her size and her need for increasing independence and mobility, from birth to three years of age. Later your baby can be carried on your back.

Riding this way, both of our children got a lot of attention from the people around us because they were carried at eye level. At that height, the children could also see what was going on around them. If I had pushed them around town in a stroller, they would have been much closer to the ground and would have seen the world from a different perspective. Probably it would not have been very interesting at this level. It could even have been disturbing in the hustle-bustle of a large store.

In addition to a backpack, I liked to use a simple "carrying cloth" made out of sturdy, natural fiber, knotted at the shoulder. When Kerry fell asleep in the car, I would fold the cloth around my shoulder and sort of scoop him into it. He would continue sleeping peacefully, and I could carry him around without waking him, which would have made him whiny. You can easily create a carrying cloth for yourself by purchasing a strong, natural-fiber fabric, hemming it to the dimensions of 32" by 100" (larger for older babies) and double-knotting it securely. Pass the knotted carrying cloth over your head so that the cloth rests over one shoulder, across your chest, and goes underneath your arm on the opposite side. Carry your baby with his head on the side of the sling going over your shoulder, so he gets good support. You may also purchase carrying slings.

Our children got a lot of attention from the people around us because they were carried at eye level.

Plastic baby seats that can be adjusted to different positions also make good sense. Many babies are awake for long stretches of the day from early in life and want to take part in what's happening in the family. From these seats, they can watch Mom or Dad cook, read or clean. They can participate at mealtimes and absorb the goings-on in their environment. However, never leave a baby in these seats unattended or misuse them as "baby-sitters." Always put them on the floor, never on a table or counter.

Diapering

Finally, a few thoughts on diapering your baby. When we bring children into this world, we tend to become more interested in its condition, which is becoming more and more polluted—by us. For the sake of generations to come, this is a good moment to consider what actions to take or avoid to enhance the health of our environment, especially where diapers are concerned.

Diapers affect our eco-system in a major way. Disposable diapers add huge amounts of nondegrading trash and chemicals to our planet. In addition, babies sometimes react to the chemicals with rashes. If you must use disposable diapers, you may want to look for diapers that are free of chemical absorbents. Ask for gel-free diapers at your local healthfood store. You might have the option of a diaper service in your community, which supplies freshly washed, cotton diapers on a weekly basis. For sources, see Appendix 2.

12

Your Baby's Birth

———————————

A baby's birth changes our lives in a moment! As parents, we can choose whether to submit passively to the experience of childbirth and let others "deliver" our baby or whether to consciously prepare for it and influence what happens. Every woman encounters pain at birth. If she has prepared herself during pregnancy with her partner, under positive circumstances she will be able to deal with any pain as a strenuous but thoroughly rewarding experience. There is no substitute for the triumph and joy of knowing "I gave birth to my baby through my own power."

Childbirth Preparation for Couples

In childbirth-preparation classes, couples learn together about the birth process and learn to trust the workings of the body. With body-awareness and relaxation exercises, couples develop a greater sensitivity for their own and their partner's body and body signals. Men in particular learn how to tune into their wives' body language and needs better. Many couples become closer than ever before—their intimacy level increases as they learn together. Although some couples may not even make eye contact with each other much on the first evening, by the end of the course they often caress or stroke each other, oblivious of their surroundings.

I highly recommend you and your partner take a childbirth-education course. Together you will learn ways to manage and ride out the pain of childbirth, often making medication during labor and birth unnecessary. Bonding can take its natural, uninhibited course immediately after the birth. Medication can affect you, the baby and the start of breastfeeding.

Childbirth classes have the advantage of giving a group of expectant parents the opportunity to share anxieties, doubts and other feelings, and process them so these issues won't get in the way of giving birth. Classes enable parents to

- explore how their lives will change and what it means for them to have a child
- clarify and reconsider their own life values
- reflect together on what it takes to rear a child to become a loving, caring, competent human being with a high level of self-esteem

Your healthcare practitioner can direct you to classes, or look in the telephone book. A group experience can be enriching personally as well as educational.

Many couples have the same questions: Will we be good parents? Can we manage everything? Will we still have time for ourselves and for each other? Parenthood is easier when we know ourselves better, because otherwise it is too easy to project our own shortcomings, pain and fears on our children unconsciously.

If you have a lot of initiative, you might form an Expectant Parents' Sharing Group. Brainstorm ways to start the group and find couples who might be compatible with you. Groups like this can become like a nurturing, extended family. Often they continue well after the babies' births and grow with the children.

How Can My Partner Help?

Bringing a child into the world is a powerful physical experience. It's probably like nothing you have ever experienced. Going through the birth process with respect for its significance, a deep consciousness of your physical and emotional role in it and with the helpful participation of your partner can give you an indescribable sense of achievement and pride.

Toward the end of labor, verbal, intellectual communication between you and your partner is hardly possible. It is not unusual to see a man suffering because of his wife's pain, squeezing her hand, wiping perspiration from her brow—overwhelmed by and in awe of the intensity of the experience she is going through. It is great if the father-to-be has learned about childbirth and has dedicated himself over time to focus his attention on birth and the little child making its way into their lives. It is great if he knows ways to help alleviate her pain. But learning "techniques" is not as important as communicating to his laboring partner that someone strong and dependable is there for her. This is a time when he can be truly and completely devoted to her with his whole body and his breath. This is easier the better they know each other physically, the more trust they have in each other and the more fulfilling their sexual relationship is.

Loving created the child in the woman. Loving ways can help bring it into the world. Snuggling, cuddling, caressing or sensual touching can bring about a miracle of relaxation, especially at the beginning of labor. If he has been able to sensitize his hands (described on page 52), he can soothe and "melt" a lot of her pain with his attentive touch, and his child may benefit from the enhanced quality of his touch, too.

When contractions get stronger, the man can accompany his partner with his own breath and communicate peace and tranquility by using a tone to make his breathing audible (perhaps an *mm*, a deep *oo*, a broad *eh* or a light *ah*). The vibrations carry from one person to the other. He also can help if you decide to use other relaxation or pain-management ideas in labor, such as showering, acupressure or massage.

In almost all hospital settings, the conventional narrow delivery tables have given way to more comfortable and accommodating birthing arrangements and aids: wide beds, birthing stools, even birthing balls. In many places, women are no longer subjected to the extremely disturbing process of being rushed from the labor room to the delivery room at the most intense phase of their labor. Instead, they labor, give birth and recover in the same room. With changing conditions in the birthing room, your partner can sit behind you and hold you in his arms so that, in the safety of his embrace and touch, you can give yourself over entirely to what is happening with your body.

What Does the Baby Experience?

Every child is confronted by pain during his birth. Dr. Fréderick Leboyer describes this impressively in his book, *Birth without Violence* (see Bibliography). A newborn is neither blind nor insensitive. Apparently people must have thought so at one time; otherwise, it is unimaginable that they routinely handled babies so roughly in delivery rooms, a common practice for decades. Anyone who has observed a newborn baby closely, has looked into her eyes and seen the way she slowly relaxes and "unfolds" after birth, understands this is an alert, extremely sensitive and feeling person.

> *After Julie was placed on my tummy, I was startled when I laid my hands on her. I had never felt such energy before. There are no words for it—I think she was completely terrified. That feeling went away quickly. My daughter grabbed my index finger as she lay there—even before she made her first sound. She opened her eyes and looked at me with deep, black, radiant eyes. I had to contort myself a little to look at her, because she lay lengthwise along my tummy. I would rather have seen her face-to-face. I felt completely open right then. Everything that happened in this early stage of our relationship has deeply engraved itself into my mind and being. Looking at my daughter for the first time, feeling her body, seeing her eyes— I can recall all of that as clearly and vividly as if it had been just a minute ago.*

For the baby, labor is a state of increasing constriction, the birth itself an explosion into limitless space. For this reason, the baby needs hands to hold him as he lies on his mother's abdomen— hands that slowly and firmly massage his back and "say" to him: "You are not alone, you can open yourself to the new—to the world."

We all know the fear of the unknown. For the newborn, *everything* is new, and he is very frightened. It is clear he needs his mother above all, her rhythms, her voice and her energy. The child knows her, she is his entire past. She remains, even if everything else has changed.

A little while ago, when attending a birth, I was allowed to bathe the little newborn baby. He had shut his eyes tightly and was completely tense. The light over the wash basin was still on—we turned it off. What a difference! The baby unfolded himself like a butterfly, stretched out his arms, opened his hands and opened his eyes. He turned his head, looked around and suddenly seemed quite satisfied.

Anyone who has come out of a dark cave into bright sunlight knows how painful the sudden flood of light can be on the eyes. For this reason, dim the lights in the birthing room somewhat for the baby's sake. The same is true regarding noise. The mother's and father's voices are familiar to the child—they can speak to him, welcome him. The others present should hold back and make as little noise as possible.

In Favor of "Gentle Birth"

Every child is different. Every child has his own past and his own future. Many babies cry as they are placed on their mother's tummy and quiet only very gradually under her hands. Others don't seem a bit disturbed, as though they move easily and dreamily from birth into life. You see by their movements, their sighs, their peaceful breathing and sometimes their open eyes that they are perfectly at ease, even if they are "suspiciously" quiet.

There are, however, situations in which a baby has difficulty getting started and needs help: after a long, difficult birth; after administration of medication; or sometimes for inexplicable reasons. Equipment your practitioner has on hand to help the baby include oxygen tanks and suction devices. Strong skin stimulation may be all some babies need to "awaken" them to the world. No conscientious doctor or midwife would waste time creating a gentle environment if such a child needed medical care or attention. Under these circumstances, any woman would understand.

Contrary to the misgivings of many obstetricians, waiting to cut the cord late, commonly done in gentle births, doesn't greatly affect the distribution of blood between placenta and baby. You can prevent the baby from cooling off too much on his mother's abdomen by covering him with a warm cloth, or by placing a heating lamp over mother and baby. "Now obstetrics is fun again!"

enthused one obstetrician with decades of experience after his hospital had converted to this more humane model of care.

"Sentimental hocus pocus" say those who close their eyes and find a thousand, petty, alleged medical arguments to discredit "gentle" birth. The emotion with which this discussion is carried out among practitioners only demonstrates more is here than meets the eye: It has to do with love, with joy, with deep openness. This is difficult for many people and causes them so much anxiety they become irrationally defensive.

Some of the anxiety expressed about gentle birth can be attributed to the way some practitioners have been taught about birth and women's bodies. To them, birth is seen as a potentially dangerous medical event that requires management. As a result, women and their babies tend to be treated as objects that need to be managed. In this scenario, the concept of gentleness during birth is seen as less important than the management of the event. But now many schools are training practitioners to look at birth as a natural event that in most cases "goes right," not wrong. And so emotion is finding its way back into the birth equation, at last.

If you have decided the way your child is welcomed into the world is important, discuss it in advance with your obstetrician or midwife. If this person is not open to your needs, you may need to consider whether he or she is really the person you want with you during one of the most intense, intimate, moving moments of your life. Find a competent, caring caregiver who respects your wishes, one whose outlook is in line with yours.

"Where Should Our Baby Be Born?"

The environment in which you feel safest is the one in which you can relax and bring your child into the world. Medical care and basic human responsibility is due you and your baby during the birth. Wherever choices are available, bear these aspects in mind when you choose the place of birth. The birth is the beginning of your baby's life and your relationship to him; it is a major event in your and his life. Take time to look around a bit, talk with other parents about their birth experiences, and check out your options. Visit different birth practitioners and facilities in your area. There may be home, birth center or hospital options.

Talk with midwives, nurses and doctors about their philosophy of and practices regarding childbirth and breastfeeding. Let them know your wishes and needs, and be aware of their reactions. Then rely on your own intuition for your final decision. Don't be afraid to change your practitioner if you don't see eye-to-eye with her. You have that right. Your birth experience should only include people whom you trust.

At Home

> *My first two children were born in Holland, at home. Then we moved to the States. I wanted to have our third child at home also. But my gynecologist was very intimidating. I also heard a lot of negative comments from people around me. In Holland, home birth had been a completely normal event—35% of all babies are born at home with the assistance of a midwife.*
> *In the States, this desire made me an "irresponsible mother." Only because I am a physician myself, could I defend myself with statistics about home birth and had researched the topic was I spared anything worse. If this had been my first child, I would certainly not have trusted myself to bring her into the world at home.*

Whether it is "responsible" to give birth at home today is discussed as heatedly as the issue of gentle birth. Why do an increasing number of couples decide on a home birth? For many, the atmosphere in the hospital can't compare with the home environment—no institution allows such intimacy, such emotional openness. Common, routine interventions of a hospital also fall away, so labor can take its natural course. Perhaps these are the reasons many studies show home deliveries, attended by a trained professional, can be just as safe as hospital births—and sometimes the outcomes are even more favorable.

For many couples, the warmth of the home environment and the closeness of people whom they trust and with whom they can let go completely, count more than the technical security of a well-equipped delivery room. During labor and birth, some women have such strong body awareness and sensitivity, and feel the experience so deeply, that they enter a highly vulnerable emotional state.

Strangers, unexpected outside influences, a hectic atmosphere in the delivery room or an impatient practitioner can upset them enough to disturb the natural birth process.

At home, many things related to labor are handled matter-of-factly. The laboring mother can walk, stoop, kneel, lean over a comfortable chair and follow her body's impulses freely. In familiar surroundings she can be more in touch with herself. She can cuddle against her partner and enter into the comfort of his breathing rhythm. Once the baby is born, his parents can welcome him into their life in a way that is right for them, without having to observe hospital routines.

On the other hand, a home birth should be considered only by a mother at low risk of complications who has had excellent prenatal care, and by a couple who would feel secure at home. If parents have anxieties about the birth and possible complications or other concerns, they are better off selecting another setting. High-risk pregnancies and risk factors such as premature labor, breech position and multiple babies belong in a hospital.

For a home birth, you will need an experienced, trained midwife. Most—where the doctors are willing—have physician backup. Your midwife should carry good supplies and have resuscitating equipment. In the rare event of a complication the midwife cannot handle, have your maternal health records and reliable transportation to the hospital available.

In the Birth Center

An alternative between home birth and hospital birth has developed in many places in the United States over the last couple of decades, called ABCs or *alternative birth centers*. In comfortably decorated birthing rooms women give birth to their babies with the help of a midwife or doctor, in a relaxed, supportive, safe environment. These rooms look like a cozy living room. The focus is on a large measure of human caring and contact, and on attending to the individual needs of the laboring woman and her family.

Technical apparatus (such as electronic fetal monitoring, suction devices and oxygen) may be available on the premises, but are only brought out when absolutely necessary. Cooperative pediatricians, obstetricians or family physicians are on call for emergencies or actually work in a birth center. Continuity of care is ensured. Women are looked after comprehensively with a wide range of services: confirmation of the pregnancy, prenatal care, childbirth preparation, birth, preparation for infant care and post-partum care. This and much more is offered either directly through the birth center or through resource and information centers, which may be connected with the birth centers. Even a small postpartum unit may be attached, although as a rule, families go home soon after birth. In most cases, the discharge time is within 6 to 12 hours.

In the Hospital

Hospitals are hiring more and more nurse-midwives. Studies have shown birth outcomes have greatly improved in those hospitals where midwives are part of the staff. Maternity departments now frequently make an effort to provide family-friendly care *and* sensitive woman-baby care. That means:

- Women are not moved from labor room to delivery room.
- Greater allowance is made for a natural birth process.
- You have the freedom to choose your own laboring and birthing position.
- Mom, dad and baby are no longer separated at birth and afterward.
- The narrow delivery table has given way to wide, comfortable birthing beds.
- Birthing chairs, birthing balls or bars to hold and steady yourself while squatting are available.

These amenities can all be found in a hospital these days. In a few hospitals, and in some birth centers, babies may even be born in a birthing tub, if you choose.

It *is* possible, even in the most structured hospital, to have a satisfying birth experience. Perhaps an essential oil (see page 60), brought from home to evaporate in a fragrance lamp can contribute to a sense of familiarity in the birthing room. See if the hospital you are interested in permits this. For example, precious rose oil is a calming, harmonizing "greeting" for the child. In Germany, aromatherapy during labor and delivery is becoming standard.

13

Bonding with Your Baby

The bond you as parents develop toward your child is the start of a lifelong nurturing and loving relationship. Your child, in turn, attaches to you, creating a good basis for his optimal development. Your baby's bond with you, his parents, is probably a model for all his future bonds. Thankfully, bonding is no longer viewed as an isolated, time-critical process right after birth, but as a continuum of experiences, affected by many factors. The continuum extends from our own childhood experiences through pregnancy, childbirth, postpartum and the early months of our baby's life.

What Happens at Birth?

The first hour after birth is extremely important for you and your baby, because it is a time of heightened sensitivity. Suckling at the breast during this hour plays an important role in the bonding between you and your child. If your baby is placed on your abdomen right after birth, you will probably want to touch him timidly at first, with your fingertips, then stroke him with your whole hand.

Above all, almost all mothers want to look into their baby's eyes and have their baby look into theirs right away. It is the most natural thing in the world. Gazing into the eyes of a newborn is regarded as one of the most powerful triggers for parenting behavior and parental love.

What does the baby see when he looks into his mother's eyes? Dr. Donald W. Winnicott, who has written about this subject, suggests the baby sees *himself* in the mother's face. The mother mimics the facial expressions of her baby and mirrors them back to her child. This is the baby's first lesson in developing a concept of self. In a test where mothers were told to keep a straight face and not to react to their babies, the babies became restless, turned away, and many started to cry.

You may or may not experience "love at first sight." Some mothers feel immediate affection for their baby, but others wonder, "Is this really *my* child, whom I am supposed to love unconditionally now?" Don't feel guilty if an all-embracing "motherly feeling" (whatever that is) doesn't appear at once or isn't always present.

Many parents are disturbed and distracted by the hassle of a busy delivery room, and some report they only "fell in love" with their child after they had quiet, undisturbed time alone together. For many new parents, this means the first days at home.

Conditions for bonding are enhanced when mothers are cared for and supported in a nurturing way themselves during labor, as Marshall Klaus, John Kennell and Phyllis Klaus describe in their book, *Mothering the Mother* (1993). Hospitals are beginning to appreciate how important this time together is and are arranging more frequently for rooming-in (babies remain with their mother trhoughout the hospital stay). Many hospitals are reducing the use of the nursery for routine baby care and are encouraging 100% rooming-in. A few progressive hospitals have closed their nurseries entirely.

Rooming-in enables constant communication between baby and parents; something many parents love to do. It seems all mothers like to talk to their babies in a high-pitched voice, and newborns react best to that. Newborns *do* recognize their mother's voice. As you talk to your baby, your baby reacts by moving to the rhythm of your voice. Though babies prefer a woman's voice to a man's, babies apparently also react to their father's voice.

Responses from their baby give parents joy, and entice them to continue talking. You will find the two of you, parent and baby, will enter into a "dance" with each other. This dialog is both interactive and self-supporting. In effect, your baby is giving a recognition signal back to you through his movements or his eyes.

And what about the baby? After an unmedicated birth, babies remain in a state of calm alertness (heightened attentiveness) for about 45 minutes. If the lights in the room are not too bright, your baby will look around with wide-open eyes. All his energy is geared toward seeing, hearing and reacting—as if he wants to soak up everything around him. Your baby will cuddle next to your body, and in direct skin-to-skin contact, his little hand will seek to touch your skin. He will gaze intently at your eyes. You will see his recognition if he is fairly close to your face. About 8 to 10 inches is optimal—the distance between the eyes of a baby and his mother's face during breastfeeding.

If Close, Early Contact Isn't Possible

Bonding during the first hour is extremely valuable, but sometimes it doesn't happen for reasons that can't be helped. In these cases, other avenues for establishing attachment and bonding are available. If you miss out on bonding with your child in the first hour after birth—because you had a Cesarean, or were strongly medicated, your child needed special care or for some other reason—you still can build a strong and secure bond with your baby over time. It takes a little longer, but the bond will grow just as strong. After all, relationship-building is a lifelong affair.

In being together with your child—in frequent contact with him or her—your love and motherliness will grow. Each one of us develops love for our new baby in our own way and at our own rate. As time goes by, almost all parents will experience unconditional love for their child.

The first breastfeeding is also an important time for you and your baby. While the baby is sucking at your breast, your oxytocin level rises, which has a tranquilizing effect on you and helps cement the tie between you. (Oxytocin also makes the uterus contract and return to its normal shape.) Incidentally, Klaus' and Kennell's studies showed mothers with prolonged first contact enjoyed greater success at breastfeeding; Swedish studies demonstrated its positive effect on the mother's desire to breastfeed and on breastfeeding duration.

From their studies and decades of observation, Klaus, Kennell and Klaus suggest placing the baby on his mother's abdomen in direct skin-to-skin contact after he has been wiped dry, looks rosy and is active. If you give birth in a crouching position, you may even pick up the baby yourself right after the delivery and place him on your body. Contact with your skin helps stabilize your baby's body temperature. Ideally you should have at least one hour alone with your baby. Routine measures such as washing and weighing can wait. Besides, babies do recognize their mother and respond unwillingly to being separated from you.

If you have a life history, difficult family, or a social condition that makes parenting seem difficult, know this initial contact immediately after birth can greatly ease the natural development of a loving relationship with your baby.

If there are no medical contraindications, parents and child should be able to room-in with each other until they are discharged from the hospital. Even if your baby is premature or ill, extensive contact as early and as often as possible is particularly important, if not critical, to his improved health (Klaus, Kennell, Klaus, 1995).

The majority of studies on initial bonding suggest beyond doubt that all parents should be offered unrestricted early contact with their newborn. It is the most natural thing in the world for mother and baby to be and stay close together. Why then, in some places, do we still separate mothers and babies after birth?

Preoccupied by the Baby

Toward the end of the pregnancy and in the first weeks after the birth, mothers experience a heightened sensitivity, which one researcher calls "primary maternal preoccupation."

> *During the last weeks of pregnancy I was absent-minded, often lost the thread in discussions, and it was difficult for me to bring thoughts to their logical conclusion. This state of mind scared me to death—I thought I was losing control. I had a hard time accepting it until I discovered in talking with other women that they had experienced something very similar.*

This preoccupation is a state of total concentration on your baby. You will barely remember it once you have recovered from it. Apparently this is Nature's way of making it easier for mothers to devote themselves entirely to their babies. Keep it mind as your due date approaches. This is obviously *not* a good time to commit to other projects!

14

The First Weeks with Your Baby

Many mothers like to go home soon after birth because that's where they feel most comfortable. At home they can organize their lives entirely around meeting their family's needs. But for some mothers, coming home means apprehension in the beginning.

Living with a Baby

No new mother and father knows everything about babies. Few of us have had any experience with a newborn before the birth of our first baby. Only slowly do we learn to tune into our children and fulfill their needs. If we adapt ourselves to the rhythm of our little baby in these early days—with joy and curiosity—we will enjoy him all the more.

Have patience with yourself. There is no such thing as "perfect parents." Just do your best! In general, "problem parents," if anything, demand too much of themselves. We all have those moments when we would gladly send our baby back where he came from! Don't feel guilty about it. Occasional negative feelings only prove we're human.

Although most of us can't find a recognizable routine in the first weeks with a new baby, a certain regularity develops by and by. Eventually we learn how best to integrate our baby's needs into our daily lives.

> *I set the alarm so it rang half an hour before my husband and the older children woke up. Then I took Elisa into bed with me and breastfed her. That way I was certain she was full and content while we had breakfast.*

Some babies need to be diapered before every meal, because too much movement with a full tummy tends to make them spit up. Others, at least in the beginning, fill their diapers during every meal, and it doesn't make sense to diaper them beforehand. Some babies are best bathed in the morning because the activity wakes them up; others are better bathed at night because they get sleepy afterward or because their father enjoys participating in the bathing ceremony every evening.

A long nap during the day may be the best time for a new mother to catch up on *her* sleep.

Most babies sleep wonderfully in the fresh air, on the porch (be absolutely sure your baby cannot slip through the railings), in a protected yard or when taken on a walk. Babies can be brought outdoors most of the time as long as they are appropriately dressed or sheltered from the weather.

Some babies always fall asleep at the breast. Others want to be rocked to sleep. For still others, a special going-to-sleep ritual is useful. It gives parents and baby a certain sense of security and identifies distinctly separate sleeping and waking phases of the day.

> *From Anya's first week, I put her in her cradle after breast-feeding and patted her gently while her musical stuffed turtle "Henry" played her a song. For Anya, that was a signal to "go to sleep now," and she always would fall asleep very quickly. By 11 months of age she was humming the melody.*
>
> *I had also composed a special "bath song" and a "breastfeeding song" for Anya (and later for Kerry as well). I sang a lot to my children, and maybe this is why they enjoy music so much.*

Singing has a relaxing and harmonizing effect—for the one who is singing as well as for the ones being sung to. If you have older children also, singing songs together can make breastfeeding times fun for everyone.

Let your baby take part in your life when he is awake. As he grows older he will observe your activities with interest and will be enchanted when you sing to him or speak with him. If he is fussy or doesn't seem to feel good, you can carry him around with you in a sling while you go about your activities. Babies who are close in proximity to their parents, with frequent contact, are often more easygoing and serene because they don't feel alone. They also develop motor and intellectual skills sooner because they are constantly stimulated by sharing in our activity.

But there are limits here too. If we adults are nervous or tense, we can transfer this feeling to our baby. On days like this, constant closeness to our child can be more of a hindrance than a help. Be sensitive to your own needs and your child's, and you will find the right balance.

Many mothers proudly report how they start cleaning house as soon as the baby is sleeping. Of course some things must be done, but other things may not be so important. Keep your priorities straight! What is essential right now? If you want to maintain a good disposition, give yourself time to rest or take a midday nap—especially if your baby interrupts your sleep at night. This makes life more pleasant for the whole family.

Nights with a Baby

> *When my husband was away recently on long business trip, I suddenly could identify with the situation of a small child at night. It had been so natural for me to snuggle against Jeff every night for all those years that I just took it for granted. If physical contact is important for a grown woman like me, then think what it must mean to a small baby who was cuddled in a tight warm space until birth! It occurred to me that our little baby must feel very lonely in her bed, out of her cozy "cave."*

Babies vary in their sleeping needs and habits. At the beginning almost all of them wake up at night, most of them several times.

After a few weeks, some babies have a relatively long sleep phase at night; others continue to wake at night for quite some time. Mothers are often asked, "Is he sleeping through yet?" This creates real pressure for some. But every baby is different; there is no "one" best way to grow. The better we understand this, so we can adjust to our baby and his rhythms in a relaxed way, the easier things will be. Attitude is important, here. Many women don't mind waking up at night. On the contrary, they enjoy the intimacy of nighttime feedings when there aren't other interruptions. They wrap themselves up and sit cozily in a rocking chair, carrying on a quiet conversation with their baby while he sucks peacefully. Then they lay him back in his cradle next to the bed, and go back to sleep.

Other women are on the verge of exhaustion if they have to get up several times a night to nurse their baby, especially if this stage lasts a long time. Just as babies in the same family can have very different sleep habits, so mothers can be different in their constitution and thus in their reactions to their baby's sleep habits. Bringing the baby into bed works well for some families. For others, it only creates other problems. Find *your* balance, and you will find what's best for your family.

> *When the twins were born, they had to spend several weeks in the incubator. When we brought them home, they cried a lot, which was very distressing. Then my husband thought of enlarging our bed. He built a frame large enough to add a twin-size mattress to our king-size one. This way both children could be close to us and get the body contact they missed at the beginning of their lives. We all got more sleep and my husband and I were able to enjoy our babies.*

Don't choose the co-sleeping option unless the bed is always very clean, smoking is never done in bed, and no violent or aggressive behavior occurs. In addition, never take your baby into bed with you if you or your partner have drunk *any* alcohol.

If your partner's sleep is so disturbed by nighttime nursing that he can't concentrate at work, you can "emigrate" out of the bedroom for nursing. Put a mattress on the floor in another room, where you take your baby to nurse. You can fall asleep while nursing and later, when you wake up, go back to your own bed again. This is also a good solution for those babies who get restless as soon as they are put back in their own beds after breastfeeding. Many children sleep more deeply, more peacefully and longer on a (washable) lambskin (source, see page 264). With a lambskin, you can bring along baby's "very own bed" wherever you go.

With older babies, frequent waking at night can become a habit that isn't satisfying for the baby and gets on his parents' nerves besides. A baby may not understand the words, but he will grasp it if you tell him clearly and firmly (but not aggressively): "I'm here for you. I love you. But right now I need my sleep so I can be there for you tomorrow. Now it is nighttime. Go back to sleep now." He might cry at first, but if he feels your strong, unshakable closeness, if he feels you won't pull back emotionally, he will calm down soon.

Perhaps Dad, who has no breasts that entice the baby to suck, can comfort the baby and take care of him at night for a while, easing him into a new nighttime sleep/wake pattern. An excellent book on this subject is *Nighttime Parenting* by William Sears, M.D. (1990).

We can also support our babies with natural remedies. Bach Flower Therapy, for example, can help deal with the emotional imbalances that can result from difficult nighttime situations. Consult an experienced practitioner to determine which flower essence could be helpful for your situation. Commonly prescribed for the baby in this situation are: Honeysuckle, Hornbeam, Impatience, Mimulus, rescue Remedy, Rock Rose, Star of Bethlehem, Vervain and Walnut. For the mother: Cerato, Elm, Hornbeam, Impatience, Larch, Olive, Pin, Red Chestnut, Vine and Willow. In chapter 7, you will find ideas for using aromatherapy (See Colic, page 120).

One old treatment that is receiving renewed attention is acupressure. You might consider consulting with a bodyworker or massage therapist trained in acupressure about helping you and your family handle this difficult time. For babies who are overexcited and can't rest, acupressure is applied to the hands or the feet. Babies under one year old should receive pressure for only 10 or 20 seconds.

As an alternative, a general, gentle massage with a mildly scented oil can help everyone immensely.

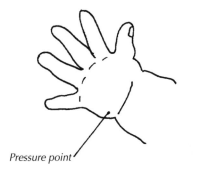

Pressure point

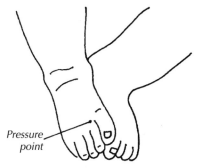

Pressure point

Father, Mother, Child

Fathers need the opportunity to build an independent relation-ship with their babies. These two need to spend private time together. Mothers shouldn't interfere in this relationship. Nor should mothers tell fathers how to handle the baby, unless of course they are doing something that could cause serious harm. Just like mothers, fathers need to be permitted to learn from and grow through their own experiences and mistakes. When parents argue over who is more competent, the argument is often actually an expression of relationship difficulties, and it should be resolved at that level.

Carrying the full responsibility of caring for her baby alone is hard on any woman. But sharing the responsibility is good for everyone. When the baby spends time with her father, her mother gains a little time for herself, restores her strength and "fills up her energy tank" so she can continue to nurture herself and the rest of the family. Father and baby get to develop their own relationship. And baby gets something a little different and special from the attention of each parent.

A Word to Fathers

Many men today prepare for their child's arrival right along with their partners. They want to experience the birth along with her. More and more frequently, men take time off work right after the delivery so they can experience the baby's first weeks as closely and intensively as possible. This is a great opportunity for you to grow together and to take those first steps as a family together.

If you have not been closely involved with the baby's progress during pregnancy, you may feel a little "behind" in bonding with your son or daughter when the baby is born. Unlike your partner, you couldn't feel your baby intimately during the last few months. But early contact immediately after birth will promote bonding in a hurry! You may even experience "love at first sight." (Don't be disappointed if this *doesn't* happen, though, because it may not.)

Extended contact during the early days and weeks after the birth is a way of making up for lost time. Spending time with your little baby now is a true opportunity for you. You may discover aspects of yourself you haven't seen before; perhaps a tender, more gentle side.

Enjoy your new baby in those first days at home. Looking at your baby as you bathe him, holding him in your arms, touching him in a nurturing way (see page 52), talking or singing to him, gazing at him—*really* encountering your child—can be a profound experience. It gives long-term perspective. Right after birth, newborns have an intense radiance—very earnest, very knowledgeable, very complete. Perhaps this is the reason your first hours or days with him will make such a strong and lasting impression.

> *When we learned Sharon needed a Cesarean section,*
> *I asked permission to be there. Ann was placed in my*
> *arms immediately—I bathed her, stroked her and talked*
> *with her all afternoon. I showed Sharon our daughter.*
> *Even now I spend every free moment with Ann.*

Men who dismiss children as "women's business," who regard it as unmanly to shower their newborns with tenderness and who prefer to wait until "you can actually do something with them" will probably be disappointed with the experience. These men miss out on a very important bonding phase. Getting to know their baby helps their baby develop a relationship with *them.* Later it may be harder to develop these deep feelings for each other.

Yes, when your baby is breastfed, feeding him or her is naturally one activity reserved for the mother. However, many expectant fathers say they plan to "hold my baby, massage him, caress him, let him feel my warmth, and talk with him a lot." The bottom line is, there are *many* ways for you to establish a relationship with your baby. Feeding is only one.

Fathers are creative playmates for their children. Often they rediscover their own joy in playing and romp wildly with their kids as they grow—more exuberantly in general than their mothers, to the delight of the children. In this way a father can complement mother's influence ideally. Of course, play expresses intimacy too, and it requires Dad to invest a certain amount of his time. But even when there isn't much time, what is important is *how* this time is spent together—quality over quantity.

You may not experience only positive feelings in those first days. It happens. Here are some of the more common negative thoughts that can pop up, consciously or unconsciously. See if they sound familiar:

- Perhaps you are jealous of your partner because she has such an intimate relationship with your child and can comfort him with her breast right away.

- Perhaps you feel shut out by their relationship.

- Are you sad you see so little of your baby because you have to work all day?

- Are you jealous of your baby because your wife spends so much time with him, leaving so little time for you right now?

- Perhaps you feel neglected because your partner's needs for tenderness and sensuality seem to be fulfilled by your baby right now.

- You may regret your lost independence.

- Do you secretly believe your wife's breasts belong only to you? Have you ever thought to yourself, "He's at the breast *again?*" or, jokingly, "Hey, leave something for me!"

You may feel ashamed for having such "childish" feelings, but you can't erase them, despite your efforts. The more you try to suppress them, the more powerful they can become. Unconscious feelings like these might be compared to threatening ghosts in a dark closet—they lose their power once they are exposed to the light. Only when you are conscious of your thoughts and feelings can you replace them with new messages (for example, "There is enough love for all three of us").

Sometimes problems do run deeper. Perhaps your partner's intense fixation on your baby does exclude you totally. Or perhaps your jealousy isn't relieved by talking things over with each other or with close friends. Then these problems are probably an expression of deeper difficulties in your relationship. They may even have roots reaching back to your childhoods. In such cases, don't hesitate to seek couples therapy, marriage counseling or other help. These services exist to provide this help. Your healthcare practitioner can help you locate the right service for you.

Be honest with your partner and let her know what you are feeling. Talk things over before you start reproaching each other. Maybe you can exchange thoughts and ideas with other parents—perhaps some of the couples you met in childbirth class. How do other men deal with this? How does your situation differ from theirs, and where are there parallels? What solutions have they found? Just hearing that others have experienced the same feelings should help you feel better. You may prefer to speak *only* with men. If no father's group exists in your area, you might organize a group yourself with the backing of The National Fatherhood Initiative (see page 259). You may also find inspiration in books. In his book, *When Men Become Fathers*, Hermann Bullinger writes:

> . . . It is important to bring your unconscious feelings to the surface. This does not only apply to envy, but also to other semi-unconscious or suppressed feelings having to do with breastfeeding. It is especially important to do so because the father—through his behavior—can influence whether and how long a woman breastfeeds.

Because emotional factors significantly influence breastfeeding, your attitude and support are enormously important to your partner (see page 47). If you become knowledgeable on the subject, you can back up your partner when she gets contradictory advice and is made to feel insecure by her environment—ranging from the hospital stay to situations in which someone expresses doubts about whether your baby is getting enough milk. It will be satisfying for you if, through your loving, caring attention, your partner is able to devote herself to your baby and create a stable basis for his healthy growth.

Consider together how you can plan time for each other in which you can love and mutually nurture each other, because your relationship is very important for the baby's sake, too. Enjoy these times to the fullest, "topping the tank" with love and strength you can radiate back to your child. Sometimes it doesn't have to be all that much—a hug, a brief, deeply meant and felt touch, a look deep into each other's eyes . . . to feel reassured that "S/he is aware of me;" "I'm important to him/her."

Brothers and Sisters

> *"May I try?" Anya asked shyly as she watched Kerry drink*
> *at my breast. Very gently she took my nipple into her mouth,*
> *sucked for a moment and exclaimed with enthusiasm,*
> *"Oh, there's sugar in it!" After that she was completely*
> *satisfied. She only wanted to be sure she could drink, too.*
> *Once she knew it was possible, she lost interest.*

Sometimes older siblings who have been fully weaned want to nurse again on a regular basis for a while (see Tandem Nursing, page 184). This is a natural form of regression the child will grow out of as soon as he has conquered his pain over the new rival. Give your older child a lot of additional closeness, cuddling and attention. The more we can respond to the needs of our older children—in a relaxed way and with humor—the faster they will regain their old self-confidence and emotional balance.

Depending on their ages and the sibling constellation, brothers and sisters can react very differently:

> *When Luke was born, Angie was 33 months old. Even during*
> *my pregnancy she showed a lot of interest in my tummy and the*
> *movement there. During the first days at home, Angie observed*
> *my nursing Luke with interest. She stood in front of us and*

watched. A couple of times she asked me to let her suck a little too and discovered her brother really had to exert himself to get something out. After three or four days, while I was nursing, Angie took her doll in her arms. Speaking very softly and gently to her, she pulled up her sweater and held the doll against her body. When I asked what she was doing, she said, "breastfeeding, naturally!"

When David was born, Angie was 4-1/2 and Luke was 19 months old. Angie accepted the baby matter-of-factly, but Luke didn't know what to make of him. He was still too small. But he learned soon enough I couldn't run after him when I was nursing. He used this knowledge to get into all kinds of mischief. He climbed up things and within minutes turned the room into a shambles.

Of course, boys can be just as interested in learning nurturing behaviors and can learn about their anatomy at this time. And girls can react negatively to a baby by pitching fits or exhibiting other acting-out behaviors. Every child is different and will need your love and support when a new baby comes along.

When your first child is born, your quiet times are over! With each successive child, the house is filled with more and more life. Children have to be able to express themselves, to unfold their spirits. Once we accept that fact, their "noise" or energy bursts probably won't disturb us anymore. Still, we have to think of how we our-selves can find a little  peace every day. Toward the end of her second pregnancy and in the first weeks after the birth, my sister-in-law lay down for a short nap in the middle of the day and gave my then-4-year-old nephew Andy an alarm clock. He was to play quietly until it rang. It worked wonderfully. Sometimes we underestimate how understanding kids can be!

Time for Yourself

You will only be able to give your children your full attention *if* you replenish your strength on a daily basis. Partly because of our socialization, we women are more capable than most men of adapting to other people's needs, even above our own needs.

> *I know the feeling of always having to be there, of doing right by everyone, of wanting to be a good mother who gives the older child just as much time as before, even though the work has more than doubled with the new baby. I'm familiar with the strong anxiety that comes from absurd guilt feelings because the older child has to share my time and love with my baby now. It's absurd, because one reason for wanting to have this baby was so the older child won't have to grow up as an only child. At the end of the day, I can't do justice to anyone because I become more and more grouchy, nervous and don't have a minute to myself anymore, with all these responsibilities.*

A self-sacrificing mother torments herself and everyone else in her environment. It is easier on everyone if you decide now what you can and cannot reasonably accomplish for others and yourself. Don't try to be all things to all people. Don't worry; the world will continue without you for a few hours! Your children will still thrive, even if you leave them with your sister for an hour while you have a long soak in the tub. Learn to take time for yourself rather than carry around the kind of unspoken resentment that could be erupt randomly at others, including your children.

Pregnancy and breastfeeding are transitional times. Use them to learn to become more centered, to enjoy your own body and to make peace with your own womanliness. You will give your children a great gift, because they will feel your joy in life.

Sometimes finding and maintaining that calm center involves a long, difficult learning process. It helps if you have someone who loves you and can spoil you somewhat. But it is just as important to be good to yourself: Take long walks, have a scented bath by candlelight, buy yourself a bouquet of flowers, listen to beautiful music, enjoy a cup of hot herbal tea. The hardest part is often to feel *entitled* to this experience. Your family will certainly support you, because they will see you come back from these times refreshed and rejuvenated—and ready to give to others again.

> *For some time, I have started my day by getting up before*
> *everyone else and taking a walk in the woods behind our house.*
> *At the end I sit peacefully for a few minutes on a patch of soft*
> *moss, feel my body and connect with this calm center in me.*
> *I think about the day ahead and take in the stillness of the*
> *woods. Then I go home. My son, who always got me out of*
> *bed early and kept me busy the rest of the day, has now*
> *accepted the fact I need this time for myself. I can truly say*
> *I am much more relaxed, more peaceful and happier now.*

15

Your Baby Grows!
The First Year

D uring his first weeks, a baby is at his mother's breast constantly; he seems to do nothing but drink in food and love. Gradually he shows more interest in his surroundings and the people he meets. This is the time of true reward for you—when your baby smiles at you, and his tiny hands gently pat your breasts while nursing. When you give, you now get a lot of attention from your baby in return, if you are open to his expressions of love: a gentle caress here, a little finger in your mouth there so you get something too, an enthusiastic cry of delight at the sight of the breast. It's a pleasure to see how your baby sucks with every fiber of his being, and how his toes, feet and hands move to the rhythm of his sucking. Perhaps with your baby's example you can rediscover how to be totally absorbed in the present moment.

As your child becomes more and more expert at breastfeeding, nursing times become shorter and shorter. He wants to be done quickly because more interesting things call him. Sometimes it doesn't go fast enough. His curiosity is so great that he turns to see what's happening when he hears a noise behind him. He may forget to let go of the nipple, and many a woman has been amazed at how stretchable it is—ouch!

The pause between breastfeeds gets longer and enables you to attend to other things again. If you have met your baby's needs with absolute reliability in the past, he slowly begins to learn to handle small frustrations—brief waits—because he knows Mom will certainly come through. He sleeps longer at night. Perhaps he even sleeps all night for the first time—and so do you. At this point, your ability to function in daily life increases again.

> *About six o'clock one morning I woke up, looked at the clock with astonishment, and then noticed the sheets were wet with milk that had leaked. My baby! Was everything all right? My heart was in my throat. I tiptoed into Anya's room. What a relief—she was breathing!*

But some babies continue to wake up just as often as they did before. And some, who had slept through the night earlier, start waking up at night again at around nine months old. For about three months, until they are a year old, these babies may be wakened several times a night by dreams and separation anxiety. They now recognize themselves as independent beings, separate from their mothers, and begin to develop a fear of strangers.

Soon your baby will not feel content any longer lying in a horizontal position in your arms. He wants to see what is happening around him. At about six months, he maneuvers himself into an upright position whenever you hold him in your arms. He will have doubled his birthweight. The peak of breastfeeding has been reached, and this often coincides with the appearance of the first tooth. From the perspective of Mom's or Dad's lap or a high chair, he'll take part in family meals and observe the action at the table.

But he won't stay in the observer's position very long—soon he'll let you know with hands and feet that he wants his share, too. He wants to snatch away your food before it gets into your mouth . . . and the glass next to your plate becomes very attractive too! Suddenly your child seems to demand the breast more often and if, after a few days of more frequent feeding, he still apparently can't satisfy his hunger (and illness or teething doesn't account for it), you'll know it's time to provide him with something in addition to mother's milk.

Introducing Solid Foods

For a time it was fashionable to give babies solid food at three months—at one point even much earlier. This is long before the digestive tract of a small baby is sufficiently mature or the mouth reflexes are sufficiently developed to handle solid food.

Mother's milk contains everything a fully breastfed baby needs for at least the first six months of life. A baby at high risk of developing allergies should be fully breastfed until the ninth or tenth month, if possible, if her doctor confirms she is thriving. Your baby will let you know when the time is right to introduce solid food. Some babies are interested in solids at five months. Others might reach this point at seven or eight months. Often an interest in solid food begins with the appearance of the first tooth. The American Academy of Pediatrics recommends breastfeeding exclusively for the baby's first six months and then supplementing breast milk with solid food until 12 months, at least.

> *On the advice of doctors and brochures, we tried to get Charlotte acquainted with something other than mother's milk at six months. She rejected it categorically. Three months later she came up with the idea herself, wanting what Mommy was eating. In no time she ate whatever the family had to eat. At about 21 months she weaned herself—one morning it just tasted "yucky."*

If you have the impression your baby is no longer getting enough to eat with breast milk alone, offer her a spoonful of mashed food— maybe banana or carrots you have cut fine and steamed briefly in water. Observe her reaction. If she doesn't resist and seems to like it, you can keep going.

Choose a peaceful time in the earlier half of the day, when your baby is well rested, to begin solid-food feeding. Pleasant, soothing background music (see page 275) can enhance a serene atmosphere. Breastfeed your baby a little first so he isn't too hungry and impatient. Put him on your lap, leaning back a bit, and let a spoonful of mashed food (maybe mixed with water or breast milk) fall lightly into his mouth. If it comes out, just ease it back in.

The American Academy of Pediatrics recommends breastfeeding exclusively for the baby's first six months and then supplementing breast milk with solid food until 12 months, at least.

Begin with small amounts—a teaspoon is enough. Pay attention to your baby's very own rhythm, and don't pressure him. Give him more if he wants it. At the beginning, you both will be a little awkward, but soon you'll become more skilled. When he is done with the solids, finish breastfeeding him. But if your baby resists solid foods vigorously, don't make a battle of it. Try again in a week or two.

First Solid Meals

It is our responsibility as parents to introduce our children to a healthful, balanced way of eating. We now know many of today's most common diseases are so-called *civilization diseases*, caused to a large extent by foods unhealthy for our bodies in the long run, such as refined sugar and flour. Eating habits are formed from infancy. A whole-foods diet helps create a body that can better withstand the environmental burden it faces in today's world. If we choose

As time goes on, breastfeeding will become less important for satisfying your baby's hunger and more important for satisfying his need for closeness and body contact.

organically grown foods—that is, foods grown without pesticides, herbicides or fertilizers, which may have long-term health effects— we even contribute to a healthier environment by supporting organic, environment-friendly farming.

At a time when allergies are increasingly common, it is recommended to begin with small amounts of a single food and to feed this to the baby for an entire week, accompanied by breastfeeding, of course. If your child shows an allergic reaction (for example, intestinal-tract disturbances, a skin rash or sore bottom), you won't need to puzzle over the cause. Simply eliminate the food from her diet and try it again when she is more than a year old. (This procedure also makes sense for the development of her taste buds.) If she tolerates one food, try another, and so on. Weeks or months later, you will find your baby can eat the same range of foods as the rest of the family. In the first year of your baby's life, you may only want to offer plant-based foods to your baby. That's OK.

At first, small portions of solid food complement the breastfeed. Gradually they'll replace one breastfeed and then another. As time goes on, breastfeeding will become less important for satisfying your baby's hunger and more important for satisfying his need for closeness and body contact. At this point, begin to breastfeed only *after* meals. Once the baby takes more than 7 ounces (200 grams) of solid food at a given meal, it will not be necessary to breastfeed in addition. However, you might want to, anyway: The American Academy of Pediatrics recommends trying to continue breast-feeding after a year, even as a supplement, because breast milk contains important preventive properties against disease.

Many mothers choose banana as a first food because most babies like it. It is easily digestible and is frequently given to young children with diarrhea. (Don't use the last inch at the bottom, opposite the stem, because it may contain the insecticide sprayed on the plant.) Carrot is also a good first vegetable. Raw carrot, finely grated or puréed in a mixer with some fluid, makes thin mother's-milk stool somewhat firmer. Lightly stewed cauliflower, aspara-gus, zucchini, broccoli, sugar peas and cer-tain beans can gradually be combined with

> Carrot is a good first vegetable. Raw carrot, finely grated or puréed in a blender with some fluid, makes thin mother's-milk stool somewhat firmer.

peeled potatoes or natural rice and some seed oil or, toward the end of the baby's first year, butter or cream. (Seed oil is added because it helps baby digest fat-soluble vitamins better, and it pro-vides essential fatty acids.) Throw everything in a blender or a food processor or just mince it and serve. Avoid eggplant because it contains too much natural nicotine. Cauliflower and broccoli are potentially gas-producing, so watch for that effect. Finely grated

apple, beet or kohlrabi with a teaspoon of cold-pressed oil can be served as a salad, combined with the foods already mentioned.

Vegetables and fruits for small children should be fresh and organically grown, if possible, because conventionally farmed veg-etables often contain too many nitrates. A small child's body cannot fully metabolize this chemical and changes it into nitrite,

Baby's First Foods

Size is important when you start your baby on solid foods. If she is at the "before-teeth" stage, she has to grind food with her gums. Her food at this stage must be able to dissolve. Chomping is difficult. Shredded fruits and vegetables are more difficult to eat at this stage than puréed foods.

If your baby has reached the "after-teeth" stage, watch her carefully. You *must* make sure that any pieces of food that break off in her mouth are small enough not to cause a choking hazard. Your child's healthcare provider will be happy to help you choose the starter foods and preparation methods that will be just right for your baby.

which is toxic. If you can't prepare fresh foods, use frozen foods. These choices are preferable to canned foods, which are low in vitamins and nutrients and high in salt and sugars. Don't reheat foods for children under any circumstances.

In the beginning you can scrape up a little apple pulp to acquaint your baby with its taste. Later you will put a slice of apple or pear, a piece of banana or a bite of ripe peach or melon in his hand, or let him pick them up on his own. Raspberries and blueberries can be appropriate, but your baby's age is a factor in this because you must watch out for choking hazards. Be cautious with apricots, grapes or plums because they have a laxative effect. After offering strawberries, you may want to observe your baby for a while because these sometimes cause allergies.

Cereals and Grains

Whole grains are especially rich in B-vitamins and should be part of your child's basic daily diet. You can make your own natural porridge cereals, preferably from organically grown grains, ground freshly in a mill—a worthwhile investment (see page 265).

Tip: To make grains more digestible and their nutrients more available, oven-dry them. Wash them briefly. Then let the slightly damp grains dry for an hour in an oven set to 140F-175F (60C to 80C). Grind dried grains finely in a food mill. (When your child is older, you can grind the grains more coarsely).

Introduce one type of grain at a time. Start with gluten-free grains such as rice, millet, corn and buckwheat. Try wheat, oats and barley only after the baby's first year.

Oats have the highest iron content. Millet, oats and rice are easiest to digest; wheat and barley are more difficult. Wheat

How to Make Natural Cereals

You may not always have time to make your own cereals, but I find it is worth the effort. If your partner likes to cook, he might become the expert at this!

1/4 cup (1 ounce) ground grain
3/4 cup (6 ounces) cold water
1 tablespoon milk or cream, optional
Unsulphured raisins, presoaked and chopped, puréed fruit or berries, optional

Soak ground grain overnight in cold water. Bring grain to a slow boil and remove from heat. Let stand briefly, until grains absorb liquid and swell somewhat. If you like, add milk or cream, raisins, puréed fruit or berries.

Note: At first the cereal must be cooked. By the end of baby's first year, however, you can prepare fresh, natural uncooked cereal from ground, oven-dried grain.

Variation 1. When your baby is 1 year old, you can add dates, yogurt and perhaps nuts—initially ground nuts, later chopped. (Watch out for possible allergic reactions!) Add 1/2 teaspoon honey, preferably organic, from time to time if you like.

Variation 2. Try a savory version of whole-grain cereal. Add chopped, fresh herbs, a few flakes of brewer's yeast, a little butter or sour cream, and mix with vegetables.

and oats are most likely to cause allergic reactions. Toward the end of the first year, you may also experiment using different grain flakes for fresh, whole-grain muesli. It is worth the effort to create your own cereals and get your older baby used to whole foods (see box, above). You may find he comes to prefer whole-grain cereals, instead of the commercial cereals so tempting to many older children, which commonly contain lots of sugar and practically zero nutritional value. When the baby is more than 2 years old, it's OK to add legumes as an excellent source of iron and protein.

Sugar

We adults often imagine we do our babies a favor when we sweeten their food. The fact is, it's no favor! Directly or indirectly, sugar causes many of our *diseases of civilization* (including heart disease, stroke, high blood pressure, obesity, diabetes and dental caries). It spoils the appetite and squeezes out other nutritious foods from the diet. The habit of using little or a lot of sugar later in life starts

Chewing

The time when the first teeth appear is important for practicing chewing, biting and gnawing. Give your baby frequent opportunities for this.

• Chewing on whole-grain zwieback feels good to painful gums. You can make your own crackers by drying bread slowly in the oven.

• Natural cheese (salt-free or low-salt), cut in cubes, is easy for the baby to eat by himself.

• At about nine months, you can introduce yogurt and cottage cheese.

• The yolk of a hard-boiled egg, perhaps thinned with some liquid, is very popular with many children and is also a good source of iron. The egg white, on the other hand, shouldn't be given until the end of the first year, because it frequently causes allergic reactions.

in early childhood. Help your child by restricting the use of sugar at your house, and by teaching other ways to make food more enjoyable to eat, such as by grilling vegetables to bring out their natural sweetness.

What about Meat?

If a diet consists of unheated, fresh produce, 1 or 2 ounces of protein a day is enough. Protein can be obtained from sources besides meat if you choose foods wisely. If you want to add meat, perhaps because it is part of your family's regular diet, add it in your baby's second year, no more often than two or three times a week. Fibrous meats (beef and lamb) can be puréed in a food processor or a special baby-food grinder.

Organ meat is nutritious and easily digested, but like veal and pork, tends to contain a high level of contaminants and for that reason should be avoided if possible. Fish is high in protein, and the filet is especially popular (look carefully for bones). Chicken is acceptable, but remove bones and skin.

Let Your Child Be Your Guide

Your child will guide you in what he needs as you explore new foods together. Children nourish themselves over time in an astonishingly balanced way, as long as their appetites are not misdirected by pressure from the adults around them, and as long as

Commercial Baby Foods

Commercial baby foods have become well established in recent decades. They used to contain mixed foods with fillers, salt and sugar added. Luckily, public attention to healthful eating has changed many baby-food products. Today, almost all are prepared without sugar, salt or starch. Some companies do make organic baby food. Look for them in your supermarket or healthfood store. Jarred baby food is convenient, but also expensive.

Check labels for content and food-to-water volume.

they are offered a wide variety of healthful, nutritious foods. Sweets or junk foods that spoil the appetite will ruin a child's natural ability to nourish himself properly.

Feeding Strategies

You can also prepare some ready-to-serve meals in larger quantities ahead of time and freeze them, portioned in yogurt cups or ice-cube trays. Just cook larger amounts of fresh produce without sugar or salt (it's better to season with herbs). Grind or blend the produce, and then freeze until needed. These meals can be unthawed and heated just before feedings. Always check any microwaved food for pockets of scalding heat.

Sometimes you encounter problems even if feeding was uncomplicated at first:

> Curtis had eaten well from the spoon at first, but suddenly he went on strike. I was worried until I decided to try something different. I put some finger food in a bowl in front of him. He grabbed it happily with his little hands and from then on ate large portions at every meal.

It takes a while before your baby can successfully feed himself with a spoon (he'll make the first independent attempts at around 15 months), but even near the end of the first year many children want to try. Give your baby the opportunity to do so and tell yourself, "Messy is beautiful!" Find a practical solution so not everything is completely covered with food in the process. It helps to cover

Your baby may show interest in eating with a spoon at around 15 months. Give your child the opportunity to try . . . and tell yourself, "Messy is beautiful!"

the floor around your baby's high chair with old newspapers or a washable drop cloth.

Drinking from a Cup

Babies get interested in drinking from a cup at around six months. Start by filling a small cup (with or without a feeding spout) or a small egg cup with clear water. Let your baby play with it for a while. Help her bring the cup to her mouth, and then let your child try it herself. When she has become somewhat adept at drinking, you can offer water mixed with other drinks, such as unsweetened apple juice.

Stay away from sweetened drinks because they can damage teeth. Avoid carbonated drinks. Go easy on fruit juices too because many contain sorbitol, which can lead to gastrointestinal problems if consumed in large amounts.

It is better not to offer cow's milk until the end of the first year. If the baby rejects cow's milk or can't tolerate it, trust his self-regulating mechanism! See if he likes soured-milk products such as yogurt, which often is tolerated better.

First Teeth

It used to be thought a mother should breastfeed until her baby gets her first tooth. But the first tooth is no reason to stop breastfeeding. Rather, take it as a sign your baby is ready for solid foods *in addition to* mother's milk. When the baby occasionally bites down on the breast, it may be to relieve her gums, which can ache so much before a tooth breaks through. When a baby bites, gently remove her from the breast (see page 76) and firmly but kindly say, "Do not bite me!" Then let her continue nursing. Generally this stops it. If a baby bites more than once, you might consider whether she wants to express something she can't in some other way.

> At six months, April got her second tooth and bit me without warning while she was nursing. I screamed, which scared us both. I wanted to put her back to breast, but she started crying. Somehow I managed to get her to nurse again, but I was afraid she might bite again. Out of confusion, I bought breast shields to protect my nipples. I followed the advice of the breastfeeding

group, too. People there suggested I give April a crust of zwieback or something similar so she could soothe her gums on that instead on my breast. When I went to put April to my breast that night, she latched on, tasted the silicon shield, looked at me furiously and started to cry. No question—she didn't want this thing! I wasn't sure how to react but finally got my courage together and said, "All right! I'll take it off, but don't bite me again, or I'll put it right back on." That worked.

During teething, sucking apparently can become so painful sometimes that babies go on strike and don't want to feed from the breast any more. They keep trying to latch on because they are hungry, but then give up, crying because it hurts. You might not understand what the problem is because you can't see the first tooth yet.

Allowing your baby to chew on a cooled teething ring or a sugar-free teething biscuit can relieve teething pain. You might massage the gums at the site where the tooth is coming in. You can also use natural remedies, such as natural teething tablets from your pharmacy. Bach Flower Therapy may also help with this potentially stressful time (the essence Walnut is used frequently for teething). If you use homeopathic remedies, Chaommilla, silicea, Calcium carbonicum, Calcium phosporicum are often used, depending on the condition and presenting symptoms of your teething child. (See page 162 for more information about homeopathy.)

Teething babies often wake more frequently at night but nurse best half-asleep. The most important, and sometimes the most difficult, thing to do is recognize what is causing the problem. Know it will resolve itself when the tooth finally breaks through.

The Toddler at the Breast

Your milk production decreases in proportion to the amount of solid food your older baby is taking. It is no longer as easy to set off the milk-ejection reflex, and your baby has to exert himself to get the milk flowing. It's quicker and easier to drink out of a cup. Quite a few children lose interest in the breast around the end of the first year. They favor drinking out of a cup now. Other babies are just beginning to discover the breast at this point and treasure the warmth and closeness it provides.

Getting Comfort from the Breast

With a 1-year-old baby, breastfeeding for hunger and thirst is a secondary need. A toddler seeks the breast primarily when

- He is afraid.
- She has hurt herself.
- He is so overstimulated by so many new impressions he can't calm down.
- She has overextended herself.
- He is sick.
- She needs attention.

Each baby has his own developmental pattern: The occasional baby takes his first step at seven months, while a few others don't walk until they are 18 months old. Some have their first tooth at four months, while others are still waiting at one year. It is the same with breastfeeding. Some children give up the breast toward the end of the first year, while others need years to satisfy their need to suck.

It would be ideal to respect the individual needs of a child and not force decisions. Given the chance to develop at his own pace and fulfill his desire for love and closeness, he won't become dependent on his mother, as so many fear. On the contrary, he will be more likely to develop into a healthy, independent and open human being. A need that is fulfilled disappears on its own.

A baby at one year of age is already his own little person and lets you know in no uncertain terms what he wants. He begins to verbalize his wish for milk ("mama," "nanny," "num-num"). If you hold your child in your arms and he wants to nurse, he wriggles until he is at breast level, pulls at your clothing, and as soon as you are undressed he "storms" the breast. While he sucks at one side, he holds the other breast in his hand, as if he were afraid he might lose it in the meantime. Before he drinks, he pats both sides to see where there is more milk, and when he has emptied one side, he throws himself determinedly on the other. Gradually he also learns to wait when you say, "No, not now. Later."

At this time, when your baby increasingly comes into contact with foreign bacteria as he crawls, walks, falls down and puts everything he finds into his mouth, don't undervalue the advantages of breastfeeding as a form of protection against infection.

The toddler at the breast

The open joy and sensuousness with which the baby sucks can cause a variety of reactions in other people. Even though on average children world-wide breastfeed for more than two years, the sight of a toddler at the breast in our culture is still uncommon and embarrasses many people. Today in the United States, according to WIC, 63% of all newborns are being nursed, and over 26% are still breastfed at five to six months of age. The higher their education and age, the more likely women are to breastfeed. In 1979, only 25% of women were breastfeeding when their baby was one week old; in 1992, it was 54%, so the interest in breastfeeding is clearly on the rise. This may be, in part, due to our increasing awareness of its incredible benefits.

The interest in breastfeeding is clearly on the rise.

When people around you get upset ("You're spoiling him!") or disapprove of the intimate, joyful relationship you share with your child, don't let it bother you too much. Nature has arranged it so that breastfeeding brings mother and child pleasure. No need to be ashamed—be happy about it!

16

Life Goes On

When you breastfeed, not only does your baby need you, but you need him as well. That is nature's way of ensuring your baby gets enough of your closeness, skin contact and attention, which encourages the development of basic trust. You may not really want to leave home at first. Many women say they feel no need to leave the "nest" in the first weeks, or if they must leave, they like to go out only briefly. This desire dovetails nicely with a baby's need to get used to his new "little" world slowly before venturing out into the "big" world.

Getting Around with Baby

The urge to be at home doesn't mean we *always* have to stay home when we have children. After a while you can get out with the baby.

> Our children always seemed to enjoy our adventures: hiking
> in the mountains slung close to Mommy's heart or carried on
> Daddy's back, walks in the woods and fields, swimming,
> picnics, camping trips with their own little beds and lambskin
> along, surprise visits with friends—our breastfed babies always
> took part, with no great problem.

Being out and about with my babies was uncomplicated for me, whether we were on a trip or I was just leaving the house for a few hours. Even when we were in a strange environment, one thing remained constant for our babies—the breast. That was enough to make my babies feel comfortable everywhere. No, come to think of it, something else was important when we were traveling: a familiar place to sleep! If your baby is used to sleeping on a lambskin, then this is often enough to create a feeling of cozy comfort and security. Practical, collapsible beds are also available, which your baby can get used to at home to make his stay in a strange place easier—unless of course your baby sleeps in your bed and can feel the reassuring warmth of your body. Then he doesn't mind where he sleeps.

However, make sure your baby's natural rhythm is not too disturbed by the activity. It is a good idea to plan your activities, especially on a long trip, so your baby's needs are still met consistently. Ask yourself these questions:

- What is appropriate for his temperament?
- What is good for him?
- What does he seem to enjoy?
- What wears him out or gets him too excited?
- What seems to disturb his rhythm too much?
- What might hurt him (for example, passive smoking at the house of a friend who smokes)?

Some babies by their very nature react more strongly to the noises and influences of their environment than others. Be sensitive about this. See that you don't overload your baby or flood him with too much stimulation.

It doesn't take much preparation to take a breastfed baby out. I always kept a few diapers and a washcloth in a diaper bag in the car, along with two changes of clothing (because the diapers always seemed to leak when we were on a trip). With these supplies along, it didn't matter whether we were in a traffic jam or got into a snowstorm or whether something else prevented us from moving right along—we didn't need to worry about the baby. (As your little one gets older, you will need to add "favorite toys" to this list.)

Breastfeeding Away from Home

It should be the most natural thing for a mother to put her baby discreetly to her breast in public. Sadly, this is not always the case. Some states still have not passed any kind of law to protect a nursing-mother's right to breastfeed wherever she needs to, without worrying about harassment. On the other hand, a number of states and provinces *have* initiated a "breastfeeding commandment" that addresses the needs of and respect for breastfeeding mothers in every environment, and all women's right to breastfeed *anywhere*.

Laws aren't really the problem for most women; it's the looks and reactions they get from some others in their own community. You have the choice to rise above it all, and do what you know is right and natural—openly and self-confidently—or to breastfeed so discreetly no one realizes it. You can choose from several options. When you put your baby to breast, turn slightly to one side; you can join the on-going activities without anyone noticing you are nursing. If you are wearing a blouse or loose sweater, these can cover the upper part of your breast; the rest is shielded by the baby. (Of course I've had the classic experience in which the baby smacks his lips so loudly that everyone in the room "participated" in the baby's feeding with a smile, anyway!) You can purchase breastfeeding tops or dresses with discreet flaps. The baby puts his face between the flaps to reach the nipple, which is shielded behind another piece of fabric. Another option is to purchase a nursing shawl that ties around your neck, shielding you and the baby from view. Of course, the shawl only works if your baby isn't interested in peeking at the outside world!

Going Out without Baby

> *A couple of months after Anya was born, I took an evening weaving course and was away for two hours at a time. I nursed Anya just before I left and put her to bed. She already had a predictable rhythm, but just in case she got hungry while I was away, I left some pumped breast milk behind. I also did that when my husband and I were invited to a party and we left Anya with a baby-sitter.*

As we've seen, long separations early in the baby's life are not ideal. Babies have no sense of time, and for them a day is an eternity. You can't convey you will really come back. But if a separation has to happen, you don't have to wean prematurely. You can pump your milk in advance, and your baby can be fed with your own milk until you come back. It's generally a good idea to keep a reserve of pumped or hand-expressed mother's milk in the freezer (see page 141).

Back to Work

Many mothers face the question of whether to go back to work after their baby has been born or whether to devote themselves entirely to their baby, at least in the beginning. On one hand, we are learning more and more about the importance of a stable primary caregiver for the development of the baby's personality and ability to love. On the other hand, women are increasingly better educated and choose professions they enjoy and in which they are successful. Also, a certain standard of living is often hard to maintain on one salary. And some women simply have no choice, as in the case of single parenting. These women need to provide for themselves and their baby. Every mother has to grapple for her own answers, at best with the support of her partner. This choice is indeed a personal one.

Unlike most industrialized countries—and many in the developing world—the United States has no universal job protection for new mothers. The United States does, however, have a federal law that allows new mothers four months of unpaid personal leave and provides a job guarantee, provided she works in a firm or agency with 50 employees or more. The federal government itself provides paid maternity leave for women in active-duty military service and enables other federal employees to "save" their annual vacations and sick leave for this purpose. Private sector firms and institutions have different regulations. Professional women are more likely to be able to negotiate leave—paid or unpaid—than women who earn less.

In Canada, you may take maternity or parental leave around the time of your baby's birth. You must have worked for pay for at least 700 hours in the prior 52 weeks. Most people receive 55% of their regular income. Maternity benefits can be taken for up to 15 weeks. They may be taken before and after the child's birth. However, you can't use the benefits later than 17 weeks after a baby is born, unless the baby is confined to a hospital. Either parent may take advantage of parental benefits for up to 10 weeks.

These benefits may be claimed by one parent or split between the two. To apply, contact your nearest Human Resource Center of Canada (HRCC).

Many women decide without hesitation to set aside their careers for a few years. Others find it difficult to commit themselves to such a major decision. Granted, it is best for the baby if his mother is able to stay with him at first. But a contented mother with a part-time job may actually be better for her child than a discontented full-time mother. Whatever you choose or whatever arrangement your personal situation calls for, know that breastfeeding and working are often compatible.

> *Because I didn't have much time for my baby during the day*
> *and missed him (I was away 9 hours), I let her spend the nights*
> *close to me in my bed. My milk production continued to be*
> *stimulated enough this way, despite my absence during the day.*
> *I nursed for nine months.*

The International Labor Organization has recommended breaks for nursing mothers since 1919; but the United States has not signed this convention. In Canada, this protection is decided on a province-by-province basis. In some settings, breastfeeding conditions while at work are poor. Piece work in a factory, a great distance between the workplace and the baby, poor or nonexistent childcare at work frequently mean a mother can't take these breaks even if she has been granted a verbal agreement to this effect. Still, some mothers do work out a solution.

In many job settings, a nursing mother can take a couple of breaks a day to pump her milk. Sometimes more flexible work times can be arranged; for example, allowing women to take longer breaks in the day to breastfeed their babies if they are near home or a day-care center. One physician I know breastfed her five children for six months each despite a full-time job. She went back to work after two months, and then breastfed twice before and twice after work, so only one bottle was necessary during the day. For mothers who go back to work after four to six months, daytime breast-milk meals can be gradually replaced by meals of solids, with nursing reserved for the morning and evening. La Leche League has other suggestions (*Practical Hints for Working and Breastfeeding*, publication number 83).

Women who know their baby is in good hands while they are at work usually don't find breastfeeding a hectic, additional burden to their outside employment. After a day's separation, most of them are happy to reconnect with their baby in this quiet, peaceful way.

> *I have fond memories of those first breastfeeds after I returned home from work. First of all, I was relieved to give up the milk at last, and breastfeeding was a good opportunity to wind down after a hectic afternoon.*

The first three years are formative for a small child. Many mothers and fathers find ways to arrange their lives, despite jobs, to alternately or jointly provide high-quality time with their little child.

Two other options are available to both you and your partner: working from home or time-sharing. Millions of people now either work for a company from their home or own their own home-based business. One of the often-reported reasons for setting up this sort of schedule is "being available for the children." Benefits of working from home include being in the comfort of your home, having a flexible work schedule and enjoying more time to play with and nurture your children. Difficulties of this arrangement tend to include too many distractions, not enough time in the day to do everything; lack of freedom from the "job" environment, and sometimes having to put off the children because of an important phone call or e-mail. These things aside, it is possible to develop a work-from-home schedule that meets everyone's needs.

Imagine you have just decided to return to work. You are comfortable with leaving your little one, but not ready (or willing) to work the long hours you put in previously. Unfortunately, only full-time positions are available at your job level. You are certain your only option is to quit. Not true! Many women have set up time-sharing with their employer and found peace of mind and happiness with that decision.

Time-sharing is a big-business concept that has allowed many women to "go part-time" in a full-time job with another employee— often another mother. Essentially you share the time you used to work with another employee who also would like to decrease his or her work schedule. Why does this work? If both of you decided to quit, the employer would lose two people; in this case the company only loses one. By sharing, the company keeps two experienced people employed, and continues to enjoy good productivity in return.

Like anything else, the answer to "Should I work?" can only be answered by *you*. Every detail has to be weighed, and every internal, thought freely expressed.

Making Love during the Breastfeeding Period

When your baby arrives, your sex life changes. Interrupted sleep, the baby's constant presence, the care you take not to wake him up will all require adjustments from you and your partner. So does an episiotomy that needs to heal and which may hurt at first when you make love, or a breast that spurts milk in an arc when you have an orgasm—it all takes some getting used to!

If your sexual life was balanced and uncomplicated until now, you probably won't experience many problems during nursing. The nursing breast can become an experience in its own right if you maintain your sense of humor and some curiosity about your own body and that of your partner. Why shouldn't your husband stroke, caress or even suck your breasts? Even when the milk squirts when you make love, it can be exciting for both of you. But that is not always the case. Sexuality is a delicate barometer for very subtle problems in relationships, and these may express themselves strongly in situations like this. If you did not enjoy the way your husband made love to you in the past, you might be tempted to use the painful episiotomy or your exhaustion from caring for the baby as an excuse to avoid sex. A husband may unconsciously feel his rejection of his wife's body intensifies when "there's milk dripping out of her breasts."

Your own life histories and your history as a couple come into play during sex. Ask yourselves, "What sort of relationship do we have with our bodies and its many secretions?"

> *It occurred to me I felt really turned off by the "disgusting mess" of pumping off my milk (a little milk escaped through the valve). In retrospect, I realize my problems with breastfeeding were caused mostly by my puritanical upbringing and negative attitudes toward my own bodily secretions—milk among them.*

One problem breastfeeding may cause in lovemaking is a dry vagina, because of hormonal changes you're undergoing that reduce vaginal secretions. A personal lubricant may be necessary.

Maybe you have turned your bed into a "family bed." In that case you may have to "move out" to make love when your baby or children are older.

Being a Woman—Being a Mother

The way we behave as parents has a lot to do with our own parents. Were they generous and loving or strict, domineering and prudish? At a more or less conscious level, a man relates to his partner who has become a mother much as he did to his own mother. Unsolved problems in his relationship with his mother might arise as conflicts in his relationship to his wife. Through motherhood, a woman is also confronted by her relationship to *her* own mother.

In our unconscious, our mother can be a very powerful and controlling figure—much stronger than our actual mother. As you and your partner become parents, it is helpful to talk with each other a lot, to go over past experiences and look together at pictures of your own childhoods. Think about what your own mother has meant for you.

- What does (did) she give you, and what does (did) she withhold from you?
- How much do (did) you love her, and why?
- What kind of love do (did) you experience?
- How are (may) you (have been) hurt by it? What makes (made) you happy?

As a society, we tend to glorify mothers and motherhood. The glorification of the mother figure carries dangers with it. If her environment influences a woman too strongly to be a mother exclusively, she may not be able to unfold as a whole person. If she herself also sees this as her only role in life, her beneficial motherly energy may transform itself into a dark and controlling energy. This makes developing an equal relationship with her husband or partner much harder. Under these circumstances, it may be hard for him to find his place in the family: Either he submits and lets himself be mothered along with his child, or he withdraws and lives his primary interests outside the home.

Bringing our womanliness and our motherliness into harmony with each other is a path, a development, that each woman has to manage for herself. We still don't have many good role models for that in our society. Ideally, motherliness is an integral part of our femininity, a matter-of-fact way of being a woman. Pregnancy and breastfeeding are a great opportunity for a woman to develop this motherly side of her personality in a most natural way.

Women who are open to having a child seem to blossom visibly. They enjoy the feeling of being so round and fertile, and they enjoy breastfeeding. Those who care for and advise mothers during this time should do everything they can to strengthen these mothers' delight and their trust in nature. May this book contribute to that!

Appendix 1

Breastfeeding Support Groups, Consultants, Organizations

Breastfeeding Support Groups

La Leche League International
1400 N. Meacham Rd.
Schaumberg, IL 60168-4079
Tel: (800) LA-LECHE
or (847) 519-7730
Fax: (847) 519-0035
Breastfeeding Helpline:
  (900) 448-7475
Website: http://www.lalecheleague.org

Nursing Mothers Counsel (NMC)
P.O. Box 50063
Palo Alto, CA 94303
Tel: (408) 272-1448
Website:
  http://wwww.nursingmothers.org
e-mail: nmc@best.com

INFACT (Infant Feeding Action Coalition Canada)
10 Trinity Square
Toronto, Ont. M5G 1B1
Tel: (416) 595-9819
Fax: (416) 591-9355
Website: www.infactcanada.ca
E-mail: infact@ftn.net

Lactation Consultants

International Board of Lactation Consultants Examiners
IBLCE International Office
P.O. Box 2318
Falls Church, VA 22042-0348
Tel: (703) 560-7330
Fax.: (703) 560-7332
Website: http://www.iblce.org
E-mail: iblceq@erols.com
International board administers the lactation-consultation certification exam.

International Lactation Consultants Association
201 Brown Ave.
Evanston, IL 60202-3601
Tel: (708) 260-8871

Canadian Lactation Consultant Association
2125-29 Avenue South West
Calgary, Alberta T2T 1N6
Canada
Tel: (403) 220-9101
Fax: (403) 244-4791

Midwifery Organizations

American College of Nurse Midwives (ACNM)
818 Connecticut Ave., NW
Suite 900
Washington, DC 20006
Tel: (202) 728-9860
Website: http://www.midwife.org

Midwives Alliance of North America (NAMA)
P.O. Box 175
Newton, KS 67114
Tel: (888) 923-6262
Website: http://www.mana.org
NAMA is an umbrella organization, which provides resources and information to midwives.

Canadian Confederation of Midwives
132 Cumberland Crescent
St. John's, Newfoundland A1B 3M5
Tel: (709) 739-6319
Fax: (709) 737-7037

Doulas

Doulas of North America (DONA)
1100 23rd Avenue East
Seattle, WA 98112
Tel: (206) 324-5440
Website: http://www.dona.com
E-mail: AskDONA@aol.com
An international association of doulas, who are trained to provide high-quality labor support to birthing women and their families.

National Association of Childbearing Centers
3123 Gottshall Rd.
Perkiomenville, PA 18074
Tel: (215) 234-8829
Website: http://www.birthcenters.org

Canadian Breastfeeding Resources

Vancouver Area Breastfeeding Hotline
Tel: (604) 737-3737

Calgary Breastfeeding Center
6628 Crowchild Trail SW
Calgary, Alberta T3E 5R8
Tel: (403) 220-9101

Hospital for Sick Children
Breastfeeding Clinic
555 University Ave.
Toronto, Ontario M5G 1X8
Tel: (416) 813-5757

CLSC de la Haute Yamaska
Breastfeeding Clinic
294 Deragon St.
Granby, Quebec J2G 5J5
Tel: (514) 375-1442

Valley Regional Hospital
Valley Breastfeeding Promotion
New Mother Resource Clinic
150 Exhibition St.
Kentville, Nova Scotia B4N 5E3
Tel: (902) 678-7381

Parenting/ Mothering/Fathering

National Organization of Single Mothers
P.O. Box 58
Midland, NC 28107-0068
Tel: (704) 888-KIDS
Fax: (704) 888-1752
http://www.npin.org/reswork/workorgs/snglmoth/html

The National Center for Fathering
P.O. Box 413-888
Kansas City, MO 64141
Tel: (800) 593-DADS
Fax: (913) 384-4665
Website: http://www.fathers.com

The National Fatherhood Initiative
1 Bank St., #160
Gaithersburg, MD 20878
Tel: (301) 948-0599 or
   (800) 790-DADS
Website: http://www.fatherhood.org
Research and education-based
organization that provides skills
and tools for fathers.

The National Parenting Center
22801 Ventura Blvd., #110
Woodland Hills, CA 91367
Tel: (800) 374-5177
Website: http://www.tnpc.com

Parents Anonymous
675 W. Foothill Blvd., #220
Claremont, CA 91711
Tel: (909) 621-6184

Depression After Delivery
National Office
P.O. Box 1282
Morrisville, PA 19067
Tel: (800) 944-4773
   or (212) 295-3994

Children in Special Situations

About Face
Tel: (800) 224-FACE (United States)
Tel: (800) 665-FACE (Canada)
E-mail: AbtFace@aol.com
Support and information organization for parents of children with cleft palate. Supports Cleft Parent Guilds, support groups of parents of children with cleft lip or palate.

The Cleft Palate Foundation
11218 Grandview Ave.
Pittsburgh, PA 15211
Tel: (800) 242-5338

National Down Syndrome Society
666 Broadway, #810
New York, NY 10012
Tel: (800) 221-4602
   and (212) 460-9330
Website: http://www.ndss.org

Premature Babies

American Association for Premature Infants
P.O. Box 46371
Cincinnati, OH 45246-0371
(513) 956-4331
Website: http://www.aapi-online.org
Provides support to parents with premature infants.

Multiple Births

National Organization of Mothers of Twins Clubs, Inc.
P.O. Box 23188
Albuquerque, NM 87192-1188
Tel: (800) 243-2276
   or (505) 275-0955
Website: http://www.nomotc.org
e-mail: nomotc@aol.com

Mothers of Supertwins
MOST
PO Box 951
Brentwood, NY 11717-0627
Tel: (516) 859-1110
Website: http://www.mostonline.org

Parents of Multiple Births Association of Canada (POMBA)
240 Graff Ave.
Box 22005
Stratford, Ontario N5A 7V6
Tel: (519) 272-2203
Website: http://www.pomba.org

Triplet Connection
P.O. Box 99571
Stockton, CA 95209
Tel: (209) 474-0885
Fax: (209) 474-2233
Website:
  http://www.inreach.com/triplets
e-mail: triplets@inreach.com

Perinatal Losses and SIDS

SIDS Network
P.O. Box 520
Ledyard, MA 06339
Tel: (800) 560-1454
Website: http://sids-network.org

SHARE National Office
St. Joseph's Health Center
300 First Capitol Dr.
St. Charles, MO 63301-2893
Tel: (800) 821- 6819
  or (314) 947-6164
Fax: (314) 947-7486
Website:
  http://www.nationalshareoffice.com

Breast Milk Banking

Human Milk Banking Association of North America
8 Jan Sebastian Way, #13
Sandwich, MA 02563
Tel: (508) 888-4041 or (888) 232-8809
Fax: (508) 888-8050
e-mail: milkbank@capecod.net
HMBANA is an organization of donor milk banks that screen donors; process donated human milk; and distribute milk to infants, children, and the occasional adult on prescription for medical needs.

Therapies: Integrated Health Practitioners

The Federation of Natural Medicine Users in North America (FON-MUNA)
P.O. Box 237
Congers, NY 10920
Tel: (914) 268-2627
Provides resources to study groups interested in anthroposophical modalities.

LILIPOH (Journal on Integrated Health Care/Anthroposophical)
P.O. Box 649
Nayack, NY 10960
Tel: (914) 268-2627
Fax: (914) 268-2764
Website: http://www.lilipoh@aol.com

Middendorf Breath Institute
435 Vermont St.
San Francisco, CA 94107-2325
Tel: (415) 255-2174
Infoline: (415) 255-2467

Complementary and Alternative Medicine Resources

American Holistic Health Association
P.O. Box 17400
Anaheim, CA 92817-7400
Tel: (714) 779-6152

American Holistic Medical Association
4101 Lake Boone Trail, Ste. 201
Raleigh, NC 27607
Tel: (919) 787-5146

Other Helpful Addresses

National Women's Health Information Center (NWHIC)
Tel: (800) 994-WOMAN
TDD: (800) 220-5446
Website: http://www.4woman.org
A gateway to a vast array of Federal (and other) health resources.

National Alliance for Breastfeeding Advocacy
254 Conant Rd.
Weston, MA 02493
Tel: (781) 893-3553
A nonprofit organization that represents breastfeeding at the policy level and provides resources for healthcare practitioners.

Wellstart International
4062 First Ave.
San Diego, CA 92103
Tel: (619) 295-5192
Helpline: (619) 295-5193
Fax: (619) 574-8159
E-mail: inquiry@wellstart.org
A nonprofit organization with trained clinical staff providing regular services to breastfeeding families. Helpline for brief telephone inquiries and consultation.

National Association of WIC (Women, Infants and Children) Directors
2001 S Street, #580
Washington, DC 20009
Tel: (202) 232-5492
This organization represents the WIC program, which provides nutrition education, breastfeeding support, supplemental foods and healthcare referrals to low-income women, infants and children nationwide.

National Women's Health Network
514 10th St., NW, Ste. 400
Washington, DC 20004
Tel: (202) 347-1140

ICEA (International Childbirth Education Association)
P.O. Box 20048
Minneapolis, MN 55420-0048
Tel: (612) 854-8660
Fax: (612) 854-8772
Website: http://www.icea.org
e-mail: info@icea.org

WHO (World Health Organization)
Website: http://www.who.ch

USAID (Population, Health and Nutrition information)
Website:
    http://www.info.usaid.gov/pop_health

Birth Works, Inc.
P.O. Box 2045
Medford, NJ 08055
Tel: (888) TO-BIRTH
Website:
    http://members.aol.com/birthwkscd/
Birth Works, Inc., offers childbirth education, teacher certification and doula certification programs.

Appendix 2

Sources
and Suppliers

Note: The sources and suppliers listed here are intended as a helpful resource;
their inclusion does not imply endorsement by author or publisher.

Breastfeeding Aids
Breast Pumps

AMEDA/Egnell Pumps
755 Industrial Dr.
Cary, IL 60013
Tel: (800) 323-8750
Website:
    http://www.hollister.com/index.htm

Avent America, Inc.
501 Lively Blvd.
Elk Grove Village, IL 60007-2013
Tel: (800) 542-8368
Website: http://www.aventamerica.com

Medela, Inc. (United States)
P.O. Box 660
McHenry, IL 60051-0660
Tel: (800) 435-8316 or (800) 363-1166
Website: http://www.medela.com

Medela, Inc. (Canada)
P.O. Box 131
Mississauga, Ont. L4T 3B5
Tel: (800) 435-8316 or (905) 795-0288
Website: http://www.medela.com

Nursing Supplementers

Medela, Inc. (addresses above)

Lact-Aid® International
P.O. Box 1066
Athens, TN 37371-1066
Tel: (423) 744-9090
Fax: (423) 744-9116
Website: http://www.lact-aid.com

*Aid for Correction of Flat or
Inverted Nipples*
Niplette ™
Avent America, Inc. (address above)

Breast Shields/Shells

AMEDA/Egnell (address above)

Avent America, Inc. (address above)

Medela, Inc. (address above)

Natural Nursing Bras and Pads

Avent America, Inc. (pads)
(address above)

Decent Exposures
P.O. Box 27206
Seattle, WA 98125-1606
Tel: (800) 505-4949
(Brochure request line)

Medela, Inc. (bras and pads)
(address above)

Nursing Pillows

Care Connection
3999 Sheriden Dr.
Amherst, NY 14226
Tel: (716) 634-0300

Maternal Instincts
439 Shaker Ridge Dr.
Canaan, NY 12029
Tel: (800) 579-6464
Website: http://maternal-instincts.com

My Best Friend Nursing
35 Leveroni Court
Novato, CA 94949
Tel: (800) 555-5522

Nurse Mate Nursing
Four Dee Products
13312 Redfish, #104
Stafford, TX 77477
Tel:(800) 526-2594
Tel:(281) 261-2291
Website: http://www.fourdee.com

Medela, Inc. (address above)

Other

La Leche League International
1400 N. Meacham Rd.
Schaumburg, IL 60173
Tel: (847) 519-7730
Website: http://www.lalecheleague.org
Publications and other products

Lactation Innovation
2415 Nottingham Ln.
Naperville, IL 60565
Tel: (888) 522-8468 or 630-357-0028
Website: http://www.mcs.net/~talmadge

Clothing
Nursing Clothing

Bravado Designs
705 Pape Ave.
Toronto, Ont. M4K 3S6
Tel: (416) 466-8652
FAX: (416) 466-8666
Website: http://www.bravado.org/
Maternity and nursing bras

Little Koala Mother & Baby Catalog
614 Bellefonte St.
Shadyside, PA 15232
Tel: (800) 950-1239
Website: http://www.littlekoala.com

Motherwear
320 Riverside Dr.
Northampton, MA 01062
Tel: (800) 950-2500 and (413) 586-3488
Website: http://www.motherwear.com

Peapods
1113 27th Ave. NE
Minneapolis, MN 55418
Website: http://www.peapods.com

Maternal Instincts (address above)

Mother's Nature on the Web
703 Main St.
Watertown, CT 06795
Tel: (888) 875-4647
Website: http://www.babyholder.com

Baby Clothing

EcoBaby
1475 N. Cuyamaca
El Cajon, CA 94583
Tel: (800) 596-7450
Website: www.ecobaby.com

Natural Baby Catalog
7835 Freedom Ave., NW
Suite 2
North Canton, OH 44720-6907
Tel: (800) 388-BABY

Moses Baskets and Bedding

Baby Bundles, Inc.
5952 Hwy 181 N.
Morgantown, NC 28655
Tel: (828) 438-4709
Website: http://www.classycre-
ations@mindspring.com

EcoBaby (address above)

The Natural Nursery
Organic Cotton Alternatives
3120 Central Ave., SE
Albuquerque, NM 87106
Tel: (888) 645-4452 or (505) 232-9667
Website:
   http://www.organic cottonalts.com
Woven bassinets and crib bedding.

Infant Advantage
Sound & Motion Sleep Unit
2420 Camino Ramon, #130
San Ramon, CA 94583
Tel: (888) 6-INFANT
   and (925) 904-0300
Website:
   http://www.infant-advantage.com

Kid Safe
7100 DeCelis Pl.
Van Nuys, CA 91406
Tel: (888) 888-4464
http://www.kidsafeprod.com
A mattress designed to help protect
against SIDS.

Lambskins

The Baby Lane
108 Strafford Rd.
Havelock, NC 28532
Tel: (888) 387-0019
   and (252) 463-0019

Slings, Etc.

Over the Shoulder Baby Holder
Theresa Lacroix
P.O. Box 5676
Kingwood, TX 77325-5676
Tel: (281) 360-1699
Website: http://www.infozoo.com/baby

NoJo Baby Slings
22431 Antonio Pkwy B190
Rancho Santa Margarita, CA 92688
Tel: (800) 440-NOJO
   and (949) 858-9496

Peapods (address above)

Pettersen Infant Products
189 Dadson Row
Flin Flon, Manitoba R8A 0C8
Tel: (800) 665-3957
   and (204) 687-8474
Website: http://www.babytrekker.com

Publications and Periodicals

**BEST (Breastfeeding Education
Support Team) Newsletter**
P.O. Box 25217
Oklahoma City, OK 73125
Tel: (405) 677-3112
Advocacy, education-research-oriented

BORN Magazine
Box 103
Huntington Valley, PA 19006-0103
Tel: (215) 675-5506

**Mothering—The Magazine of
Natural Family Living**
P.O. Box 1690
Santa Fe, NM 87504
Tel: (800) 984-8116
Website: http://www.mothering.com

New Beginnings
La Leche League Breastfeeding Journal
1400 N. Meachum Rd.
Schaumburg, IL 60173
Tel: (847) 519-1730

Nurturing Magazine
#373, 918 16th Avenue NW
Calgary, Alberta T2M 0K3
Website: http://www.nurturing.ca

Pregnancy Today
P.O. Box 1724
Evanston, IL 60204
Tel: (800) 444-0064
Website:
    http://www.pregnancytoday.com

TWINS Magazine
5350 S. Roslyn St., Ste. 400
Englewood, CO 80111
Tel: (888) 55-TWINS
Website:
    http://www.TWINSmagazine.com

Food Mills

VillaWare
1420 E. 36th St.
Cleveland, OH 44114
Tel: (800) 822-1335
Food mills and grain mills

Baby Foods

Earth's Best, Inc.
P.O. Box 28
Pittsburg, PA 15230-9421
Tel: (800) 442-4221
Website: http://www.earthsbest.com
Organic baby food, available in
healthfood stores

Gerber
445 State St.
Fremont, MI 49413
Tel: (800) 4-GERBER
Website: http://www.gerber.com
"Tender Harvest" line offers some
organic foods, as well as non-organic
with no added sugar or starch.

Diapering

Check the yellow pages for local
services, or try:

Earthwise Basics
214 Elliot St., Ste. 2
Brattleboro, VT 05301
Tel: (800) 791-3957 or (802) 254-2235
Website: http://www.ediapers.com

**National Association of
Diaper Service Referral**
994 Old Eagle School Rd., #1019
Wayne, PA 19087
Tel: (800) 569-1462
    and (610) 971-4850

Tushies Diapers
675 Industrial Blvd.
Delta, CO 81416
Tel: (800) 34-IMDRY
    and (800) 344-6379
Website:
    http://www.ecomall.com/biz/tushies

Natural Remedies for the Family

National Center for Homeopathy
801 N. Fairfax St., #306
Alexandria, VA 22314
Tel: (703) 548-7790
Fax: (703) 548-7792
Website: http://www.homeopathic.org
How to select a homeopath; nation-
wide addresses and homeopathic
pharmacies for a small referral fee.

**National Association for
Holistic Aromatherapy**
P.O. Box 17622-7622
Tel: (800) ASK-NAHA
    or (313) 963-2071
Fax: (314) 963-4454
Website: www.naha.org
E-mail: info@naha.org
For help finding a certified aroma-
therapist.

Nelson Bach USA, Ltd.
Wilmington Technology Park
100 Research Dr.
Wilmington, MA 01887-4406
Tel: (978) 988-3833
Website: http://www.nelsonbach.com
Official Bach Flower distributor;
referrals; information.

Flower Essence Services
P.O. Box 1769
Nevada City, CA 95959
Tel: (530) 265-9163
Website:
   http://www.info@floweressence.com
Preparation and distribution of
California Research/FES
Quintessentials.

WELEDA, Inc.
Anthroposophic, Homeopathic and
Natural Personal-Care Products
175 North Route 9W
Congers, NY 10920
Tel: (800) 241-1030
Website: http://www.weleda.com
Treatments, some by prescription
only, may be ordered direct from
WELEDA. Baby-care products and
products for the mother.

Aroma Vera
5901 Rodeo Rd.
Los Angeles, CA 90016
Website: www.aromavera.com
Tel: (213) 280-0407

Holistic Health Information

National Institutes of Health
OAM (Office of Alternative
Medicine) Clearing House
P.O. Box 8218
Silver Spring, MD 20907-8218
Tel: (888) 644-6226
Website: http://altmed.od.nih.gov
OAM facilitates research and
evaluation of unconventional
medical practices and disseminates
information to the public.

LILIPOH Magazine
P.O. Box 649
Nayack, NY 10960
Tel: (914) 268-2627
Website: http://www.lilipoh@aol.com

Baby and Natural Health Products

Herbs for Kids
151 Evergreen Dr., Suite D
Bozeman, MT 59715
Tel: (406) 587-0180
Herbal products for children.

Appendix 3

Bibliography, Videos and Music

Breastfeeding and Nutrition

Bumgarner, Norma Jane. *Mothering Your Nursing Toddler*. Schaumburg, IL: La Leche League International, 1982.

Dalley, Jill. *The Meat & Potatoes of Breastfeeding: Easy Nutritional Guidelines for Breastfeeding Moms*. Coppel, TX: Footprint Press, 1997.

Gotsch, Gwen. *Breastfeeding Pure & Simple*. Schaumburg, IL: La Leche League International, 1994.

Huggins, Kathleen and Ziedrich, Linda: *The Nursing Mother's Guide to Weaning*. Boston, MA: Harvard Common Press, 1994.

Johnson, Roberta (ed.). *Whole Foods for the Whole Family: La Leche League International Cookbook*. Schaumburg, IL: La Leche League, 1981.

Kippley, Sheila. *Breastfeeding and Natural Child Spacing*. Cincinnati, OH: Couple-to-Couple League, 1989.

Kitzinger, Sheila. *Breastfeeding Your Baby*. New York: Alfred A. Knopf, 1989.

La Leche League International. *The Womanly Art of Breastfeeding*. Schaumburg, IL: La Leche League International, 1997.

Lawrence, Ruth. *Breastfeeding: A Guide for the Medical Profession*. St. Louis, MO: Mosby, 1994.

Mohrbacher, Nancy, and Julie Stock. *Breastfeeding Answer Book*. Schaumburg, IL: La Leche League International, 1997.

Moody, Jane, Jane Britten and Karen Hogg. *Breastfeeding Your Baby*. Tucson, AZ: Fisher Books, 1997.

Moore-Lappé, Frances. *Diet for a Small Planet*. New York: Ballantine Books, 1991.

Pryor, Karen and Gale. *Nursing Your Baby*. New York: Pocket Books, 1991.

Renfrew, Mary et al. *Bestfeeding—Getting Breastfeeding Right for You: An Illustrated Guide*. Berkeley, CA: Celestial Arts, 1990.

Riordan, Jan, and Kathleen Auerbach. *Breastfeeding and Human Lactation*. Boston, MA: Jones & Bartlett Publishers, 1993.

Walker, M. *Summary of the Hazards of Infant Formula*. Evanston, IL: International Lactation Consultant Association, 1992.

Pregnancy and Childbirth

Balaskas, Janet. *Active Birth: New Approach to Giving Birth Naturally*. Harvard, MA: Harvard Common Press,1992.

Bing, Elisabeth. *Six Practical Lessons for an Easier Childbirth*. New York: Bantam Books, 1982.

Crawford, Karis, and Johanne Walters. *Natural Childbirth After Cesarean: A Practical Guide*. Cambridge, MA: Blackwell Science, 1996.

Curtis, Glade, MD. *Your Pregnancy Week by Week*. Tucson, AZ: Fisher Books, 1997.

Gaskin, Ina May. *Spiritual Midwifery*. Summertown, TN: Book Publishing Co., 1990.

Janus, Ludwig, et al. *The Enduring Effects of Prenatal Experience: Echoes from the Womb*. Northvale, NJ: J. Aronson, 1997.

Johnson, Jessica, and Michel Odent. *We Are All Water Babies*. Berkeley, CA: Celestial Arts, 1995.

Kitzinger, Sheila, and Marcia May (photographer). *The Complete Book of Pregnancy and Childbirth*. New York: Alfred A. Knopf, 1996.

Kitzinger, Sheila. *Homebirth: Essential Guide to Giving Birth Outside of the Hospital*. New York: Dorling Kindersley, 1991.

—*Giving Birth: How It Really Feels*. New York: The Noonday Press, 1989.

Klaus, Marshall, John Kennel and Phyllis Klaus. *Mothering the Mother*. Reading, MA: Addison-Wesley, 1993.

Klaus, Marshall, et al. *Parent-Infant Bonding*. St. Louis, MO: Mosby, 1982.

Leboyer, Frederick. Birth without Violence. Rochester, VT: Healing Arts Press, 1995.

Martin, Margaret. *Pregnancy & Childbirth: The Basic Illustrated Guide*. Tucson, AZ: 1997.

Odent, Michel. Birth Reborn. New York: Pantheon Books, 1994.

Odent, Michel and Christine Hauch (translator). *Entering the World: The Demedicalization of Childbirth*. New York: M. Boyers, 1984.

Parsons, Betty. *Preparing for Childbirth: Relaxing for Labor, Learning for Life*. Tucson, AZ: Fisher Books, 1997.

Stukane, Eileen. *The Dream Worlds of Pregnancy: How Understanding Dreams Can Help You Bond With Your Baby and Become a Better Parent With Your Mate*. Tarrytown, NY: Station Hill Press, 1994.

Verny, Thomas, and Pamela Weintrab. *Nurturing the Unborn Child: A Nine-Month Program for Soothing, Stimulating, and Communicating With Your Baby*. New York: Delacorte Press, 1992.

Preparing Children for the Birth of a Sibling

Cole, Joanna. *How You Were Born*. New York: Morrow Junior Books, 1993.

Davis, Jennifer. *Before You Were Born*. New York: Workman Publishing, 1998.

Lansky, Vicki, and Jane Prince (illustrator). *A New Baby at Koko Bear's House*. New York: Bantam Books, 1991.

McBride, Will. *Show Me: A Picture Book of Sex for Children and Parents*. New York: St. Martin's Press, 1975.

Mendelson, Morton J. *Becoming a Brother: A Child Learns About Life, Family, and Self*. Cambridge, MA: MIT Press, 1993.

Nilsson, Lennart, and Lena Katarina Swanberg. *Preparation for Birth: How Was I Born?* New York: Delacorte Press, 1994.

Sandra Van Dam Anderson and Penny Simkin. *Birth through Children's Eyes*. Seattle, WA: Penny Press, 1981.

Parenting, Living with Children and Family Life

Berends Berrien, Polly. *Whole Child/Whole Parent*. New York: Harper & Row, 1983.

Brazelton, T. Berry. *To Listen to a Child: Understanding the Normal Problems of Growing Up*. Reading, MA: Addison-Wesley, 1992.

Bolster, Alice. *Motherwise: 101 Tips for a New Mother*. Schaumburg, IL: La Leche League International, 1997.

Carroll, David. *Spiritual Parenting*. New York: Paragon House, 1990.

Curran, Dolores. *Traits of a Healthy Family*. Minneapolis, MN: Winston Press, 1984.

Dix, Carol. *The New-Mother Syndrome*. New York: Doubleday, 1988.

Ewy, Donna. *Preparation for Parenthood: How to Create a Nurturing Family*. New York: New American Library, 1986.

—*Guide to Parenting: You and Your Newborn*. New York: E. P. Dutton, 1982.

Jones, Sandy, et al. *Guide to Baby Products (5th Ed.)* Vol 1. Yonkers, NY: Consumer Reports Books, 1996.

Kitzinger, Sheila. *The Crying Baby*. New York: Penguin Books, 1990.

Klaus, Marshall, and Phyllis Klaus. *The Amazing Newborn*. Reading, MA: Perseus Books, 1998.

Leach, Penelope. *Your Baby and Child: From Birth to Age Five*. New York: Alfred A. Knopf, 1997.

Lewis, Deborah Shaw. *Stress-Busters for Moms*. Grand Rapids, MI: Zondervan Publishing, 1996.

Lowman, Kaye. *Of Cradles and Careers: A Guide to Reshaping Your Job to Include a Baby in Your Life*. Schaumburg, IL: La Leche League International, 1985.

Mindell, Jodi A. *Sleeping through the Night: How Infants, Toddlers, and Their Parents Can Get a Good Night's Sleep*. New York: HarperCollins, 1997.

Montessori, Maria. *The Absorbent Mind*. New York: Holt, 1995.

Placksin, Sally. *Mothering the New Mother: Women's Feelings and Needs After Childbirth: A Support and Resource Guide*. New York: Newmarket Press, 1998.

Sears, William. *Growing Together: Parent's Guide to Baby's First Year*. Schaumburg, IL: La Leche League International, 1987.

—*Nighttime Parenting: How to Get Your Baby and Child to Sleep*. Schaumburg, IL: La Leche League International, 1985.

Sears, William, and Martha Sears. *Parenting the Fussy Baby and the High-Need Child: Everything You Need to Know: From Birth to Age Five*. Schaumburg, IL: La Leche League International, 1996.

Thevenin, Tine. *The Family Bed, An Age-old Concept in Childrearing*. Garden City Park, NY: Avery Publishing Group, 1987.

—*Mothering and Fathering: The Gender Differences in Child Rearing*. Garden City Park, NY: Avery Publishing Group, 1993.

Walker, Peter. *Natural Parenting: A Practical Guide for Fathers and Mothers Conception to Age 3*. New York: Interlink Books, 1990.

Nurturing Your Baby, Massages, Etc.

Auckett, Amelia D. *Baby Massage: Parent-Child Bonding through Touch*. New York: Newmarket Press, 1989.

Field, Tiffany M. (editor). *Touch in Early Development*. Mahwah, NJ: Lawrence Erlbaum Associates, 1995.

Heller, Sharon. *The Vital Touch*. New York: Henry Holt, 1997.

Leboyer, Frederick. *Loving Hands: The Traditional Art of Baby Massage*. New York: Newmarket Press, 1997.

Ludington-Hoe, Susan. *Kangaroo Care: The Best You Can Do to Help Your Preterm Infant*. New York: Bantam Books, 1993.

Montagu, Ashley. *Touching: The Human Significance of the Skin*. New York: Perennial Library, 1986.

Streri, Arlette, et al. *Seeing, Reaching, Touching: The Relations Between Vision and Touch in Infancy (Developing Body and Mind Series)*. Cambridge, MA: MIT Press, 1994.

Walker, Peter. *Baby Massage: A Practical Guide to Massage and Movement for Babies and Infants*. Schaumburg, IL: La Leche League International, 1996.

Becoming a Father

Brott, Armin A. *The Expectant Father: Facts, Tips and Advice for Dads-to-Be*. New York: Abbeville Press, 1997.

Goldman, Marcus Jacob. *The Joy of Fatherhood: The First Twelve Months*. Rocklin, CA: Prima Publishing, 1997.

Hill, Thomas, and Patrick Merrell (illustrator). *What to Expect When Your Wife Is Expanding*. Kansas City, MO: Andrews & McNeel, 1993.

Sears, William. *Becoming a Father: How to Nurture and Enjoy Your Family*. Schaumburg, IL: La Leche League International, 1986.

Couple's Relationship

Downing, George. *The Massage Book*. New York: Random House/Bookworks, 1998.

Gray, John. *Men Are from Mars, Women Are from Venus: A Practical Guide for Improving Communication and Getting What You Want in Your Relationship*. New York: HarperCollins, 1992.

Kitzinger, Sheila. *Woman's Experience of Sex*. New York: Putnam, 1985.

Twins and Multiples

Bryan, Elizabeth M. *Twins, Triplets and More: Their Nature, Development and Care*. New York: St. Martin's Press, 1992.

Gromada, Karen. *Mothering Multiples: Breastfeeding and Caring for Twins*. Schaumburg, IL: La Leche League International, 1985.

Noble, Elizabeth. *Having Twins: A Parent's Guide to Pregnancy, Birth and Early Childhood*. Boston, MA: Houghton Mifflin, 1991.

Novotny, Pamela Patrick. *The Joy of Twins and Other Multiple Births: Having, Raising, and Loving Babies Who Arrive in Groups*. New York: Crown, 1994.

Self-Care and Health—Physical, Emotional and Spiritual Self-Nurturing and Growth

The Boston Women's Health Collective. *Our Bodies, Ourselves for the New Century: A Book by and for Women*. New York: Simon & Schuster, 1998.

Andrew Goliszek. *60-Second Stress Management: The Quickest Way to Relax and Ease Anxiety*. Farhills, NJ: New Horizon Press, 1992.

Barnett, Libby. *Reiki Energy Medicine*. Rochester, VT: Healing Arts Press, 1996.

Dychtwald, Ken. *Bodymind*. Los Angeles, CA: J.P. Tarcher, 1986.

Elias, Jason, Katherine Ketcham. *In the House of the Moon: Reclaiming the Feminine Spirit of Healing*. New York: Warner Books, 1995.

Levine, Arlene Gay, and Karen Kroll (illustrator). *39 Ways to Open Your Heart: An Illuminated Meditation*. Berkeley, CA: Conari Press, 1996.

Sheldon Z. Kramer. *Transforming the Inner and Outer Family: Humanistic and Spiritual Approaches to Mind-Body Systems Therapy* Binghampton, NY: Haworth Press, 1995.

Michael, Sky. *Breathing: Expanding Your Power & Energy*. Santa Fe, NM: Bear & Co., 1990.

Middendorf, Ilse. *The Perceptible Breath* (book and two exercise audio cassettes). Available from the Middendorf Breath Institute (*see* Appendix 1 *for contact information*).

Parady, Marianne. *7 Secrets for Successful Living: Tapping the Wisdom of Ralph Waldo Emerson to Achieve Love, Happiness, and Self-Reliance*. New York: Kensington Books, 1995.

Ruhnke, Amiyo and Anando Wurzburger. *Bodywisdom: An Easy-To-Use Handbook of Simple Exercises and Self-Massage Techniques for Busy People*. Boston, MA: Charles Tuttle Co., 1996.

Natural Remedies/Complementary and Alternative or Holistic Medicine

Bach, Edward. *Collected Writings of Edward Bach*. Hereford, England: Bach Educational Programme, 1987.

Barnard, Julian. *The Healing Herbs of Edward Bach: An Illustrated Guide to the Flower Remedies*. Hereford, England: Bach Educational Programme, 1988.

Castro, Miranda. *Homeopathy for Pregnancy, Birth and Your Baby's First Year*. New York: St. Martin's Press, 1993.

Collinge, William. *American Holistic Health Association Complete Guide to Alternative Medicine*. New York: Warner Books, 1996.

Dooley, Timothy R., ND, MD. *Homeopathy Beyond Flat-Earth Medicine: An Essential Guide for the Homeopathic Patient*. San Diego, CA: Timing Publications, 1995.

Elias, Jason, and Katherine Ketcham. *Feminine Healing: A Woman's Guide to a Healthy Body, Mind, and Spirit*. New York: Warner Books, 1997.

Fischer-Rizzi, Susanne, et al. *Complete Aromatherapy Handbook: Essential Oils for Radiant Health*. New York: Sterling Publishing, 1991.

Fischer-Rizzi, Susanne. *Medicine of the Earth: Legends, Recipes, Remedies, and Cultivation of Healing Plants*. Portland, OR: Rudra Press, 1997.

Gardner, Joy. *Healing Yourself during Pregnancy*. Freedom, CA: Crossing Press, 1987.

Gladstar, Rosemary. *Herbal Healing for Women*. New York: Simon & Schuster/ Fireside, 1993.

Hammond, Christopher. *The Complete Family Guide to Homeopathy: An Illustrated Encyclopedia of Safe and Effective Remedies*. New York: Penguin Studio, 1996.

Idarius, Betty, and C. Hom. *The Homeopathic Childbirth Manual*. Ukiah, CA: Idarius Press, 1996.

Jackson, Judith. *Scentual Touch: A Personal Guide to Aromatherapy*. New York: Fawcett Columbine, 1987.

Kaminsiki, Patricia, and Richard Katz. *Flower Essence Repertory*. Nevada City, NV: Flower Essence Society Division of Earth Spirit, Inc., 1994.

Kramer, Dietmar. *New Bach Flower Remedies: Healing the Emotional and Spiritual Causes of Illness*. Rochester, VT: Healing Arts Press, 1995.

—*New Bach Flower Body Maps: Treatment by Topical Application*. Rochester, VT: Healing Arts Press, 1996.

Lockie, Andrew. *The Family Guide to Homeopathy*. New York: Dorling Kindersley, 1995.

Mole, Peter. *Acupuncture: Energy Balancing for Body, Mind and Spirit*. Rockport, MA: Element,1992.

Gary Null. *The Woman's Encyclopedia of Natural Healing: New Healing Techniques of 100 Leading Alternative Practitioners*. New York: Seven Stories Press, 1996.

Romm, Aviva Jill. *Natural Healing for Babies and Children*. Freedom, CA: Crossing Press, 1996.

Scheffer, Mechthild. *Mastering Bach Flower Therapies*. Rochester, VT: Healing Arts Press, 1996.

Scott, Julian. *Natural Medicine for Children: Drug-Free Health Care for Children from Birth to Age Twelve, plus a Practical, Comprehensive Guide to Herbs, Homeopathy*. New York: Avon Books, 1996.

Scott, Julian and Susan Scott. *Natural Medicine for Women*. New York: Avon Books, 1991.

Sullivan, Karen C., and Norman Shealy (editor). *The Complete Family Guide to Natural Home Remedies*. Rockport, MA: Element, 1997.

Ullman, Dana. *Homeopathic Medicine for Children and Infants*. New York: J.P. Tarcher/Perigee Books, 1992.

Ullman, Robert, ND, and Judith Reicherberg-Ullman, ND. *Homeopathic Self-care: Quick and Easy Guide for the Whole Family*. Rocklin, CA: Prima Publishing, 1997.

Weed, Susun. *Wise Woman Herbal for the Childbearing Year*. Woodstock, NY: Ash Tree Publishing, 1989.

Weiner, Michael, and Kathleen Goss. *The Complete Book of Homeopathy*. Garden City Park, NY: Avery Publishing, 1989.

Special Circumstances

Diamond, Kathleen F. *Motherhood after Miscarriage*. Holbrook, MA: Bob Adams, Inc., 1991.

Good, Julia Darnell, and Joyce Good Reis. *A Special Kind of Parenting: Meeting the Needs of Handicapped Children*. Schaumburg, IL: La Leche League International, 1985.

Lothrop, Hannah. *Help, Comfort and Hope after Losing Your Baby in Pregnancy or the First Year*. Tucson, AZ: Fisher Books, 1997.

Murphy-Melas, Elizabeth, and Diane Tate (illustrator). *Watching Bradley Grow: A Story About Premature Birth*. Atlanta, GA: Longstreet Press, 1996.

William, Sears. *SIDS: A Parent's Guide to Understanding and Preventing Sudden Infant Death Syndrome*. Boston, MA: Little, Brown, 1996.

Videos

Birth and Parenting for the 21st Century. Services for the Nurturing of Children, 1100 Irvine Blvd., Ste. 173, Tustin, CA 92680-3596

Breastfeeding Your Baby: A Mother's Guide. Available through Medela and La Leche League.

Breastfeeding with Pleasure—Breastfeeding Support Services. Halton Health Department, 251 Main St., Milton, Ontario L9N 1P1. Tel: (416) 878-7261.

Colic Relief: A Chinese Pediatric Massage Approach. Healing Arts Productions, P.O. Box 10714, Portland, OR 97210. Tel: (800) 328-1751. E-mail: info@healartspro.com

Music for Meditation and Relaxation

Classical:

Tomaso Albinoni: *Adagio in G Minor*

Johann Sebastian Bach: *Air; Brandenburg Concertos; Concert for Flute, G-major, Largo*

Johann Pachelbel: *Canon in D-minor*

Antonio Vivaldi: *Concert for Violin and Lute, D-major, Largo*

Relaxation, Instrumental and Other:

Diamond, Neil: *Jonathan Livingston Seagull.* Sony Music, 1988.

Enya: *Shepherd Moons.* Reprise Records, 1996.

Gallagher, Cheryl: *Pregnant Pause.* Publications Services, Inc., 8803 Tara Ln., Austin, TX 78737. Tel: (888) 514-7253.

Gardner, Kay. *Drone Zone: Healing Music* (Healing Music Series). Relaxation Company, 1996.

Halpern, Steven: *In the Key of Healing* (Healing Music Series). Relaxation Company, 1996.

Horn, Paul: *Inside the Taj Mahal 2; Inside the Great Pyramid.* Kuckuck Records, 1990; 1995.

Kitaro: *Best of Kitaro, Vol. 1.* Oasis Records, 1997.

Kobialka: *Moonglow; Going Home Again; When You Wish upon a Star; Relaxation Music for Children.* (Li-Sem Enterprises, P.O. Box 746, Daly City, CA 94017-0746.)

Salmon, Keith: *Angels of Love and Healing.* Bluestar Communications, 1997.

Appendix 4

Homeopathic Remedies List for the Postpartum Period

For a full discussion of using homeopathic remedies, see page 162.

Note: Use this list as a reference. You might take it along to guide your discussion with a homeopath or naturopath about any breastfeeding problems you may have. Your practitioner will suggest appropriate dosages.

Homeopathic remedies are successful in many situations, but with medical conditions, consultation with a physician is essential.

These brief descriptions are not meant to replace thoroughly studying the appropriate literature or consultation with practitioners experienced with homeopathy.

Mother's Problems

Not enough milk

Bryonia C6: The mother is upset (perhaps about the hospital or her partner), but doesn't let her anger out, justified or not. She is extremely thirsty but has a limited milk supply; has headaches.

Calcium carbonicum C6: The mother has fears, feels overwhelmed, everything is too much; after birth she perspires unusually strongly, perspiration often appearing on her neck and face. She has cold shivers, frequently has cold feet. The baby only sucks a little, appears phlegmatic.

Ignatia C6: Mother and baby are separated (the baby may be in intensive care, or rooming-in is not available around the clock), she tends to be critical of herself; has high expectations and idealized views. Now everything is different than she had imagined; she feels that there is something she hasn't done right. She is in despair, bewildered.

Pulsatilla C6: The mother is sad and cries a lot; for example, about her inability to produce enough milk. She seeks frequent advice from the nurses, feels like a child in need of help herself. She feels in despair; has noticeably little thirst.

Zincum metallicum C6: Despite having little milk, mother has breast pains. She experiences noticeably great restlessness and nervousness; she can't sit still, her legs and feet are constantly in motion; she says she is too restless to breastfeed.

Too much milk

Phytolacca C6: The breast is very full and painful. There's a great deal of milk coming from the mother's breast; the pain spreads into her shoulders.

Pulsatilla C6: There is abundant milk flow. The mother is overjoyed and effusive, at the same time she is needy. She wants everyone to see her baby. She weeps frequently and intensely. She has noticeably little thirst.

Sore nipples

Castor equi C6: The mother's nipples are so sore and painful that she can hardly wear a nursing bra, she can't even tolerate loose clothing. The left breast is often more strongly affected than the right. Peculiar feature: The pain is accompanied by extreme itching of breast and nipple; scratching brings temporary relief but makes the skin even more sore. Skin and nipples are frequently very dry.

Graphites C6: There are cracks around the nipples, often small blisters also, from which comes an amber-colored liquid. Frequently there is eczema on the nipples.

Phytolacca C6: There are cracks on the nipples. Pain is felt throughout the breast when the baby sucks; in many cases pain is felt throughout the body. The mother feels exhausted overall and depressed; feels a strong inner restlessness.

Plugged ducts

Conium C6: There is a reddened area on the breast, very sensitive to touch; the area is hardened. There is a stabbing pain; pressure from the bra is hard to bear. Frequently only the right breast is affected. Mother has circulatory problems—even turning over in bed makes her dizzy.

Nux vomica C6: The milk ducts feel plugged. Mother is annoyed at the nurse for not giving enough attention, she could explode with anger. This is felt in the stomach and causes pressure.

Phytolacca C6: Milk is backed up; the breast is red and hard in some places, painful to the slightest touch. The breasts feel extremely heavy.

Breast Infection

Note: Homeopathic remedies may be useful in treating a breast infection, but should not replace consultation with your doctor, or be used long-term in place of conventional medicine. Remember, if you don't see results *within hours*, the remedy has not worked for you.

Belladonna C6: The infected area is bright red; the infection develops quickly, usually manifesting red stripes fanning out from the center of the infection. The mother has a high fever. She sometimes has a hot face accompanied by cold feet and hands. She is greatly sensitive to touch.

Bryonia C6: The breasts are hard and heavy. The slightest movement hurts. Even breathing in causes pain in the breast. Breast pain is stabbing and is frequently accompanied by a headache. The mother is irritable and wants to be left alone; she doesn't want visitors. She has a strong sense of being "dried out," combined with great thirst.

Hepar sulfuris C6: Only warmth feels good. Cold is extremely uncomfortable; the mother is freezing. Warm, damp compresses are helpful.

Weaning

Phytolacca D1.

Problems with the Baby (See also chapter 13)

Homeopathic remedies may be given to babies in some instances, such as colic, nursing strikes and aversion to the breast, and newborn jaundice. Obtain the expert advice of an experienced practitioner. And always let your baby's doctor know what homeopathic remedies you plan to give your baby.

Acknowledgments

I am very grateful to have been able to serve woman- and mankind with this book and hopefully contribute to making this world just a little bit better place. I am in awe and sometimes can't quite believe that so far, nearly 750,000 copies of this book have been sold worldwide. I want to thank my many readers who have helped spread the word. My great appreciation goes to the women and men who shared their personal experiences. I heard over and over again how those in the midst of a crisis, dilemma or problem felt inspired and encouraged by stories of others in a similar situation: "I am not alone. If they managed, I'll manage too."

My heartfelt thanks to the people who generously and lovingly supported me during the research and initial writing of this book—the late Drs. Niles and Michael Newton, the Founding Mothers of La Leche League, Dr. Gregory White and Elizabeth Hormann; also to my co-pioneers and early La Leche League leaders Olivia Wacker, Sylvia Brunn and Welda Hoerz for their solidarity and sharing, as well as to Dr. Adriane Elbrecht for her counsel and editing of the first version. I warmly thank my friend Mechthild Fuchs for her interest and accompaniment of the book from conception through birth and its many life phases.

Thanks to all those who in recent years have contributed to our knowledge about the incredible benefits of breast milk and the management of lactation, as well as other important factors relating to breastfeeding, and particularly to Kittie Franz, Chele Marmet and Ruth Lawrence, from whose work this book has benefited.

Thanks to the many who have counseled me for this edition—Dr. Elien Rouw, Marsha Walker, Helen Armstrong, Betty Crase and others at La Leche League for sharing their immense knowledge on breastfeeding and breast milk; Dr. Toni Drähne for contributing his wisdom on homeopathy in obstetrics and pediatrics; Dr. Claudia Monte for commenting on and complementing the chapter on Bach Flower remedies, and aromatherapist Susanne Fischer-Rizzi for her advice and tips regarding the application of aromatherapy for pregnant and nursing women and their children. Thanks to Dr. Marshall Klaus for his assistance on the chapter on bonding, Kitty Ernst for her review of the birth chapter, Ashisha of Mothering Magazine for taking the time to answer many questions regarding the American situation, Rosemary Boudreaux, Pat Sturgis and many others. Thanks to Dr. Donna Ewy for being my friend for more than 20 years. Thanks to Elizabeth Hormann for the translation and to Karen Salt and Sarah Trotta for their commitment as editors.

Above all, I want to thank Rob, my husband of 31 years, who feels that he has probably become the world's best-informed, non-medical male expert on breastfeeding. He enthusiastically embarked on research for the new edition, spending many, many hours on the Internet, reading through and highlighting research material and interviewing experts for me. He not only was a tremendous help with this book, but without his support and caring I certainly would not have been able to dedicate myself to bringing about positive changes in our society to the degree I was able to. Last but not least—thank you, my now grown-up children Anya and Kerry, who have kept on challenging me to new growth experiences and perspectives. Without you, this book would not have come about.

Hannah Lothrop

Index

F-G